12/3/76

Very special regards to
my sister, Eleanor —

Elizabeth Simmons Howard

The Vagabond Dreamer

"There is a story in every life, in every tree and flower, in every dancing sunbeam or passing cloud, in the cry of the little child or the moaning of the beggar."

M. W. H.

"I had rather be a vagabond, wandering about in God's beautiful mountains, or beside His gurgling streams and sweeping oceans, dreaming my dreams, than to be chasing the will-o-the-wisp of fame, power, achievement and money in the great marts of commerce."

M. W. H.

"I am the evergreen optimist, the eternal dreamer."

M. W. H.

THE

VAGABOND DREAMER

BY

ELIZABETH S. HOWARD

THE STRODE PUBLISHERS, INC.
HUNTSVILLE, ALABAMA 35802

FORT PAYNE BICENTENNIAL COMMITTEE

ALABAMA BICENTENNIAL COMMISSION

This publication has been endorsed by the Fort Payne Bicentennial Committee and the Alabama Bicentennial Commission.

To my husband, Max J. Howard—
who shared the eager beginning . . .
but is not here now to read the book

Contents

Preface

I did not know Milford Howard. He passed this way long before my own Howard came to this beautiful north Alabama area to hang out *his* shingle for the practice of law. But of all the legendary figures of local history, the Colonel has appealed, more than any other, to my imagination and curiosity. Yet there appeared to be very little documented information relative to his many exploits and endeavors. So for the past four years I have searched for the scattered pieces of the immense puzzle of this intriguing life which began over eleven decades ago. This task has continued even as the book was being published, but a few of the missing parts have remained undiscovered. However, the surprise has not been in the number of fruitless efforts but rather in the scope and the high percentage of the successful pursuits.

I have attempted to present Colonel Howard's life as he lived it—neither embellishing his admirable traits nor magnifying his faults. This, I believe, is as he would have wanted it. He did, however, have a very great desire that he not be completely forgotten, and I think he will not be.

Different conclusions may be drawn as to Colonel Howard's contribution to our heritage. He lived in a time—almost forgotten now—when individuals, not governments, bore the major responsibility for a community's progress. In such an era, he constantly stood out as a leader of vision. Unfortunately, however, he was rarely practical. He also had many human frailties. As one of his contemporaries expressed it, "Colonel Howard was a man with feet of clay."

But, oh, how he reached for the stars!

Acknowledgments

Many people have made valuable contributions toward the total time, effort, and material required to produce this biography. I am especially indebted to several good friends for their great assistance. Mrs. David Bare became a specialist at reading the Colonel's handwriting (an achievement itself) and "transcribed" whole manuscripts for me. She also helped with research and spent hours and days performing an excellent job of proofreading. Mrs. Margie Gravitt traveled with me over the highways and back roads of Alabama and Georgia, helping me gather much of my most necessary data. Miss Myrtle Cash and her brother, Grady Cash, have supplied priceless old pictures of members of the Howard family and have helped me locate other people who had valuable information.

Others who have furnished photographs or material include the following: James R. Kuykendall, Tom McCurdy, Jerry Whittle, Mr. and Mrs. Mack Hamilton, Mrs. Annie Young, Mrs. L. H. Ferguson, Mrs. Rose Pickens, Mrs. Willie Morgan, Mrs. O. C. Cochran, Woodrow Biddle, and Judge W. M. Beck, Sr., all of Fort Payne; Mrs. Charles Willard, Silver Spring, Maryland; Mrs. John R. Walsh, Jackson, Alabama; Col. C. M. Howard, Columbus, Georgia; Mr. and Mrs. James Floyd Cordell, Rome, Georgia; Mrs. Lucile Webb, Gadsden, Alabama; James Sulzby, Jr., Birmingham, Alabama; and Mr. and Mrs. Frank Kirk and Max Cash, Mentone, Alabama.

Those who supplied useful information (some on many different occasions) include Mrs. Mary Davenport, Mrs. Sarah P. Sawyer, J. A. Downer, Willie Culpepper, Judge W. J. Haralson, Mrs. Maude Pendergrass, Judge Richard Hunt, Bill Garrett, Dee

Gilliam, and John B. Isbell, Jr., of Fort Payne; Mr. and Mrs. B. C. Wester and Paul Crow, Mentone; Dr. Brady R. Justice, Enterprise, Alabama; and Milford Lankford, Gainesville, Florida.

For help with research, I am indebted to Mrs. H. E. Smith, Mrs. J. W. Hawkins, Mrs. Kenneth Parker, Erskine Davenport, Mrs. Louise Tribble, Ed Ladd, Mrs. John B. Isbell, Jr., Mrs. John B. Isbell, III, and Mrs. Charles Isbell.

Special credit is due to Mrs. H. M. Everett, Jr., for helping to design the cover; to Mrs. Leon White for assistance with typing; and to Mark Moore for some excellent photography.

Finally, to my family and friends, whose unfailing loyalty and kindness have constantly provided inspiration throughout my darkest hours, I wish to express my thankfulness and love; without their support I could not have completed this story.

Foreword

I knew Colonel Howard personally and visited him often. While sitting on one of the porches at Alpine Lodge, we had many long conversations. He related many incidents of his life in an unreluctant manner from time to time and it often appeared to me that the Colonel just needed someone with whom to talk. From my recollections of the gentleman it seems I have never known a man to fail at more endeavors, yet overlook the past and have such visions of the future.

With *Vagabond Dreamer* Mrs. Elizabeth Howard of Fort Payne (no relation to Colonel Howard) has brought to life an interesting biography of the Colonel. Mrs. Howard is regarded as a very thorough researcher. Most amateur historians are known for their accuracy; this is the case with Mrs. Howard. She has discovered and shown that the business enterprises and ventures of Colonel Howard throughout life were "separate but equal," a sequence of disappointments and failures; but that's the way his life went. Colonel Howard, a dreamer, moved quickly, facing every responsibility with "hit or flop" concepts. Mrs. Howard makes it clear her subject "was no success story."

The author actually makes the story of Colonel Howard read more like a novel than the simple tale of his life. A reader is prone to read ahead to see what else could happen to the man. Had this publication been labeled as one of fiction, the title could easily have been *Success at Failure*. With his background as a lawyer, a congressman, a writer, a lecturer, and an outstanding leader in his community, his life in part is somewhat a mystery.

There are some good lessons which may be learned from Mrs. Howard's story. It should be understood that Colonel Howard was most willing to identify himself with projects for the betterment of Fort Payne, DeKalb County, the DeSoto Park area on Lookout Mountain, and mankind in general. His love for the mountain was ever present. He was successful in acquiring vast acreage on the mountain; he harnessed the water power of Little River near the lodge; he made every effort to establish permanently the Master School for the education of the underprivileged mountain youth; he envisioned the Scenic Highway atop Lookout Mountain from Gadsden to Chattanooga and began its construction. Colonel Howard took pride in the erection and completion of the chapel, a memorial to his first wife. Though he was a dreamer, I do believe Colonel Howard wished to succeed in everything he undertook. The Colonel admitted his inability to hold on to money, and, as the account of his life is told by Mrs. Howard, he very seldom had any to manage.

Knowing Colonel Howard as I did, I had admiration for the few things counted as successful in his world of material accomplishments, but some of his failures should be admired also. Whether a success or a failure, his memory lives on.

Mrs. Howard has contributed greatly in the interest of local history. She is well known as an amateur author who does a professional job in writing of the earlier days of DeKalb County. This is her fifth publication in five years, four of which were under the sponsorship of Landmarks of DeKalb County, Inc.

James F. Sulzby, Jr.
Past President and Current Secretary
Alabama Historical Association
Birmingham, Alabama

Scars Of Early Childhood

When Milford Wriarson Howard arrived as the first-born child of a poor north Georgia tenant farmer, Abraham Lincoln was serving his second year as president of a country torn by civil conflict. The date was December 18, 1862, less than a week after the Confederate victory at Fredericksburg and three days before the beginning of the long Battle of Murfreesboro, which was won by Union troops.

His father, Stephen Oliver Howard, was the son of Thomas and Elizabeth Howard, whose families had long eked out a living in the southern Appalachians. Poor non-slaveholders, with little formal education, the Howards nevertheless supported the Confederacy and several brothers marched off to war. But Stephen, lame since childhood, remained on a farm in Floyd County with his wife, Martha Maddry Howard. Martha, descended from the Maddry and Betts families of North Carolina, was a kind but high-strung, extremely sensitive woman. Stephen, however, was a stern religious zealot, embittered by the shackles of poverty and the pain of crippling rheumatism.

Milford loved and revered his mother, whom he described as having "the soul of an artist, the sweetness of a garden of roses . . . and the purity of a Madonna." He did not love his father, who was soon aware of his young son's lack of affection, as well as his rebelliousness against the austere disciplinarian.

Stephen Howard's word was the law of the family, with implicit obedience demanded at all times. His decrees were repeatedly enforced by unrelenting blows of the rod. "If I can't

11

make you love me," he often told his son when preparing to punish him, "I'll make you fear me." Many were the times when the spirited youngster returned from an encounter with his father, blood trickling down his legs below his long flannel shirt, as he sought tender comfort from his compassionate mother. Always she kissed away his tears and eased the pain; but the bitterness remained and the imaginative mind of the physically battered boy fashioned wild dreams of retribution and plans of revenge.

The silently suffering and uncomplaining mother was completely dominated by the dictatorial and uncompromising father, eight years younger than she. The youngest of a large family and always petted and spoiled as a child because of his physical affliction, Stephen had emerged the victor the one time Martha had expressed opposition to his wishes. When she, at the age of 29, declined to marry her 21 year old suitor,[1] the enraged young man, in a fit of frenzy, attempted to kill himself rather than accept her rejection. The prompt attention of a physician prevented Stephen's bleeding to death and he prevailed upon Martha to marry him after all, on February 18, 1862. He was never to be a good provider for his wife and the children they were to have. And he would become more bitter, cruel, and inflexible with the passing of time.

Memories of Milford's early childhood, which molded the complex man of later life, consisted primarily of sad and traumatic events. The psychological scars from his youth were to cause recurring periods of melancholia throughout his entire life. His chief defense against unpleasant periods or episodes—his escape by means of imaginative dreams—helped develop a very creative, but unrealistic person.

There was near tragedy. One of Milford's earliest memories was that of a three year old tumbling into the darkness of an open well, of sinking to the bottom of the cold water, of rising to the top and desperately grasping a board which protruded from the wall. Other children ran screaming to his mother, who was aided by neighbors in rescuing the drenched lad from his perilous predicament.

---

[1] *Stephen Oliver Howard was born July 21, 1840, Martha A. Maddry on July 4, 1832.*

There was chastisement. When only four years old, Milford was attending some sort of brief neighborhood school and studying the A B C's from the old blue-back speller. Momentary frustration on the part of the young scholar, combined with a nagging schoolmarm's wagging finger, brought about the sudden biting of the finger by the small boy. Escaping from the infuriated teacher, the confused and frightened child ran home where he was summarily punished by his father, who returned with him to school and proceeded to lash him again before the other pupils.

There was unnecessary punishment. To Milford's father, enjoyment and pleasure were synonymous with sin. Because of his son's fondness for butter and the great enjoyment he displayed while eating it, Stephen once attempted to bring an end to such pleasure by pushing the butter dish toward Milford and commanding him to eat it all. The boy soon felt he had had enough butter but his father remained adamant and insisted that he could not stop until he had finished. However, Stephen's action failed to have the desired effect, as butter remained one of Milford's favorite foods.

There was extreme disappointment. At the end of the war Milford often saw soldiers on the streets of Rome. He knew that these men in blue uniforms, carrying guns with bayonets, were Yankees and he had absorbed enough of the talk and emotions of the period to hate them and to revere those who had been Rebels. At this time, a big event in his life was the arrival of his Uncle Samuel Milford Jemison Howard, for whom he had been named, for a visit. A former Confederate captain, released not long before from prison at Johnson's Island, the older Milford was the boy's idol. He listened to every word his 28 year old uncle spoke, learning some choice "cuss" words he had never heard before.

Milford's father and uncle decided to go fishing and the boy wanted to go with them more than he had ever wanted to do anything in all his life. His Uncle Milford wanted him to go and it was only a short distance to the river, but his father said no and could not be persuaded to change his mind. Milford had to stand in quiet rebellion at such a cruel injustice as the two men walked down the lane toward the river. Finally, he gave a loud, piercing scream in a last vain attempt to be permitted to join the men; but his father did not even look back.

The small barefoot boy was a forlorn figure as he tearfully watched the two men disappear from sight. Even his new cuss words could not adequately express his futile anger. But how could a little boy retaliate for the hurt caused by a great big man?

He ran down the dusty path to the orchard and struggled to break a large limb from an apple tree. Then he proceeded to give his father a dreadful whipping, a vicarious punishment by which he was suffering in his father's place. The rough limb battered his shoulder, his back and his bare legs until the flesh was torn and blood streamed down his legs. He fell exhausted to the ground, finally, mixing red soil with his blood and tears, a miserable and lonely four year old, already a victim of his ability to substitute visions for reality.

His mother found him there, and—gently lifting the dirty little head—mixed her tears with his.

And there was the suffering of others. When Milford was five years old his family migrated to Arkansas by means of a covered wagon. By this time there were two more children, Andrew, who was three years old,[1] and Ada, who was just a baby.[2] They traveled over the rough roads all day and camped by the way whenever night came, building a log fire on which the mother cooked the evening meal.

One night while Milford's mother was busy preparing the food, the tired and fretful baby began to cry. The father gruffly took command of the problem and undertook to stop the crying. The two boys were well aware of his method, but the babe in arms had not yet become acquainted with it. "You must always conquer a child," Stephen Howard often declared, "and after that you can control it." His method of conquering was to spank the child until it quit crying and this had been quite effective with Milford and Andrew.

On this occasion he decided that Ada was old enough to be "conquered" and he immediately set about his task. The mother pleaded in vain as Milford and Andrew silently wept and prayed and the determined father insisted that Ada must be

---

[1] *Silas Andrew was born February 9, 1865.*
[2] *Ada was born January 18, 1867.*

conquered. The spanking began, along with harsh commands to hush crying, but the screams grew louder and echoed through the darkness.

Finally supper was ready and the eager and distressed mother sought custody of the child at last. But even then the frenzied father continued to strike the child, feeling he must conquer her now that he had set out to do so. With a sickening ritual fervor, he spanked and commanded quiet—spanked and commanded, stopping only to order the others to eat while he completed the job. The two frightened boys and the anguished mother, unable to swallow any food, waited for what seemed like an eternity as the baby's screams gradually subsided and became heartbreaking, hysterical sobs. Then the father announced that his task was finished; he had now conquered all three of his children.

Life In Arkansas

Stephen Howard ended his western trek in the northeastern section of Arkansas in a desolate and almost abandoned town which had at one time served as the county seat of Randolph County. Six small houses in various stages of disrepair stood around the square where the remains of the old log courthouse gave silent testimony to livelier days gone by. This was Old Jackson, so named because of its antiquity, rather than as a differentiation between it and a "New Jackson." It was 12 miles from the new county seat and the nearest post office at Pocahontas.

Here, in rural Arkansas, Milford was to mature rapidly, contributing long hours of hard physical labor toward securing the family's bare necessities. He would obtain a small amount of "schooling," develop an intense desire for more knowledge, and choose his future profession. Here, he would suffer his greatest humiliation, experience a spiritual awakening climaxed by participation in a mass baptism in Spring River, and lose his heart to his first love. Milford learned much about life and people and also made discoveries about himself and his capabilities during the decade he lived in Arkansas. And all the while, he delved intermittently into the world of fantasy, which the pain and suffering of real life could not penetrate—fashioning at first images entertaining and amusing to a small boy, but gradually envisioning the more serious dreams of a young man.

Soon after the Howards had settled in one of the log

cabins which still had a roof on it, Stephen salvaged logs from the old courthouse to build a blacksmith shop. An expert at shoeing horses and making wagons, Howard ran a thriving business, for a few days at a time, when westward-moving wagon trains came through. He made the shoes and nails and shod many horses and mules headed for western Arkansas and Texas.

Milford soon had his own imaginary herd of horses, wild ones which he drove to the hills in the spring to fatten on the succulent grass. And in the fall he drove them back to the sheltered river bottom to feed on cane during the winter. This semi-annual roundup of his horses was a great event, which took place almost daily. For his saddle horse, he chose the wildest one, which was also the swiftest runner. He mounted his steed and went like the wind to overtake and lasso any horse in the herd. Often his favorite charger reared and plunged and threw Milford high in the air, or over a cliff. But always, he scrambled to his feet, seized the clamoring animal by the bit, and brought him to his knees. His brother Andrew was his constant companion, riding by his side on his own thoroughbred "stick" horse, which became real flesh and blood, with a sleek, glossy coat and distended nostrils and flashing eyes.

While attending his second—and last—three month term of school at Old Jackson, Milford acquired a nickname which stayed with him until he left Arkansas. His mother, who spun the thread, wove the cloth and made all the family's clothing, had saved enough white cotton from some other purpose to make Milford some trousers, then called "britches." Rather than have white ones, he gathered some walnut hulls and persuaded his mother to dye them. The pants came out an unusually bright yellow or "yaller," and as he appeared on the school grounds the other boys began to sing and shout, "Yaller Jacket! Yaller Jacket!"

During noon recesses at the brief and infrequent school sessions, the boys played town ball, bull pen, and chase the fox, while the girls played hide the switch, prisoner's base and William Trimbletoe until the schoolmaster shouted, "Books! Come to books!"

A special program was always presented at the end of school and Milford appeared in his "yaller britches" on the last day of this session to recite a poem. Stepping out on the improvised platform with heavy feet, numb limbs and a pounding head, he cleared his throat and began with a voice which sounded hollow and far away:

You would scarce expect one of my age,
To speak in public on the stage.

Looking about him wildly, he doubted very much that anyone did.

And if I should chance to fall below
Demosthenes or Cicero
Don't view me with a critic's eye
But pass my imperfections by.

He realized that he was, without a doubt, falling far below these famous orators. In fact he seemed to be falling down a great yawning chasm, but he made a desperate attempt to continue.

Tall oaks from little acorns grow—grow—grow
Tall oaks from little acorns—acorns—acorns . . . . .

Surely he would reach the bottom of the chasm. His head spun. He stopped and stood still for ages as the room appeared to become dark. Then it was suddenly bright again and from the sea of grinning faces arose a burst of laughter. In a trembling voice he mechanically started again:

You would scarce expect one of my age
To speak in public on the stage.
Tall oaks from little acorns grow . . . . . .

He floundered once more, giving up in despair. Never again, throughout his many periods of sadness and tragedy would he feel quite the anguish of that moment as he ran through an audience rocked with laughter and fled from the building feeling shamed and disgraced. Little would he have dreamed—later as he lay crying upon his trundle bed—that he would one day become a famous speaker and lecturer, favorably compared with the best orator of his time—William Jennings Bryan, and featured on the same platform with Clarence Darrow. But he would never become completely free of the terrible pangs of stagefright which the "Yaller Jacket" suffered at Old Jackson.

The six months of schooling Milford had acquired at the age of 14 had aroused an insatiable thirst for knowledge and a deep longing for the opportunity of a formal education. But the only books he had access to at this time were a blue-back speller, a McGuffey's Reader, the Bible, and a hymn book. Around 1870 a star route was established which provided Old Jackson with mail delivery twice a week. Milford's father was appointed postmaster and kept the office in their home. This provided Milford with a new source of reading material, as he eagerly devoured all the sample papers, periodicals, and advertisements which arrived at the new post office.

Stephen Howard "felt the call to preach" while at Old Jackson and became an ordained Baptist minister. The Howard home became the religious center of the community and Milford's attention became focused upon the Bible. Martha Howard organized a Sunday School and Milford joined the other children in spending the whole Sabbath each week at the little school house a mile from the Howard home. There were Bible study and hymn singing in the morning and lessons from the blue-back speller after lunch.

In learning Bible verses to recite on Sunday mornings, Milford made the discovery that he had the very unusual ability of being able to memorize whole chapters without difficulty. The more he committed to memory, the easier the process became. During the summer nights he read and memorized by the light of a tallow candle; in the winter it was a pine knot blaze. His daylight hours were used for work and not for study, but the nights were his own. He was excited by the scope and power of his memory and cherished it with a secret joy. He could read a section of the Bible, close it and repeat it almost *verbatim* after a single reading. He read chapter after chapter and lay awake after going to bed, silently repeating what he had memorized. In this manner he secretly memorized enough Bible verses to amaze his mother at Sunday School by reciting one morning for about two hours without stopping. Before long he had memorized the four Gospels of Matthew, Mark, Luke, and John, hundreds of hymns and all the reading matter in the speller, in addition to learning how to spell all the words.

During this period of intense Bible study Milford had many deeply religious experiences which played a significant role in shaping his character and personality. When he was 12 he joined the Baptist Church at a brush arbor revival conducted by a traveling evangelist and was the youngest of a large number of repenters who were baptized at Imboden Ford on Spring River. Yet he soon found the fundamentalist tenets of the primitive Baptist Church in conflict with his own view of a loving and compassionate deity. His variance with the narrow beliefs taught during his childhood formed the basis for recurring periods of questioning and doubt which at one time brought him near agnosticism before he returned to the faith of his childhood. In religion as in political and social philosophy, Milford Howard was ever the irrepressible rebel.

The six months of school and his study of the Bible, the hymn book and the blue-back speller constituted Milford's "book learning" up to the age of 15. But he was also learning a lot from "the school of hard knocks."

Though Stephen Howard worked hard, he was a poor manager and received nothing for his work as a minister so the family was always wretchedly poor. Martha found time to do religious work, along with all her demanding household chores, and gave birth to three more children. Wallace Warren was born July 8, 1870, William Edgar on October 14, 1872, and Octie Eugenia March 15, 1875. Unfortunately Martha's frail body was not as strong as her will and she became a semi-invalid.

Malaria was common in their section of the state of Arkansas and sore eyes raged as a regular epidemic. Quinine and Thompson's Eye Water were two popular medicines used by the Howards, who were sometimes all confined to their beds at the same time.

Milford began hard physical labor at an early age and was blowing the bellows and striking with a sledge hammer in his father's blacksmith shop even when he had to stand on a large block of wood to reach the anvil. When he was 11 and Andrew was nine, they made a two-horse crop. Milford also helped with the washing and ironing in order to lighten the load of his failing mother. During the cold winter of 1874, when Milford was 12, he got a job at a cotton gin and walked the mile to work and back in early mornings and late afternoons. His 30 cents a day salary was collected by his father in goods at the store of the merchant who owned the gin.

During the summers Milford and Andrew worked like two grown men at their crops but they remained boys at heart and engaged in frequent skinny dipping in Spring River. They also became very adept at bareback riding and would stand with their bare feet on their horses' backs while galloping them full speed down Old Jackson's only street. The boys waved their hats and yelled like Indians to the startled inhabitants of the little community. But such happy experiences were far outnumbered by sad and tragic episodes during these years.

The single saddest memory of Milford's childhood which always stood out for its tragic pathos, as no other incident ever did, was that of Christmas eve, 1873. Seemingly always in dire poverty, the Howards were at this time without any money, and almost without food. The younger children had talked for weeks about Santa Claus and had hung their stockings, quite certain they would be filled. Their mother, who always worked at spinning or mending until late into the night, sat for hours this Christmas eve before the big log fire. Milford feigned sleep as his beloved mother, weary from toil and worry, read the Bible and then, with tears on her cheeks, kissed his brow as she stooped to see whether he was asleep. Then, going to the nearly-empty flour barrel, she scooped all that remained, added the other ingredients, and carefully kneaded some dough. Adding some home-made sorghum, she patted out little round cakes. Milford peeped with one eye as she pulled live coals from the hearth, placed a small oven with the cakes inside on the coals, piling more on top, and then sat down to wait for the cakes to bake. When they were done, she put one in each stocking, put the oven back in place, swept the embers from the hearth and quietly slipped into bed.

The next morning Milford arose first to "discover" the wonderful sweets—made by Santa's wife just for them and boasted to his brothers and his sister that they must be especially favored to receive such a treat. The younger children appeared to be happy with their presents and Milford's mother tenderly placed her hand on his head, giving him a look of deep gratitude which he would not have exchanged for all the plaudits of the world.

In 1875, when Andrew was 11 years old, he suffered an accident which permanently impaired his health and eventually brought about his death when he was a young man. He and Milford had gone to the field with their father for a load of seed cotton and were on their way to the gin with their father driving the team of horses. As the two brothers and close companions lay on their backs on the cotton, imagining what they could see with their eyes closed, there was a sudden lurch of the wagon as one side dropped into a deep rut. Milford heard an anguished scream from his father and opened his eyes to see that Andrew was gone. Leaping from the wagon, he raced up the hill toward the crushed, still body which the wagon had passed over. Before his father could get there, he had lifted Andrew in his strong arms and was screaming his brother's name into a pale, expressionless face. They quickly placed Andrew in the wagon and as his father drove rapidly home, Milford held his brother, talking to him, praying and sobbing. There was no sound from Andrew except a heartbreaking moan.

The nearest doctor, summoned from 12 miles away by horseback, arrived after several hours and pronounced that the lad might live. However, all the ribs were broken loose from the breast bone on one side and might be pressing against the lungs and the doctor feared serious consequences. Though the unfortunate boy recuperated, he was to grow up appearing deformed, with one side of his chest caved in and would develop the dreaded tuberculosis some years later.

When Milford was about 13, a seemingly insignificant incident occurred which fired his lively imagination to new heights and determined his future career. Among the hodge-podge of jobs undertaken by Stephen Howard was that of justice of the peace at Old Jackson. During the winter of 1875, two neighbors, engaged in some sort of legal conflict, had hired lawyers from Pocahontas to handle their cases in Howard's court. The weather was bitter cold and the only suitable building, adequately large and warm to hold the expected crowd, was the gin where Milford was working. Court was held, therefore, on the second floor of the cotton gin, with spectators sitting on a pile of cotton seed. Milford was allowed to attend the unusual trial where his father presided with sternness and dignity from his seat upon a wool sack. The technical aspects of the case made no impression whatever on the young ginner but the personal appearance of the lawyers, in their store-bought clothes, and the eloquence of their speeches, held him spellbound. Listening enraptured to every word, noticing every intonation of voice, and following each gesture, Milford forgot all about poverty, forgot time and place, and for one brief hour enjoyed life as few boys ever do.

When the impressive men concluded their arguments, Milford left without waiting for the verdict, flying home on eagle's wings, with his mind racing madly, his imagination aflame, feeling a new inner power, an ability to reach any height. He announced to his mother that he was going to be a lawyer and the fledgling barrister began at once to try cases in an imaginary court. Though he had never seen a courthouse, a judge or jury, he drew mental pictures of himself making such persuasive appeals that jury members shed tears and even the judge on the bench had great difficulty in controlling his emotions.

Never for a moment would he ever doubt that he would one day stand before real judges and juries. Never would he lose the vision he caught that day in the old gin house in Arkansas. An ignorant country boy, without any prospect of getting an education, would become a member of the learned legal profession; there would be no difficulties or obstacles too great to overcome.

Milford practiced on the trees, the corn and the cotton fields, the horses, mules and cows, even on the blue sky and the twinkling stars. They all succumbed to his eloquence and logic as he continued his imaginary forensic battles until his father decided to return to Georgia in the fall of 1876.

Martha Howard was happy with the decision, as she longed for the red hills of northern Georgia and the scenes of her childhood. Most of the children were also enthusiastic over the prospect of moving. But 14 year old Milford was downcast and dejected at the thought of going away, never to see a certain person again.

She was his first love; she was 16 and her name was Sally

23

Phillips. He had fallen madly in love with her during their last three months school and she had often smiled at him from behind her book, sometimes even winking slyly. This had been the extent of their courtship. Still, Milford knew, with all the positiveness of a teen-aged boy, that she was the one girl in all the world for him. His imaginary law practice fell off and he closed his office, hanging out a sign which read, "Died of a broken heart."

He could talk to no one about his terrible problem. Finally he summoned the courage to write the object of his affection, telling her the cause of a boy's broken heart. He promised to write her often and asked her to wait until he became a lawyer and could return to make her his wife. Carefully hiding the letter, he awaited an opportunity to send it to Sally. He was never to have the opportunity. The letter disappeared and Milford had a dreadful feeling that it would fall into the hands of his father—which is what had happened after his sister Ada had found it.

A week passed while Stephen Howard quietly observed Milford's restless anxiety. Then he called everyone into the family circle one night after supper, cleared his throat and slowly drew the paper from his pocket as his son's face reddened. The father announced that he had an important matter to present to the family and proceeded deliberately and cruelly to read all the words which had poured forth in a passionate torrent from a young boy's heart, as his younger brothers and Ada giggled and his mother shared his suffering.

During the next few days Milford's brothers and sister tormented him by repeating an ardent expression of love from the letter. He finally ended the agony by whipping them all, one at a time, and then licking them all again until they promised not to tell on him. However, Sally never saw the letter and never knew of his love for her.

Milford helped load the covered wagon and the Howards were soon on their way back to Pleasant Valley, in north Georgia, with no more in material possessions than they had when they left a decade earlier. The number of children had increased from three to six and his mother's health had been permanently broken. His father had become an ordained minister, though he exercised his calling only spasmodically and

24

would not preach at all during the last twenty years of his life.

There was one member of the Howard family, though, whose life had been profoundly affected by the time spent in Arkansas and his experiences there. Milford had met Sally Phillips; he had had a brush arbor conversion, and had seen the two lawyers wearing store-bought clothes. At 14, he had chosen his profession and looked toward a bright, exciting future, though he had already suffered periods of depression and melancholy.

Upon reaching the Mississippi River, the tired travelers crossed the water on a steam operated ferry boat and camped near a railroad just outside of Memphis. During the night Milford heard a train for the first time in his life and stood in the dark watching the moving lights and listening to the puffing of the engine. The next morning Milford and Andrew listened to the singing of the telegraph wires and wondered if they could throw a stick and knock the messages off the wire, then pick them up and read them. Milford tried it, striking the wire with such a resounding blow that they became frightened. Deciding that the noise might be heard in Memphis or New York and a man sent by telegraph to catch them, they ran away as fast as their heels would go.

At last the Howards reached Georgia and there was great rejoicing on the part of everyone except Milford. He told no one of his sadness, but secretly grieved over the shattering of a beautiful dream. He knew that he had left Sally Phillips, as well as the "Yaller Jacket," behind forever.

Becoming A Lawyer

After the Howards' return to Georgia in 1876, Milford was to spend four grueling years helping his father farm. Cutting wood, building fires, shucking corn and feeding stock, milking cows and performing other regular chores before daylight, he then put in a man's work in the fields. But he never lost sight of his dream of being a lawyer and deeply longed to add to his six months of schooling. However, most of his education was to be gained through private reading and by his stubborn efforts to gain knowledge at every opportunity.

The Howards lived for a year at the old Maddry homestead, on a rather poor and neglected farm which was Martha's unmarried sister's home. Stephen and the boys went to work turning land, hauling leaves from the woods to make compost, clearing out sassafras thickets, filling gullies, rebuilding fences and making other repairs. With the coming of spring, their first crop was planted, with Milford, who was already tall and strong at 14, assuming the heaviest chores. His literary achievement for the year was the reading of Dickens' *Bleak House* and Bunyan's *Pilgrim's Progress*. The battered old copy of *Bleak House*, with the title page and first chapter missing, was a surprising discovery in a house where the reading of fiction was considered wicked and sinful. It was a number of years before Milford would know who the author of this fascinating book was, but he acquired a taste for Dickens' writing from his surreptitious reading of this volume. He also read with real enjoyment and appreciation the copy of *Pilgrim's Progress* which had been in his mother's family for many years.

After the crop was "laid by" in the fall of 1877, Milford's father leased a threshing machine which they used for wheat and oats throughout the community in order to add to their meager farm income. While engaged in this work, Milford chanced to meet Julia Boyd, the beautiful daughter of a country doctor, and Julia soon took Sally's place in his affections. However, his bashfulness prevented his giving any indication of his admiration for her. Indeed, his painful timidity at this age was of increasing concern to him.

In 1878, Stephen bought a farm on credit, hoping to raise enough cotton to make payments on the land and to feed and clothe his family. Milford worked harder than ever but realized that, at age 17, time was running out for his chance to continue his education. He persuaded his father to let him attend another three months school three miles from their home after the crop was finished.

The big barefoot boy walked the three miles each way gladly. He was so anxious to study, so eager to learn, that a kind and intelligent Professor Lawson took a special interest in him, lending prized books from his personal library to this avid reader. Milford's gratitude was boundless upon being permitted to keep indefinitely a large leatherbound copy of *Shakespeare's Complete Works*. Long after the others were asleep, he read by the light of a pine-knot blaze and explored a storehouse of wisdom and dreams in a new world far from the poverty of his life on the farm.

At the close of the short school term Milford delivered "Mark Antony's Oration Over the Dead Body of Caesar" and was pleased that he was much more successful than with his previous effort at "Tall Oaks From Little Acorns Grow." He even gained the confidence to write a letter to his beautiful, stately Julia Boyd, telling her of his admiration, of his ambitious plan to be a lawyer and asking the favor of a reply. He was quite chagrined at her failure to answer and became all the more determined to be an outstanding success. Some day the haughty Julia would be proud to say she knew him during his early struggles!

The first cotton crop on the new farm fell short of expectations and the Howards were unable to make their payments, but were given a year's extension. Milford slaved away by day, in his old handmade clothes, going barefoot except during the coldest weather, to help his father pay for a home. He was still dwelling in two distinctly different worlds, one filled with work and poverty and the other a land of books and dreams.

After completing the ponderous Shakespeare volume, Milford borrowed a large book of Blair's lectures on rhetoric, then a copy of Burns' poems and letters. He memorized much of Burns' poetry and would later quote him often during speeches and in his writing. Along with his literary pursuits during this period, he also nurtured a fledgling neighborhood debating society which he had organized and for which others showed little sustained interest.

With a total of nine months' schooling behind him, Milford had the opportunity in the fall of 1880 to begin another three months term. Weighing 175 pounds, the six-foot boy still had to walk to school barefoot, wearing a homemade shirt and pair of trousers, held up by suspenders his mother had made from cotton cloth. Yet the big fellow strode down the road with a buoyant spirit, the happiest young man around, for two reasons. One of the reasons was a sweet, demure little girl named Mattie Taylor, who had recently taken the place in his heart scorned by Julia Boyd. He never told her of his love, presuming that she and the whole world must know of it. He was filled with joy, too, at returning to school to learn more from the textbooks he had studied by himself since the last term. He had even obtained a Latin book and had taught himself quite a vocabulary of words, including *amo, amas, amat*, which to him meant Mattie Taylor.

Three weeks before this school ended, Milford's father shattered his state of euphoria by abruptly announcing one night that the fodder was ready to pull and his help was expected the next day. Just that afternoon Milford had said good-by to Mattie at the forks of the road, thinking how fortunate he was to be completing his fourth three month school session. It was not fair that this should be denied him! Shedding bitter tears that night, an act he would repeat often during his life, he determined to leave home and work somewhere so he could go to school and get an education. The next morning he announced his plans to his mother, who became so upset that he abandoned the idea of leaving home and went to the fodder field instead.

In spite of all their work, however, Milford's father found that he still could not make his land payments that year and have any money left for necessities. The sympathetic landowner agreed to take the land back, to cancel Stephen Howard's debts, and even to charge no rent for the two years he had farmed. As he now had a little money left from the crop, Milford's father consented to let him attend the Hearn School of Cave Spring during the winter, if he would walk the four miles back and forth rather than pay board. No tuition was charged for a minister's son, so this meant that his only expenses would be for books.

On cold and icy mornings Milford arose before daylight to make fires and feed the stock, eat breakfast and then gladly walk the four miles to school. He soon found, however, that he was ill prepared for the courses in which he had enrolled. He gamely struggled for four months with Greek, Latin, English, algebra, geometry, and analytical arithmetic before his father moved to a tenant farm fifteen miles from Cedartown.

By cotton planting time Milford had decided that he could never hope to get an education by attending school, that he would have to read law at home while making a crop if he ever became a lawyer. He had heard of an outstanding Cedartown lawyer, Major Joseph A. Blance, who had lost an arm while serving as a major in the Confederate army. He determined to go to see Major Blance as soon as possible to solicit his help.

The next Friday a heavy rain fell and Milford knew it would be too wet to plow the next day. He got his father's permission to go to Cedartown and early Saturday morning began a great adventure by walking the three miles to Cave Spring before the stores opened. Here, he looked up a Mr. Tilley who carried mail to Cedartown and talked him into letting him drive his hack that day. He was to leave the team at a livery stable to be fed while he spent several hours in Cedartown before bringing the return mail back. With a great deal of joy and excitement, Milford drew rein and set out for Cedartown. He had never been there before, had never been inside a lawyer's office or courthouse, had never seen a law book. He had no idea as to the course of reading required for admission to the bar. But at last he was taking his first step toward becoming a lawyer.

Upon reaching Cedartown, Milford left the mail bags at the post office and fed his horses at the stable. Then he found the law office he sought and soon found himself trembling with excitement as he stood before Major Blance. He was impressed immediately by the kind and gentle voice of the man who greeted him and offered him a chair. When asked, "What can I do for you?" Milford answered without hesitation, "I want to read law, Major Blance. Will you please lend me the books and examine me occasionally on what I read?"

The major silently visualized the gawky country boy, clad in homespun clothes and brogan shoes, reading law. With a slight twinkle in his eye he began, in a kindly manner, to ask questions intended to reveal the impossibility of Milford's entering the legal profession. "How much education have you had? Does your father own his farm?" These and other questions elicited answers which satisfied the lawyer that he would give the right advice.

He admonished Milford to give up his foolish dream. A boy who had attended school less than two years, whose father was poor, who had no chance of going to school or college could not succeed at law, even if he could get admitted to the bar. He would starve. The major admired his ambition but would be doing him a cruel injustice, he said, if he encouraged him. A warm-hearted emotional man, he blinked back a tear as he saw the boy's disappointment as he talked. He arose from his seat, as a signal to end the conversation. "Don't you think I'm right?" he asked.

Milford stood groping for words. He wanted to tell the major that he had read the works of Shakespeare, the immortal poems of Burns, the classic *Pilgrim's Progress*, that he had memorized the four gospels of Matthew, Mark, Luke and John and a hundred grand old hymns, that he could spell every word in the blue-back speller, that he was not totally ignorant. He wished he were able to express his desire to be a lawyer. If the major only knew that he had already been a lawyer since he was twelve, that he had tried hundreds of cases and delivered the most eloquent of orations, that he had kept debating societies going so he could give expression to something struggling inside him. But he was yet too timid to make these revelations to a stranger who thought him merely a yokel.

He stammered determinedly, "Major Blance, I—I'm going to read law. Will you lend me the books if I will take good care of them?"

"You mean you still want to read law?" the astonished man asked.

"More than ever!" Milford answered.

"Then perhaps I am wrong," he admitted. "Yes, I will lend you the books, and help you in any other way I can, if I see that you're succeeding."

They then agreed that Milford would return two weeks from that day, if his father would allow him to, for his first examination, and he left carrying the first volume of *Blackstone's Commentaries*, happier than he had ever been before.

The sky became overcast and Milford rode against a steady rain most of the way back to Cave Spring where Mr. Tilley willingly promised to let him drive the mail again in two weeks. Gray skies gave way to darkness by the time he was half way home and he stumbled blindly through the darkness in mud up to his ankles for the last two miles. All the time he held tightly to the precious volume of Blackstone, wrapped securely in a piece of oil cloth and felt as though he were marching triumphantly to an enchanted land.

His mother smiled happily as Milford showed her the book and exuberantly recounted the day's events. He quickly ate the supper she had kept warm for him, opened his new treasure, and began to read. His excitement grew as he turned page after page. Instead of being dry and difficult to understand, it was interesting and easy. He marveled at the beautiful, smooth flowing English as the author traced the foundation and development of English common law. It was more fascinating than any fiction he had ever read and it was midnight before he realized it. He had already read a hundred pages of Blackstone.

Major Blance had suggested that he write down the legal principles formulated by Blackstone and familiarize himself with them. Having no money to buy blank note books, Milford obtained a number of free patent medicine booklets from the proprietor of the drug store. On one side of the pages were "before and after taking" pictures, with one side blank for the druggist to make notes. One of these little booklets would fit perfectly in his trousers pocket while he plowed. At the end of each row, while the mule turned around, he grabbed the booklet and read over a principle. By the time he reached the other end of the row, he was not only familiar with it, but knew it *verbatim ad literatim*. Each night he read until his father ordered him to bed and the next day he memorized what he had written the night before. On Sundays he sought the solitude of the woods and read Blackstone all day.

After two weeks of intensive study, Milford so impressed his father with his first knowledge of law that he was given permission to go back to Cedartown. He could hardly wait to receive his examination that Saturday. Major Blance asked how much he had read and was incredulous at the answer.

The major sat down and began slowly and patiently phrasing some questions, which were answered quickly and exactly. Then he started firing questions in rapid succession as Milford shot the answers back, the words fairly tumbling out. He knew every word of it and had repeated it a hundred times as he had followed his mule across the cotton field. For an hour he was questioned and he answered eagerly.

"My boy, have you done anything besides read Blackstone for these two weeks?" the major asked, after complimenting him.

"Yes, sir. I have plowed every day, except on Sunday," Milford answered.

"I don't understand it. But I'm proud of you," he said, rising and shaking Milford's hand firmly.

After Blackstone, Milford studied *Greenleaf on Evidence*, pursuing the same method of study, memorizing every rule of evidence until he could close the book and repeat the rules in the order they appeared. Then he mastered *Stephen on Pleading*.

By November, with most of the crops gathered, Milford began thinking about a place to begin his practice after he had been admitted to the bar. During the summer his father had made a trip to Sand Mountain in north Alabama, where he had rented a farm for the next year. He had spent one night in Fort Payne, the new county seat of DeKalb County, and had learned there were only three lawyers there, two brothers in one firm and one without a partner. His father did not remember the lawyer's name, but Milford decided he would go into partnership with this man he had never seen and whose name he did not know.

The rest of the family would be moving to the new farm, located only twenty miles from Fort Payne, around January. They all agreed that Milford should go as soon as possible and get established by the time the others reached their new home. Stephen Howard bought his son a new suit, the first "store-bought" clothes he had ever had and gave him $30.

At noon on November 6,1880, Milford bade his mother, brothers and sisters good-by and left in a buggy with his father, planning to spend the night with a relative in Cherokee County. At dusk, as they passed through the little village of Centre, with its antiquated courthouse and jail, Milford wondered if the men in front of the courthouse were lawyers.

Late in the afternoon on November 7, they arrived in Fort Payne and spent the night at a boarding house run by a man named Payne, who was also the postmaster. The next morning Milford's father left for home and left him alone in this strange town where he knew no one, with $30, the suit of clothes he had on, and the little bundle packed by his mother which contained shirts, underwear, handkerchiefs, a comb, a brush, and a Bible.

Room and board was $10 per month but the landlord agreed to charge Milford only $25 for three months, if he would pay in advance. By a strange coincidence, chancery court would convene in Fort Payne on January 7, 1882, and he could be examined for admission to the bar at the end of three months.

Sheriff Pat Frazier, a popular Irishman, and other county officials made him feel welcome at Fort Payne. The sheriff's cousin, L.A. Dobbs, was the lawyer without a partner and had quite a lucrative practice for that time. The two other attorneys, Wallace Jehu Haralson and Henry C. Haralson were the brothers, the senior member of the firm having served as judge of the circuit court for two terms.

Milford talked to Colonel Dobbs about his ambition to become a lawyer and secured his permission to use his office and law books, for which Milford would make fires, clean the office and make himself useful whenever possible. As Colonel Dobbs advised him to study the statutory law of Alabama, Milford spent much of his time studying the code.

Fort Payne had four or five small stores, a printing office, a railroad depot, and several dozen houses. It didn't take the dashing prospective attorney long to meet most of the people, including some attractive young girls. But his heart was still back in Georgia with Mattie Taylor, whom he had not seen in over a year.

He decided to write a letter, which would be a master-piece, revealing a heart aflame with divine passion for her. Then she could respond with an expression of the love that had been pent up in her heart for months. He wrote her, telling of the great love he had nursed all this time, until he could obtain a high goal. He told her he would be a lawyer in a short time and could offer her security along with his love.

Many days later he received a sweet little letter, telling him she appreciated his love, of which she had never had the slightest suspicion, and that she would shortly be married to one of the most prosperous young farmers of the community. As he finished reading, the big homesick boy sat down and cried for his mother.

Milford managed to pass the three lonely months by studying hard for the bar examination and also by reading some borrowed books, including *The Adventures of Tom Sawyer* and *Ivanhoe*. When the chancery court convened at Fort Payne on January 7, 1881, Milford Howard, who had observed his nineteenth birthday the month before, applied for admission to the Alabama state bar, and became one of the youngest men ever admitted.

Chancellor Graham, who presided, appointed a Mr. Dunlap of Gadsden and a Mr. Phelan of Chattanooga, along with Milford's sponsor, Colonel Dobbs, to examine him. Beginning with his usual timidity and stage fright, the young applicant answered five or six questions hesitatingly but correctly before gaining confidence and answering quickly in a strong, clear voice. At the conclusion of a conscientious examination on the general principles of law and equity and the rules of pleading and practice, Milford was heartily congratulated by the chancellor and members of the bar. Then he took the oath of an attorney, which had been prepared by Thomas H. Smith, register in chancery, and also editor and proprietor of the Fort Payne *Journal*.

Leaving the two-story brick courthouse, Milford strode briskly against the cold winter wind, nodding happily to new acquaintances on Main Street and pausing to hand a bent woman beggar his last coin. A bright gleam had replaced the sad, haunted look in his eyes; a cocky tilt of his head and a swaggering gait supplanted for the moment the inferiority complex which plagued him. He had now realized his greatest dream. What did it matter at that moment that he was a lawyer without a penny or a single client and whose paid board expired that very day?

Milford And Sally

Lacking even a postage stamp to send his mother the good news that her son was a full-fledged lawyer, Milford conceived a proposition to make to the postmaster. He would meet the train twice a day, carrying mail to and from Payne's office in the courthouse, in return for stamps. The proposal was readily agreed to by Postmaster Payne, who gave him enough stamps in advance to mail a letter to his family.

His next problem of finding a place to live was solved through the generosity of "Uncle" Jimmy Hawkins, who lived east of Fort Payne at the base of Lookout Mountain at what was later known as Hawkins' Spring. Milford was invited to join Hawkins, his wife and their four children, Ben, Jim, Susie, and Ruth, at their home, a big two-story farm house. Here he was treated as one of the family for several months while he paid them whatever he could collect in small fees for his board. When not at work Milford often enjoyed hunting trips with the boys, tracking raccoons, squirrels, and rabbits over the mountainside and occasionally shooting at wild goats which lived in the bluffs and gorges.

Another enjoyable pastime was visiting with Thomas Smith, the intellectual newspaper editor who owned the best library in Fort Payne. They spent many a glorious evening discussing literature and reading aloud their favorite poems by Burns. Then Milford would depart with several selected books to enjoy at leisure until he called on his friend again.

Always a keen observer of the opposite sex, Milford took

special notice of all eligible females in Fort Payne. One day as he stood in the doorway of the courthouse, an attractive, slender 15 year old girl bounded up the steps and looked around in an uncertain manner. As he stood admiring the gorgeous creature's spun-gold hair and luminous deep brown eyes, she shyly asked him where the post office was located, saying she had not been there since it had been moved to the courthouse. Milford gallantly offered to show her where it was and stood by rather awkwardly as she asked if there were any mail for Sally Lankford. He then introduced himself and was flattered to learn that she had heard of him. He was also enraptured by her vibrant, musical voice and her glorious expressive eyes and knew instantly that she was the most wonderful girl in the world.

Milford walked down Main Street with Sally, making a conscious effort to match her short steps with his own long legs, as he inquired as to where she lived. Luckily, she lived some distance south of Fort Payne, giving him time to become better acquainted. They reached the railroad and continued walking down the track for a mile, a simple, unsophisticated young couple engaged in rapt conversation. He learned that her mother had died when Sally was three years old, that her father had gone west and remarried, leaving her and her two brothers, Bob and Jeff, with their Grandmother and Grandfather Griffith and their Aunt Nannie Griffith. They lived on a small farm which provided few advantages for a teenaged girl, but Sally impressed him as a person of brilliant mentality and natural refinement. He was completely captivated by the time they reached the trail which led to her home on a high hill. He watched as she stepped lightly up the path, looking back at him once before turning with a blush to disappear on a winding path through a pine thicket.

Their courtship was to last almost two years while Milford sought to improve his financial affairs. When he first asked her to be his wife, Sally confided that she had known the first time they met that she would marry him. She was completely willing to wait for him to build his law practice.

Colonel Dobbs had taken Milford into his office promising nothing definite other than whatever small cases he didn't want himself. Such assignments often included trifling cases in country justice courts which required him to walk fifteen or

37

twenty miles to court and back. Meanwhile, Colonel Dobbs was helping him make acquaintances in the area and to build his own practice. He would never forget the kindness of this benefactor.

Colonel L. A. Dobbs was a large, nice looking man of middle age, who had served four years in the Confederate army, spending the last months of the war in a federal prison. He, too, was a self-educated man, as well as a truly generous person and he was more than fair in his dealing with the young man who had gained his sympathy and friendship when he first sought help.

By the winter of 1882, Milford felt he was prospering sufficiently to move back to town, where he obtained room and board at the Wills Valley Hotel, operated by Mrs. Sophie Ward. Though she catered to traveling men, whom she charged $2.00 per day, Milford paid only $10 a month and was not required to pay in advance. Even then, it was sometimes difficult to keep the landlady paid. On one occasion, he had to walk three miles before daylight to borrow Sheriff Frazier's horse and then ride to Valley Head to track down a client who owed him $10 before finally returning late at night, tired and hungry, to pay Mrs. Ward on the last day of the month.

Before long, Colonel Dobbs had his office stationery inscribed "Dobbs and Howard, Attorneys and Counselors at Law," and admitted Milford to a nominal partnership with no stipulated division of fees. About the same time, Milford's name appeared in the Fort Payne *Journal* as local editor on the page carrying Fort Payne news. His writing brought in no money at all, but increased his popularity with young people who enjoyed seeing their names in print.

Finally, after two difficult and lean years, Milford felt his financial position adequately improved for him to embark on the great adventure of marriage. On December 23, 1883, five days past his twenty-first birthday, Milford and 17 year old Sally took their wedding vows, blessed with good health, youth, enthusiasm and love. They rented the only available house in town at $4.00 a month. With only two rooms, it provided ample space for all they owned as they first set up housekeeping, feeling—in spite of their meager belongings—quite important.

After his marriage Milford was given a one-third division of all fees, which he considered a generous share, based on Colonel Dobbs' large and profitable clientele. Then, within two years, he was admitted as a full partner, with an equal share of fees. Each advancement came at his partner's suggestion, rather than at Milford's request.

During 1884, Milford and Sally bought a lot and built their own two-room house, planning to enlarge it when they could. Their family grew first, however, when his brown-eyed, golden-haired, girl-wife gave birth the following June to their first child, Clyde. Milford then bought a larger house which had been recently built and moved his wife and son to it.

Meanwhile, Stephen Howard had at last obtained a farm of his own by home-steading 160 acres on Sand Mountain, about 25 miles from Fort Payne. As it was located deep in the woods, Milford helped clear land, in addition to giving his family what financial help he could. Making life easier for his mother, father, brothers and sisters seemed to become an obsession with him as his income grew larger. After boarding Andrew while he attended school in Fort Payne for a year, Milford furnished him with money to start a small country store on their father's farm. He also helped care for Sally's grandparents during their last years.

Just as it appeared he might win his long war against poverty, tragedy began to strike. Clarence, their second son, died from a sudden illness in June, 1888, when he was only nine months old, leaving an ache in the young couple's hearts which remained even after the birth of their third son, Claude, two years later. Soon afterward Sally's beloved grandfather and grandmother died. Then one day a messenger brought word that Milford's sister, Ada, was very ill. Before they could drive their horses over 25 miles of country roads, she was already dead.

Milford also found tragedy and drama while pursuing his law practice. As he walked into the circuit clerk's office on February 22, 1884, H. C. Haralson was arguing with a client named Roe who suddenly lunged at his neck with a knife, severing his jugular vein. As Haralson fell, Milford caught his fellow lawyer and laid him on the floor. Then he ran after Roe, who dashed down the steps, jumped on his horse and sped toward Lookout Mountain before anyone could catch him. Though

Haralson died, his murderer was never apprehended.

A dramatic episode, with an ironic ending, occurred soon afterward at the old log jail in Fort Payne. One day Milford heard the prisoners shouting and creating a great disturbance. Rushing from the courthouse to the jail, he heard a prisoner cry that a man was hanging himself. He was a desperate outlaw named Tatum who had been jailed for horse stealing. The jailer was gone and by the time his wife found the keys for Milford to open the jail door, a crowd had gathered. The inside of Tatum's cell was so dark that no one else wanted to go in and urged Milford to wait for the sheriff. But Milford struck a match and stepped inside the room to peer into a hideous, distorted face with protruding eyes. Grabbing his knife from his pocket, he lifted the body with one arm and slashed at the rope with his free hand, carried the body out and laid it on the ground. The "body" suddenly showed signs of life, to his great surprise. Two local physicians soon appeared on the scene and worked with him for about an hour, finally reviving the shaken prisoner. Then Milford, who had been appointed county solicitor, successfully prosecuted the man for horse stealing and sent him to the penitentiary.

All this time Milford had nurtured his private world of books and dreams. As soon as he could afford them, he began buying books and planning a personal library of the world's best literature. One of his first acquisitions was a 15 volume set of Dickens, which cost less than $10. Then he obtained the works of Scott, Bulwer, Hugo, Balzac, Dumas, Hawthorne, and many others, as well as books of poetry, histories, biographies, and essays by Emerson and Carlyle. A rapid and omnivorous reader, Milford also continued his law studies and kept up with supreme court decisions. With his ability of almost total recall, he soon became the local "walking encyclopedia" of law.

His doting wife was swept along in Milford's overwhelming desire for culture and self improvement. She, too, had been denied the advantages of much schooling and he eagerly sought to help develop her intellectual faculties. For her literary advancement, he presented Sally with a beautiful volume of Milton and suggested that she memorize one of the great classic poems as an aid to her vocabulary and her memory development. As all cultured ladies should know music, he purchased a piano and contracted to pay Miss Nimmo Green $50 a month to live with them and instruct Sally in music.

She worked heroically at the piano and laboriously memorized lines from "Paradise Lost." At night after supper, she played her repertoire and recited Milton, sharing Milford's happiness at her accomplishment. Little did it matter to him that their natures were very different, their talents and interests far apart. Failing to consult her wishes, it was some time before he realized how difficult the music was for Sally, or how dull the sonorous lines of Milton. For a while he was happily blind and self contented, until his frustrated wife eventually laid Milton aside and closed the piano forever to spend more time with her two sons and to pursue her own interests in flowers and the great outdoors, in travel, in business enterprises—and in politics, which attracted them both.

The beginning of Milford's stormy political career came in December, 1886. After a special act of the legislature created the office of county solicitor for DeKalb County, Milford Howard became the first person to serve in this office when he was appointed to a four-year term by Governor Thomas Seay. He proved to be a vigorous prosecutor and prospered under the prevailing fee system, especially when an increased volume of criminal cases was brought on by Fort Payne's boom period.

Colonel Howard
And The Boom

In the autumn of 1887, before Howard reached his twenty-sixth birthday, he helped launch the great industrial boom at Fort Payne. With his aid and encouragement, northern investors made grand plans for a dream city, built as a manufacturing center in the midst of scenic beauty and bountiful supplies of coal and iron. As factories were built and the city began an astronomical growth, Howard's mind reeled at all the possibilities for financial fortunes. Along with wealthy speculators, he invested in a variety of business ventures, buying and spending with boundless zeal, becoming—for a brief, exhilarating period—a very rich young man. Then suddenly his fortune was lost, his dreams shattered and his heart embittered when the boom ended, with millions of dollars lost in a very costly and ill-advised Yankee venture.

Before the boom Fort Payne was a little country town with only two streets. One ran east and west from the courthouse to the depot, with the other crossing it and going from the jail northward to an open area known as Duncan Field. Nearly all the vacant lots belonged to Dr. A. B. Green, the original owner of most of the town property.

One day a stranger got off the train, stood for a few minutes looking over the few stores and dusty streets and walked toward the courthouse. He aroused considerable curiosity as he strode by in his immaculate clothes, a black Prince Albert coat, gray striped trousers and black homburg hat. He was Major C. O. Godfrey, age 55, of Taunton, Massachusetts, formerly chaplain of the Union army. He was looking for a certain lawyer he had heard of. As all southerners admitted to the bar during this period automatically received the honorary title of "Colonel," it was Colonel Milford Howard for whom he asked.

As he introduced himself in his crisp, New England accent, Colonel Howard looked down at the stocky, square shouldered man who was a foot shorter than he, grasped his chubby, stubby-fingered hand, and wondered what had brought him to Fort Payne. A distinguished looking man, with his glossy white hair, neat mustache and Van Dyke beard, Godfrey immediately impressed Howard as being a man of much culture and education. The major's large blue eyes peered intently through thick glasses in a manner which indicated a serious and "all business" attitude. He spent little time on pleasantries and explained his promotional scheme.

John C. Gault, the general manager of the Queen and Crescent Railroad System running from Cincinnati to New Orleans was a personal friend of his, Godfrey said. It was he who had suggested Fort Payne as a possible site for an industrial town Godfrey wished to promote. He had already obtained, through Gault's influence, a 12 months option on several thousand acres of railroad lands which samples had proven to be rich in coal and iron. He needed an option on certain lands for 12 months in order to be sure of space for his town site.

Colonel Howard was thrilled with the whole startling idea and assured Godfrey he would help in any way he could. He was certain he could get options on most of the land, he told Godfrey, but the owners of the Duncan farm lived in Gadsden and could pose a problem. Upon being told that this property was the most essential part, Colonel Howard promised to go to Gadsden himself to negotiate for the option.

He made the trip and succeeded in obtaining the option, but had to pay $50 for it out of his own money. When he returned, proud of his accomplishment, Godfrey thanked him heartily, told him he would have lots of opportunities to make money, and left. Chagrined at his failure to get back his $50, Colonel Howard attempted to persuade Colonel Dobbs and also his brother, the local agent for railroad lands, to share his expense. But they jeered at their naive friend and reminded him that a fool and his money are soon parted. Then, as weeks and months went by, he took more razzing from acquaintances who predicted he would never see his "slick Yankee" again.

The 12 months option was nearly up and Howard was sick of being asked, "What do you think of the boom now, Colonel?" Then one morning a fast train sidetracked some sleeping cars and a diner from Boston and a group of expensively dressed, silk-hatted New England Yankees stepped off behind Major Godfrey. Colonel Howard was notified that they were ready to take up the options and start building the city. A vacant store room was quickly rented and improvised fixtures arranged for Fort Payne's first bank. New England businessmen were soon counting money out on empty crates and paying off options for land.

Colonel Howard was anxious to tell his wife the good news but he no longer lived near town, having recently traded his home and one-half interest in a store and livery barn for a beautiful farm several miles north of Fort Payne. At noon he raced his horse and buggy through the outskirts of town to his farm. After a quick lunch, Sally returned with him and joined a gathering crowd of curious onlookers outside the store-front bank.

Major C. O. Godfrey, former Congregationalist minister, now a financier and promoter of boom towns, was ready to build his industrial city. He had brought with him many wealthy business and professional men, mainly from New England. They included W. P. Rice, Kansas City banker, Henry B. Pierce, secretary of state of Massachusetts, and Governor D. H. Goodell, of New Hampshire. Thus it was, that in November, 1888, the Fort Payne Coal and Iron Company was organized, with Major Godfrey as manager.

The company's capital was established at $5,000,000, with $4,000,000 worth of stock being placed on the public market and sold in New England in less than five weeks. The city of Fort Payne was incorporated the following February and surveys were made for streets and parks on the company's 32,000 acres of land. Sites were chosen for two furnaces, a rolling mill, and many other industries as well as the huge DeKalb Hotel and Rice's Opera House.

The population rose from 500 to several thousand within a few months as speculators and laborers arrived on every train.

Temporary tents covered the ridges on both sides of town and two 30 room barracks were built by the company, as houses could not be built fast enough. The first year 13 miles of streets were graded and houses were started on streets before they were ever made.

Fort Payne became a New England city in the deep south. There was a New England Shoe Shop, a New England Barber Shop, and a New England Clothing Store. Lodging could be found at the New England House and medicine was sold at the New England Drug Store. The large park opposite the hotel was named Union Park and the first mayor of the new city was Massachusetts' illustrious Major Godfrey.

Real estate business was brisk and many older residents received fabulous prices for their property. It was a sellers' market and the "natives," as they were called, usually fared well at both ends of the boom. As an example, John B. Stetson, the hat manufacturer, paid John McCartney $11,000 for a lot and sold it back to him later for $100.

Colonel Howard joined the speculators. He began buying options on parcels of land and selling them at big profits to reinvest the money. Paying $40 a front foot for one lot on Main Street which he could have bought at $4.00 before the boom, he broke ground for a two-story brick, the first brick store building in Fort Payne. With feverish enthusiasm, he set about obtaining modern store fixtures, determined to own the best dry goods store between Chattanooga and Birmingham for his brother, Andrew, to run.

To help finance this enterprise, he sold most of his country estate except for his home and journeyed to New York with his wife, their small son Clyde, and Sally's Aunt Nannie, to buy stock for Howard Brothers. Adding pleasure to business, Colonel Howard included a few days' visit to Niagara Falls. He felt an overwhelming surge of excitement as the train raced through Canada, where he first stood upon foreign soil. They arrived late one August afternoon and the eager Alabamian hurried from his hotel on the American side to see the famous falls, standing in awe at the beauty and magnitude of the roaring giant until the shadows fell. Later, as he and Sally sat on a rustic park bench near the falls watching the moon climb higher and higher in a clear sky, Colonel Howard marveled at the thought of how his own personal fortunes had risen since he scrounged for a postage stamp less than nine years before.

After its $50,000 stock arrived in Fort Payne, the new store was soon filled with customers. Andrew, who had no previous business experience other than that of a few years in his small country store, employed a number of clerks who were equally inexperienced to help him. As everyone seemed to be prosperous in a town where money flowed freely, credit was granted for the asking, with hundreds of customers and thousands of dollars placed on the books. Cash fairly rolled in and most bills could be paid when they became due. It was still necessary at times for Colonel Howard to write checks to supplement the firm's bank account. Instead of realizing profits, he continued to furnish additional capital anytime his brother needed more money. Yet he took pride in the idea of building an establishment which would take care of his father's family and educate his brothers and sisters. In addition, there was the excitement of doing business on a grand scale—and the gratification of his enormous pride and vanity.

When a spacious ten-room house was offered for sale in Fort Payne, Colonel Howard bought and furnished it and moved the Howard family from their Sand Mountain farm to the new home. He then employed a servant so that his mother could at last be free from work and care. Then he placed Wallace, Edgar, and Octie in school.

Soon the indefatigable Colonel Howard was working 18 hours a day carrying on his law practice and running a real estate office for his land transactions. As part of his real estate business he handled the sales for the 262 lots in what is still known as the Thomas and Howard Addition, including Walnut, Cedar, Chestnut, Oak, and Pine Avenues and Thomas and Howard Streets in southeast Fort Payne. He also became involved in a number of the boom industries, serving as director for the Fort Payne Coal and Iron Company, the Journal Publishing Company, the Fort Payne and Eastern Railroad and the Fort Payne Basket and Package Company.

Becoming a compulsive speculator, Colonel Howard even invested in other boom towns, including Bridgeport, Alabama and Middlesboro, Kentucky. Then he organized a land and development company incorporated as the Pell City Company,

46

to buy out the "town" of Pell City, which consisted primarily of several hundred vacant lots and two hotels. In April, 1890, he became general manager of the company at $4,000 per year and left for Pell City to promote a manufacturing center there. In May his wife spent several weeks with him in his new location and commented favorably on the little town. By June, however, he had given up on his grand plans for Pell City and left for Fort Payne, with Howard Avenue[1] remaining as the only permanent reminder of his sojourn there.

Far from being discouraged over this business failure, he rushed into another, buying a corner lot on Main and Gault (later occupied by the Southern Hardware Company) for $200 per front foot. He paid two-thirds of the $20,000 in cash, giving a mortgage for the balance, and hired an architect to draw plans for a three-story building with one corner section designed as a bank. He was going to organize a bank—the Howard National Bank. He planned to keep the majority of the stock for himself and hand the institution down to Clyde and Claude.

Then, at the height of his dreams of establishing a financial empire, disaster struck. First, a staggering psychological blow came when he learned that his mother was dying. The one tender and understanding person in his early life, she—for whom he had planned and toiled—was slipping away just as he could finally give her so much. After his mother was gone, Colonel Howard, whose spirits either soared with eagle's wings or sank in deep despair, fell to the depths of melancholia. He was hardly prepared for the second stroke of fate's heavy hand.

Rumors were heard to the effect that all was not well with the Fort Payne Iron and Coal Company. Some businessmen were becoming disenchanted with Major Godfrey, who spent considerable time promoting another boom town in Tennessee. Most industries began dismissing some of their men and spending was watched with more caution. Then Godfrey returned to Fort Payne assuring everyone of continued prosperity. The boom just needed a little boost, he said. The great promoter would plan another excursion, a huge sale. There would soon be more money flowing in.

---

[1]*The main street of the town, it was later changed to its present name, Cogswell Avenue.*

The big sale was planned for a week in October, 1890. A huge tent, 150 feet wide, was put up behind the DeKalb Hotel. Engineers spent weeks carefully painting a map 50 feet long and 14 feet wide to show each lot to be sold. "The City of Fort Payne" was written in bold, neat letters, with the name Fort Payne taking five feet of space. The sign was finished and the canvas nailed to a giant billboard inside the tent. Everything was ready for a successful sale.

The excursion train arrived with 54 Pullman cars late one Monday afternoon and the visiting New Englanders made the rounds of the industries, visited Manitou Cave and looked at the mountain scenery. The auctioneer began selling lots at 2:30 Tuesday afternoon, but was halted at 3:30. The prices were disappointingly low and only $40,000 worth had been sold in an hour's time. The sale was to resume the next day—after the investors had dined and listened to sales talk that night.

The next morning a rain and wind storm lashed at the tent until Major Godfrey feared the whole thing might blow away at any minute. Employees who were instructed to save the big map hurriedly cut the huge canvas at the top, rolled it into one big wrinkled mass and rushed it to an empty building. There the engineers spread their sign out to dry, shaking their heads dejectedly at the smeared paint and the frayed edges of their once-beautiful map.

On Wednesday Godfrey asked his men to display the map as best they could in the Opera House. A middle section was cut out to fit the width of the stage and was fastened to a curtain. The sales that day were as disappointing as those on Tuesday had been and Colonel Howard knew that the boom was ending while he was overexpanded and his own financial condition was unstable. Even his law practice, which could have provided ample income, had been neglected.

Early in the boom W. N. Ewing, a well-educated lawyer who spoke several languages, came to Fort Payne from Virginia and joined the firm with Dobbs and Howard. In March, 1891, Colonel Howard withdrew from the firm and moved into an office on the second floor of his new brick building. That fall Ewing accepted Colonel Howard's offer of a partnership and took over his office while the senior partner embarked on yet another adventure.

His impressive court room arguments and increasingly frequent political talks had rekindled Colonel Howard's yearning to excel as a public speaker. Also, a change in his hectic life as a businessman seemed advisable at this time, due to the effects of the strain he had undergone. So Colonel Howard answered an advertisement and enrolled in the School of Oratory and Dramatic Expression in Washington, D. C. for a three-month course beginning in October.

Applying himself with the same dedicated fervor he had put into his study of Blackstone, he even arranged for private lessons between regular classes. He memorized great orations, and dramas, studied voice and practiced gestures. He played Hamlet and Macbeth and became as stagestruck as any aspiring actor.

Then he returned to Fort Payne to become more active in politics, to practice law briefly once more and to attempt to straighten out his tangled finances. He could remember with regret his wife's sound advice in the midst of the boom to sell all his holdings, invest in a blue grass farm in Kentucky and go abroad for a long rest. Now even men with thousands of dollars worth of property had difficulty in paying their household expenses. His only consolation was that he was not the only foolish man in town.

When the Fort Payne Bank was reorganized in 1892, with a capital of $50,000, Colonel Howard was made a director and vice-president. But although he would remain connected with this bank for several years, most of his financial involvements during this time dealt with dissolving businesses and paying off debts.

Stephen Howard had exchanged his Sand Mountain farm for property in Jackson County and had moved there. Colonel Howard sold his country home, moved into the house he had bought for his father's family, and sent Wallace, Edgar, and Octie to boarding school.

The large stock of goods at Howard Brothers was advertised for sale at half price in papers in adjoining counties as well as in the *Journal*. Most of what was not sold locally was shipped to Middlesboro, Kentucky, where several thousand dollars worth was sold before a fire destroyed the rest of the uninsured stock. Some goods were sent to Attalla, where Andrew ran a store for a short time before closing out to a local merchant for $2,500 in December, 1892, and returning to Fort Payne quite ill with tuberculosis.

The firm had managed to pay off all its debtors except one dry goods firm in Louisville. Few who owed Howard Brothers paid their bills, however, including one local man who prospered later when Colonel Howard was in desperate need of money. Of those who joined the mass exit from town, only one person, a man from Kansas, ever sent back the money he owed the store. In order to pay his last debt, Colonel Howard gave the Louisville firm the deed to his house, which had cost him as much as the amount of the debt and also $2,500 in gold and silver which he could have held on to in secret. He and Sally rejoiced though, at paying off the last indebtedness of Howard Brothers, and moved into a rented house with nothing left but household goods, the long-silent piano, and his law library.

The brick building had been sold to pay a note he had endorsed, merely as an accommodation, for the basket factory. Though he had served as a director, he had never helped operate the plant. The corner lot which cost him $20,000, of which two-thirds was paid in cash, had been sold at a foreclosure sale for $500, and a judgement was taken against Colonel Howard for the remainder. All his other real estate holdings were also gone.

He turned to lecturing and signed up with the National Entertainment Bureau, of Washington, for a tour of lectures on "Ambition." With his natural dramatic flair, his great booming voice, and his new knowledge of the finer points of lecturing, Colonel Howard became an outstanding speaker. The familiar wave of panic always seized him as he first stood before his audience. But he would soon develop a sense of great strength and confidence as he watched his listeners sit in rapt attention, changing moods and expressions according to the content and delivery of his orations. Upon the stage he performed like an actor, enunciating in a slow deliberate tone, or shouting with climactic emphasis, pacing, gesturing, smiling, grimacing. He was the great maestro, the audience his orchestra. He was in full command, the man of the moment in an era of oratory. He savored every minute of attention. And the applause—the thundering rounds of acclamation—gave wings to his spirit and balm to his ailing psyche.

After eight weeks of travel and lectures in 1893, Colonel Howard sent for his wife to join him in Washington. Sally arrived the first of December and stayed until mid-January, attending some of his lectures and enjoying sight-seeing trips through the city. She returned to Fort Payne shortly before his tour ended.

Back in Fort Payne once more, Colonel Howard contemplated his future, drifting in a mental fog of uncertainty and depression and filled with a spirit of rebellion against the economic depression which he believed to be the fault of congress. One Sunday afternoon, as he sat thinking about the scandals and Washington gossip he had heard during his months there, he remembered a book he had read about some shocking affairs in Chicago. He had been amazed at the revelations made by W. T. Stead in his book, *If Christ Came to Chicago* and held the author in high esteem for his daring and honesty.

Always quick to copy any idea he liked, Colonel Howard determined to write a similar book about Washington. He would expose the capital's social evils, the corrupt influence of the lobbies, the intrigues of the money power and, in general, the rule of the strong and corrupt and the impotence of the weak and honest. He could satisfy a desire to write, strike a blow at the politicians responsible for the nation's problems, and perhaps make some money, too.

During the afternoon he formed a mental outline for his story and created his characters. He announced to Sally that he was going to write a book and discussed the plot with her. As usual, he received her encouragement. Packing his clothes again, he made plans to return to Washington the next day for local color and the latest gossip about important government officials and Washington society.

On the train he took out his pencil and the yellow paper he always preferred to write on and began the first chapter of his book. Writing rapidly, as was his custom, he never paused to proofread or to make changes. In this and all his other writings which were to follow he let everything stay as originally written, never once revising any part of his manuscript.

By the time he reached Washington his story was well underway and all his characters introduced. He was ready to

51

search newspapers daily for choice tidbits of yellow journalism and to listen attentively to local experts expound on the latest capers of well known politicians. While there he also watched Coxey's famous army of unemployed workers mill around Washington and heard other radicals bewail the country's plight. He obtained his scandals to weave into the stories in his book and increased the bitterness with which he wrote it.

Within four weeks from its beginning the book *If Christ Came to Congress* was published. The newspapers were soon printing reviews and excerpts and Washington society was discussing the sensational charges. The author intended for Washington to furnish the major market for his books and sales there were very successful.[1] He made no effort to promote its sale back home, where he returned shortly.

Andrew, who was growing weaker daily in the last stages of tuberculosis, had been living with Milford and Sally for several months. Colonel Howard attempted to make his brother's final weeks as pleasant as possible. He bought Andrew a horse and buggy and kept a boy available to drive him around whenever the weather permitted his getting out. He left reluctantly on speaking engagements, fearing Andrew's condition might worsen before his return. A two-day engagement at Rogers, Arkansas was almost canceled, but Andrew objected, promising he would be there to welcome Milford back home.

As Colonel Howard boarded a train for the trip, he insisted that Sally send him a telegram if there were any change in Andrew's condition. After he completed his lectures and was leaving his hotel, he gave silent thanks that no telegram had arrived. But the return train was so slow that he became restless, extremely nervous, and almost ill. Then the locomotive was involved in an accident which was to delay it for hours. In a frantic attempt to make his connection, Colonel Howard changed his route, going hundreds of miles out of his way, by Louisville, Kentucky, hoping to make his Alabama-bound train. He just missed it and waited in agony for 24 hours, feeling a terrible premonition that Andrew was worse.

Indeed, Andrew was dying. On August 12 he clung to life

---

[1] *The entire edition of 25,000 copies was sold out by the end of the first month.*

by sheer will power until Sally returned from the depot without his brother, looked up in disappointment and was gone. The next day at that hour Colonel Howard returned, weary, haggard and mentally exhausted, to learn at the depot that his fears were true. When he reached home this man of many tears wept over his younger brother: "Ah, Andrew, we swam rivers and swollen streams together in boyhood, but you had to cross the last dark river alone and I could not hold your hand when you embarked."

As often happened after traumatic experiences, Milford Howard again changed directions. Just as news about his book, and a few much-sought-after copies of it reached Fort Payne, the man who had made such bitter attacks upon the members of the senate and house of representatives announced that he would run for congress.

Part II

If Christ Came to Congress

The general tone of *If Christ Came to Congress* is revealed in the dedication, written with more precision of purpose than of grammar:

This Little Volume
Is Unwillingly and Without Permission
Dedicated To
Grover Cleveland, President of the United States,
Certain Corrupt Members of His Cabinet,
And The Horde of
Drunken, Licentious Senators
And Congressmen and Their Mistresses,
Herein Referred To.

Most of the book consists of interwoven tales based in part on some actual incidents and real characters, but is based mainly upon embellished capital gossip, colored and magnified by the author's political beliefs at this period of his turbulent life. The main characters include the Honorable Joseph Napoleon Bonaparte Clay and the Honorable William Henry

Snollygoster, two married congressmen who are more preoccupied with wine and women than with legislation; Miss Madeline Rollard is Clay's scheming mistress; Miss Gertrude Sweet, a middle-aged spinster presides over an assignation house; and Jennie Harmon, the beautiful daughter of an impoverished farmer, seeks a career in Washington after being encouraged to do so by her congressman—the lecherous Snollygoster, who seduces her.

Although permeated with the author's bitter fanaticism, this book provides glimpses of a polished refinement and consciousness of effort Colonel Howard would never repeat in his later books. He was no master of dialogue and in this, as in other fictional works, his characters deliver stilted speeches instead of engaging in realistic conversation. He was at his best with descriptive phrases and the creative and imaginative portrayal of scenes and events. His writing ability can be detected from the following description of an iron furnace as it was viewed at night:

> ... Thousands of coke ovens sent up their black smoke, writhing and coiling like the folds of a huge serpent, while the flames from the tops of the ovens rose and fell, showing the blackened, begrimed faces of the workers. The furnaces belched forth great rivers of glowing, sizzling, bubbling, burning iron, and the huge engines thundered and roared, while the men, stripped to the waist, shouted and cursed like demons, and as they ran here and there, drawing off the steaming red hot masses of iron, with their faces, arms, hands and bodies discolored with the smoke, with the fiery red glow shining upon them, the scene was that of Vulcan and his helpers at their forges in the bowels of the earth, making weapons for the gods.

Colonel Howard's two-fold purpose was to expose the great disparity between the nation's poor and wealthier classes and to indict a majority of federal government officials and most of Washington society on myriad moral and criminal charges. With seething invective he utilized his vivid imagination and vast vocabulary in his private war against widespread poverty and governmental corruption. With a confident command of the English language the self-educated writer dashed off such words as peccadilloes—bagatelle—eclat—stentorian—allegorical—libation—mendicants—bacchanalian—putrescent—amanuensis—cadaverous—capacious—celerity—seraphic—profligacy—escutcheon—soubriquet—virago—cabal—excrescence.

Nor was he at a loss for words to describe the national capital. Washington was declared to be a "hot bed of licentiousness, libertinism, fraud, dishonesty and theft." The average congressman was said to have two objectives, "to have a good time," and "to get all the money" he could. As this was two decades before the adoption of the seventeenth amendment to the constitution, the senators were still chosen by state legislatures, thereby making it possible, according to Colonel Howard, for wealthy men to "buy" this office. A fictional congressman declares the senate to be a house of plutocrats. "Many of the senators are millionaires," he says, "and if Christ came to Congress they would not associate with him because of his poverty and lowly position." He also thought Christ would "scourge this old dragon and horde of satellites and subsidized Senators from the Capital as he scourged the money changers from the temple at Jerusalem."

Attorney General Richard Olney was labeled "the best friend of the trusts and combines in the United States." Colonel Howard decried the influence of the money power upon the house of representatives, the senate and the president—and drew a comparison between Grover Cleveland and Benedict Arnold. The Smithsonian Institution, the agriculture department and other government departments were alleged to exist primarily to provide jobs for relatives of congressmen. There was even more "corruption and rottenness," according to the irate author, in the census office, dubbed by Colonel Howard as the "National Whore House." He called by name "one of the worst, vilest, most bestial and debauched men in Washington," who worked in the treasury department and warned that a certain southern senator and the married daughter of a deceased president should be more discreet.

In a thinly veiled reference to undenied gossip about Cleveland, Howard relates the sad tale of the illegitimate daughter of a United States president. A member of the president's cabinet is described as he enters a "boarding house" of ill repute, accompanied by a beautiful young Washington lady. Indeed, the ladies of Washington society receive their share of Colonel Howard's vitriolic accusations. It was averred that "One-half of the wealthier women of Washington have their lovers, their secret affairs, their private meetings." Jurists and clergymen also allegedly participated in the "fraud, lasciviousness, drunkenness, bribery and debauchery" which Christ would have found in Washington. Tales are told of an illegitimate daughter of a supreme court justice (born to a young relative of the jurist's wife), of an illicit romance between the wife of a prominent citizen of the capital and a Presbyterian minister who headed a female college, and of a Catholic priest whose housekeeper was his mistress.

Through the words of a congressman who is describing Washington to a foreigner, the Capitol is averred to be "the NATIONAL ASSIGNATION HOUSE as well as the NATIONAL SALOON;" this authority on life at the capital declares that "under the dome of the Capitol ten thousand guilty liaisons" between congressmen and women of ill repute had begun. The "fraud and hypocrisy" and the "mock piety" of congressmen are condemned and these "barefaced hypocrites and frauds" are charged with receiving from $25,000 to $50,000 for important votes.

His scathing denunciations gained momentum and seemed totally devoid of any restraint as the name calling continued: ". . . prostitutes . . . moral lepers . . . embezzlers . . . whoremongers . . ." Nothing was too derogatory to be said of the "gigantic trusts and monopolies, rich corporations, bloated bondholders, millionaires and plutocrats." He predicted there would arise a Moses to deliver their victims, the starving and suffering people. A revolutionary movement would begin unless there were reforms and it would make the recent Coxey uproar seem like only a ripple.

The experiences found at the extremes of the social structure, according to the author, were "poverty—pain—labor—toil—sorrow—death," on one hand, and "wealth—luxury—peace—rest—joy—life" on the other. The poor of Washington were at a worse disadvantage than those elsewhere, as there were only two ways to get a job in Washington—by the use of money or of personal charms. In the book little children starve because their mothers are refused jobs unless they will submit to the desires of their benefactors. Colonel Howard writes of "poor little half-starved, half-clad children . . . upon pallets of rags, moaning in their sleep." To him, even the "interminable click of the revolving wheels" of a train departing from Washington seems to say "hunger, poverty, death, hunger, death."

Near the end of the book is an event based on a famous case, Madeline Pollard vs. W. C. P. Breckinridge. In the book it is Madeline Rollard who sues her "Star of Kentucky," Joseph Napoleon Bonaparte Clay. The congressman, who had remarried after his wife died and had attempted to sever his relationship with Miss Rollard, loses a breach of promise suit.

The main story ends with Jennie Harmon carrying the child of Congressman Snollygoster, who has deserted her. Jennie is discovered by her father and childhood sweetheart while drowning her sorrow with wine in an assignation house. Upon realizing what the congressman has done to his daughter, the enraged father delivers a sad and impassioned monologue which includes the exclamation, "May he be cursed while living, tortured while dying and damned when dead!" Jennie runs barefoot through a Washington snow storm, jumps into the icy waters of the Potomac and drowns.

A number of times Colonel Howard indulges in somewhat overdone sketches of horrendous imagery. Such is the case preceding the death of Snollygoster, who goes mad after seeing Jenny's body.

> . . . What is this thing here with its arms fastened about my neck, raining foul kisses on my lips? Oh, it is the rotting, reeking corpse of the ruined child! Go away, in God's name! Take your putrid lips from mine—your fleshless cheek; oh, that horrible, rotting cheek, take it from my face! Close those sightless, staring eyes, for I cannot endure their reproachful gaze! Unclasp your decaying limbs, from which skin-worms and vermin protrude from around my body!

The twenty-sixth chapter was Colonel Howard's big shocker. He not only described the section of Washington, D.C., allegedly known as "the Division," as the location of saloons and brothels, but showed each house of ill fame on a map. According to the author, this district, bounded on the north by Pennsylvania Avenue, on the south by C Street, on the west by 15th Street and on the east by 11th Street, contained 80 houses of prostitution and assignation. He named the proprietresses, designated the houses as either white or Negro, and listed the number of "inmates" in each. No explanation was given as to how he obtained this detailed information.

In the thirtieth and final chapter Colonel Howard writes of a vision he had while asleep, in which the Capitol was blown up by bombs placed in it by members of "The Black Knights," a small secret society; every congressman and senator was killed. The poor of Washington were then led to the treasury, where doors were battered down and vaults blown open. Even the guards joined in the looting which followed. The whole country became paralyzed; the trusts and combines and the money power were swept from the land.

In a second vision, the author saw a happy country, with damage to its capital repaired and with better and more honest men in congress. Then came the author's version of a happy ending: "No more did the laugh of the money God echo through the halls of Congress!"

The Political Maverick

Colonel Howard was no political novice. He had been known for several years as one of Alabama's most promising young Democrats and had an impeccable record of party loyalty. Two years after being appointed as DeKalb's first county solicitor he had been elected chairman of the DeKalb County executive committee and had been reelected in 1892 and 1894. As head of his party, Howard had called the first primary the Democrats ever held in DeKalb County in order to eliminate the free-for-all races which had taken place in previous general elections. In 1892 he had been elected as an alternate delegate to the state convention in Montgomery which nominated Thomas Goode Jones, whom Colonel Howard supported, for governor.

After a faction of the party backing Reuben F. Kolb, the Farmers Alliance candidate, met at the Montgomery Opera House and nominated its own ticket under the label of the Jeffersonian Democratic Party, Colonel Howard had remained with the "Organized Democrats," as they were called by the more liberal wing. Along with A. L. Woodliff, Colonel Howard had served as a delegate from the seventh congressional district to the Democratic national convention in Chicago, where both cast votes for Grover Cleveland. After directing a successful campaign in the county for Cleveland and for William H. Denson, the regular Democratic candidate for congress, he had written a letter, published in the Fort Payne *Journal*, thanking the people who had supported Cleveland and Denson.

Referred to as "the young Democratic Goliath" by the Attalla *Herald*, Colonel Howard had been recognized throughout the district as a clever and efficient political organizer. He had been in good standing with the leaders of his party and counted as one of its most loyal members. He had been, as he phrased it, "a shouting Democrat."

Then, in September, 1894, Colonel Howard sent shock waves through the county when he renounced the Democratic Party and pledged allegiance to the Populist Party, a temporary fusion of agrarian groups in the southern and western states. He was going to seek that party's nomination for congressman in order to unseat William Denson of Etowah County. Democratic leaders were incensed at his treachery. His father refused to listen to any of his speeches and bitterly declared that he would have preferred to have made Milford's coffin with his own hands, and to have buried him, than to have had his son desert the Democratic Party. Former friends who had attended political meetings at his office became his worst enemies.

Colonel Howard's bolt from the Democratic fold was to unleash four years of the most virulent and abusive political battles in Alabama's history. The Democrats and Populists of the district were to engage in slander, threats of arson and assassination, fights and beatings and public stand-offs, where pistols were drawn by impassioned and irrational men. There were those on both sides whose actions would be less than honorable. The district which Colonel Howard sought to represent in 1894 would live up to its reputation as "The Bloody Seventh."

The reasons for Colonel Howard's defection from the Democratic Party were largely economic. He himself had lost most of his material possessions the previous year. He could well sympathize with the debtor farmers who appeared to bear the brunt of the 1893 financial panic and the depression which followed. As a boy he had experienced the long hours of toil required to produce a cotton crop—a product selling in 1894 as low as three cents a pound or $15 a bale. Many farmers and some laborers began to look to the government to ease the tight-money situation by printing more money backed by silver, rather than to adhere to the gold standard, which protected the high value of money for those few who had it. Colonel Howard and others who had supported Cleveland had hoped he would be persuaded to aid those who suffered because of a money shortage.

But Grover Cleveland was not their man. Just as had other presidents before him, he refused to regard the problem of business recovery as the direct responsibility of government. He did, however, consider it best for the country to maintain the gold standard. It was his belief that the basic cause of the panic had been the depletion of the nation's gold supply and the legal requirement of backing a certain amount of treasury notes with annual silver purchases. Calling congress into special session, Cleveland sought the immediate repeal of the Sherman Silver Purchase Act, passed during Harrison's administration in order to secure tariff support from western silver-mining states. This action infuriated agrarian groups, to whom a strict gold standard meant low prices and continued agricultural distress.

No one was more angry than Colonel Howard. He had helped nominate Grover Cleveland and had campaigned for him in north Alabama. After the election of 1892, he had joined other DeKalb County Democrats in a victory celebration at the Opera House. There had been band music, fireworks and political speeches predicting prosperity under the Democrats. Colonel Howard had confidently expected Cleveland, upon his return to office, to help the debtors rather than the creditors of the nation. Now it appeared that the president had made matters worse for all the poor. Colonel Howard's denunciation of Cleveland's money policy was furious. He began a personal crusade against the Democratic president, aimed not only at his policies but also at his integrity.

While in Washington, early in 1894, writing his book and venting his ire upon both the president and congress, Colonel Howard had met H. E. Taubeneck, chairman of the Populist Party's executive committee, with whom he discussed the political situation in Alabama.

During the previous summer, John H. Bankhead and William H. Denson had been severely criticized by conservative Democrats for having attended several meetings held by Jeffersonian Democrats and Populists. There had been persistent rumors that Denson and several other Alabama congressmen might even join the Populist movement. Taubeneck assured Colonel Howard that Denson did indeed intend to change parties and was expected to help campaign for the populist nominee for governor, R. F. Kolb.[1]

After being invited to join the party himself, Colonel Howard had a conference with Denson and several other congressmen whose party preferences were vascillating. They all agreed to follow Senator John T. Morgan, if he would lead the revolt, and then to work together to carry the state for the Populist Party and free silver. Colonel Howard made an evening call upon the old senator, who had been in politics long before Howard had been born, and he was courteously but firmly turned down. He would not blame the others for making the move, the senator said, but he did not feel, now that he was near the end of his political career, that he should leave the party which had so highly honored him.

When Colonel Howard reported to the congressmen they all decided to stay with the Democratic Party, except for Denson, who wavered for some time and then attempted to gain the support of both the Democrats and the Populists. A sincere advocate of free silver, he thought that by not interfering in the governor's race between Kolb and Oates he would have a clear shot at the Populist endorsement. In staying out of the campaign for governor, Denson simply announced that he would "tote his own skillet."

Though some conservative Democrats opposed him, Denson received his party's nomination at the Cullman convention on September 4, 1894, when he was nominated over John W. Inzer of St. Clair and W.W. Haralson of DeKalb. If he could obtain either the nomination or endorsement of the Populist convention in Attalla two weeks later, his election would be practically assured.

But some Populist leaders, disappointed at Denson's failure to openly join their party, were determined not to support him. They looked about for a candidate who might possibly defeat the incumbent congressman and decided upon Milford W.

---

[1]*In a letter to the state chairman of the Populist Party, written on September 10, Taubeneck said that Denson had backed out of his promise to campaign for Kolb after returning to Alabama and canvassing his district.*

Howard, who had spoken to their chairman of his disenchantment with his party and its president. At the time, Colonel Howard and his wife were in New York making arrangements for another lecture tour.

Dr. John B. Harris, a fiery Guntersville Populist, wired Colonel Howard, asking him to return in order to become the nominee for congressman. Although flattered, Colonel Howard replied that he had just signed a contract for a lecture series which would require several months to fulfill. However, Dr. Harris continued sending telegrams and Colonel Howard yielded to the temptation of the challenge, hurriedly packed and caught a southbound train.

Speaking at Lebanon on September 8, he startled a group of farmers with the sensational charge that Denson had accepted $500 from the Populists to support their candidate for governor. If he were to overcome Denson's 2,000 majority vote two years before, Howard had to fight hard and he had started swinging. Several days later he reiterated his charges to the *Journal* editor and added that he had an unsigned paper condemning William Oates, which was in Denson's handwriting. He also confided that he would appear before the Attalla convention and seek the Populist nomination.

Both Denson and Howard were invited to speak at the Populist meeting on September 18 and it was predicted to be a lively affair. When the time came for the two protagonists to appear before the assembly, Denson demanded that Howard speak first to repeat his charges and to produce the papers he claimed to have as proof. "I have come," the congressman proclaimed, "to meet my traducers!"

Colonel Howard arose and held a receipt which he calmly proceeded to introduce as evidence, as though in court. It was a receipt for $500, signed on July 11, 1894, by Denson, he announced. He then showed the delegates the indictment of Oates, which he claimed was written by the same hand which had signed the receipt. He read, with careful emphasis upon the derogatory statements, the paper which he said was supposed to have been delivered as a speech by Denson explaining why he was supporting the Populist candidate against William Oates. After a few other brief remarks Colonel Howard returned to his seat.

Then William Denson arose, flushed with anger. One of the best speakers in the state, a highly intelligent man with a strong physique and magnetic personality, he was quite an adversary for his youthful accuser. He acknowledged receiving the money to come to Alabama to speak, but it was from the Bimetallic League for his support of the free and unlimited coinage of silver, he exclaimed. Branding the statements made about him as willful, malicious lies, he furiously charged Colonel Howard with twisting the facts and assaulting his honor. No man could go over the district impugning his character and *live*, he warned as he threateningly shook his finger in Colonel Howard's face and denounced him as "a liar blacker than hell!"

At this point a young friend of Colonel Howard's sprang to his feet and started toward Denson with his hand in his pocket and a fierce expression on his face. Pat Frazier, a relative of Sally's who had served four terms as sheriff of DeKalb County, quickly caught the enraged youth and commanded him to keep his head and to calm down. The atmosphere remained explosive as a number of men exchanged hostile glares and revealed the bulges of their concealed pistols and the chairman quickly declared a recess in the convention's proceedings.

As Colonel Howard and a friend sat on the sidewalk talking shortly afterward, Denson strode by them, then suddenly turned back and stood before his hated accuser with a steely gaze as he clutched at a pistol in his hip pocket. Three times he moved the weapon only slightly, then dropped it back into the pocket, before letting his better judgment rule as he turned and stalked away. Then Colonel Howard withdrew his own pistol from his coat pocket, where it had been pointed at Denson all this time. After showing it to his friend, he replaced it with a heavy sigh of relief.

After the adoption of a platform that night, the convention prepared to receive nominations. Several state leaders had previously favored Denson but realized now that his endorsement would cause a serious split in their growing party. Many were still not ready to back the young upstart who had assailed Denson, however. Some supported Thomas W. Powell, of Cullman, and others were behind George F. Gaither or W. B. Beeson, both of Etowah County. With 54 votes being cast, 28 were necessary for nomination. The first ballot gave the following results: Howard 18; Powell 13; Beeson 10; and Gaither 7. It was not until the seventh ballot that Howard received the necessary plurality, with 31 votes being cast for him.

As he had no money with which to finance a campaign, Colonel Howard decided to sell his law library and Sally willingly consented to contribute her piano to the cause. With the proceeds they would gamble on the chance of his election to a $5,000 a year job. Then he utilized his bountiful energy in waging a determined uphill political struggle, with Sally enthusiastically taking over the responsibilities of campaign manager. Together they compiled lists of eligible voters and Sally then proved to be very proficient at writing letters and making personal contacts. Of course an office seeker's main activity was that of making speeches several times a day, at every town, village, and crossroads. Day after day there were speeches, speeches to entertain as well as to inform, serious ones and funny ones, and most of the time—long ones. Colonel Howard was right at home.

Meanwhile, his opponent was having some difficulty within his own party. The Montgomery *Advertiser*, which had supported him before he had become linked so closely with the Populists, backed a plan to force him off the ticket. The Cullman Democratic Club was very active in a move to replace him and many Democrats in Franklin and Etowah Counties threatened to stay away from the polls if he remained in the race.

With the Democrats thus divided, Howard saw a good possibility of victory if he could win the support of the Republicans. Arrangements were made with John J. Durham and other Republican supporters for him to be extended an invitation to address a Republican mass meeting at Fort Payne on September 27. When Durham made the motion to invite him, Captain Joe J. Nix, chairman of the DeKalb County executive committee, made an adamant speech against such action. John T. Blakemore, who was considering running on the Republican ticket, claimed that there were Populists among them who should not be at the meeting in the first place. After a peppery debate, engaged in by almost everyone present, the original motion was amended to include Blakemore in the invitation and it was approved.

In Colonel Howard's address he advocated a protective

tariff, a pet issue with the Republicans, and also demanded a fair ballot and an honest count, which they usually maintained they didn't get. He naturally reiterated his stand for the free coinage of silver, calling attention to the need of the people for more money. He ended by asking for the convention's endorsement.

Blakemore did not second the motion. He began his talk by calling attention to the fact that he had been born in Alabama and also reminded his listeners that he had been a life-long Republican. On the other hand, Blakemore insisted, no one knew just where to place Howard. "He has been a Democrat, a Jeffersonian, a Populist and a Republican all in the short space of six months," he asserted.

At the close of his impassioned opposing arguments, however, the majority of those present voted in favor of a resolution endorsing Colonel Howard's candidacy and reaffirming their allegiance to the principles of the Republican Party. The same action was taken the following week by the Republican executive committee of the district. After both Nix and Blakemore again denounced Colonel Howard and opposed his endorsement, the district committee voted for him, but by the most narrow margin possible, a majority of one.

Congressman Denson was not standing still. As he agreed with Colonel Howard on the silver question, he looked for another issue. When *If Christ Came To Congress* gained sudden notoriety he knew he had one. At the end of a speech in Fort Payne late in September, Denson paid his compliments to Howard's book, reading the title page, the dedication, and several passages which he commented on. Then he delivered an eloquent and glowing tribute to Mrs. Cleveland and defended her against imputations which he claimed had been made upon the character of "this noble and virtuous wife and mother." His speech was well received, with the tribute to the first lady eliciting the loudest applause. A few days later, in a speech at Gadsden, he repeated his moving tribute to Mrs. Cleveland and again defended her character against the alleged assaults.

Actually, Colonel Howard had made no references to the beautiful 29 year old Mrs. Cleveland, but had woven lurid tales of various women in Washington society. Included was "one of the first ladies of the land, a beautiful and accomplished woman," with the claim that, should he mention her name, "it would cause a thrill of horror to run from Maine to California." But he vehemently denied that he meant *the* first lady, as claimed by his political opponent.

If Christ Came To Congress remained a popular subject with the press throughout the stormy congressional campaign. It provided ample opportunity for the acrid editorial comment indulged in by most newspaper men of this period. The Gadsden *Times-News* was certainly not reticent in regard to Colonel Howard or his book.

The following is one of four separate articles concerning the book which appeared in one October issue of the *Times-News*:

> The question is being frequently asked, "Who is Mr. Howard?" The only reply this writer can make is that his only acquaintance with Mr. Howard is through his book. He seems to have reached his highest point of public notoriety in the slums of Washington City. If we may judge from the long list of the names of the keepers of houses of ill fame, white and colored and his map showing the situation of said houses, we would suppose him to be an agent for these parties, employed to advertise their business and whereabouts. Mr. Howard certainly has gained notoriety; he has shown himself to be notoriously immoral, if we may judge him by his book.

Another caustic comment was: "Mr. Howard quotes a great deal of scripture in his book. So the devil quoted scripture when he tempted Christ."

After the post office department barred the book from the mails because of its alleged obscenity, the *Times-News* editorialized that congress should go further in regulating obscene literature and should prohibit its sale at news stands and on railroad cars—or even prohibit the publication of "such stuff." A prediction that "If the *Times-News* is not being much mistaken Mr. Howard will wish, before the campaign is over, that he had never written a book," undoubtedly came true.

The attack upon Colonel Howard's book branched out into ingenuous and varied accusations designed to finish off his reputation. Handbills were circulated containing affidavits charging Colonel Howard with a number of assorted crimes and indiscretions. Among the charges were: being expelled from a church in Georgia after being caught stealing cotton; gambling with Negroes in Fort Payne; leading a mob to beat up Negro voters; and paying $5.00 to have a Republican Negro assaulted. According to the handbills, there were other offenses committed by Colonel Howard which were so vile that the post office would refuse to mail the material if they were printed. Some Democrats reasoned that Colonel Howard had indulged in character assassination at the very beginning; but they would show him how to play the game.

It was difficult to disprove all the last minute accusations, but W. N. Ewing, Colonel Howard's law partner, succeeded in proving that the cotton-stealing charge was false. According to his detractors, the reason Colonel Howard came to Alabama in the first place was because he had gotten into trouble for stealing cotton from a man named LaFayette Sutterlin. Ewing went to Georgia and brought back an affidavit from Sutterlin which declared the story to be totally false and stating that, although he was a life-long Democrat, he would vote for Colonel Howard if he lived in his district.

The handbills, the newspapers, and the political speakers together did a very thorough job of publicizing the comparatively unknown Milford Howard. All across the shoe-string district of the old seventh, reaching from the Georgia line to the Mississippi boundary, throngs of curious gathered to see and to hear this morally depraved monster. Huge crowds gathered in the cities and towns of Cherokee, Etowah, St. Clair, DeKalb, Marshall, Cullman, Winston, and Franklin Counties to hear the man whom Congressman Denson was lambasting and to see the author of "that book."

He had been furnished with an audience and a stage; and Milford Howard knew how to perform. The tall, handsome orator held his listeners spellbound as his strong, resonant voice echoed through the city streets or country lanes. He spoke the language of the farmers and laborers as he sympathized with their problems; he expounded on the benefits to be derived from a free-silver policy and a protective tariff; he tossed about all sorts of impressive figures and percentages and threw in a few Biblical quotations or borrowed phrases from the literary masters. As to the personal attacks of his opponent, he ignored them, presenting nothing but a show of respect for all who opposed him. Even the *Times-News* was impressed by his demeanor when he spoke at Gadsden.

Frustrated at their inability to ruffle him, the more lawless element often attempted to provoke a fight with him or his companions and there was even talk of assassination plots on several occasions. Once, in Russellville, in Franklin County, a local attorney heard of a scheme to cause trouble after Colonel Howard's speech there. Although the man was a prominent Democrat, he personally escorted Colonel Howard down the street, warning that if there were any killing, he would be in on it.

At last November 6 arrived and Colonel Howard was relieved to see the constant danger end. He and Sally waited anxiously to see whether they had won or lost his first political race. Colonel Howard led from the beginning. Even the city precincts, where Denson was strongest, showed a trend in the challenger's favor. The next day he was certain of victory. He had won with a majority of 3,460 votes, carrying every county except Franklin, which he lost by 80 votes.

There had been, however, a sharp decrease in the number of voters as compared with the presidential election year of 1892, with almost 8,000 of the more than 20,000 voters staying home on election day. Although some drop could have been expected, there had evidently been a large number of men who agreed with the Montgomery *Advertiser*, which had declared that neither Denson nor Howard deserved to be elected.

The opposition press did not let up on Colonel Howard after his election and he cooperated in furnishing headline material. Shortly after his victory he made a trip to New York, where he was interviewed by reporters. After giving a predictable answer as to the prospects for the future of the Populist Party, he launched into a newsworthy plan to investigate the means by which the Sherman Silver Act had been repealed. Then he promised to try to find out how President Cleveland had amassed a fortune within five years.

The Atlanta *Constitution* called Howard "a wild young man" who was "preparing to cut a wide swath in Congress," and declared, "This young man promises to be a second Tom

Watson."
The Gadsden *Times-News* had harsher words.

Mr. Howard, congressman-elect from this congressional district, has taken a big job on his hands when he gets to congress. He proposes to investigate into Mr. Cleveland's business methods in order to ascertain by what means he has managed to accumulate an alleged $4,000,000 in his possession. We suppose that it is simply the effervescense of youth and inexperience. If he undertakes it he will be the "most flattened" young man that ever turned his trumpet loose in the halls of congress. Only pigmies propose to do great things in advance, and he will find it a hard road to travel. Being devoid of the necessary brains to legislate for the people, he proposes to keep himself in notice by sensational methods. If Mr. Howard carries out his intentions, or attempts to do so, he will only hang himself politically.

Colonel Howard was referred to a few days later in this paper as "a young hopeful, without a single well digested idea on any public question." But the editor found comfort in the following confident but mistaken prediction:

That Mr. Howard will make his exit two years hence, goes without question.

Congressman Howard

Congressman-elect Howard was 32 years old, eager, and ambitious. He had big plans for his political future, great expectations of what he could now accomplish. He was anxious first to heal the wounds inflicted during the vicious campaign and was confident of then becoming an outstanding statesman. He would do neither.

In January it was Colonel Howard who presided over a mass meeting held at the courthouse in Fort Payne to make plans for securing a cotton mill for the city. The crowd was large and responsive. With his leadership they could foresee success. A movement was started to attract other industries as well.

The first few weeks of 1895 found the Howards more relaxed and hopeful of a return to normal activity in Fort Payne. But the momentary pause of quiet and tranquillity ended with a sensational fight in front of the Opera House.

It was February 22, and the regular Friday afternoon exercises of the Fort Payne Institute were being held in the exhibition hall of the Opera House. Ben Jacoway stood before the assembled students, faculty, and visitors to read a paper entitled, "Purity in Politics." Then he proceeded to specify some of the impurities of the recent election, citing the allegations that Colonel Howard was an anarchist, a libertine, and a slanderer of women. Sally Howard and her young brother-in-law, Edgar, were infuriated. A small and dainty woman, Mrs. Howard was known, nonetheless, for her explosive temper. It now flared beyond control at the schoolboy's condemnation of her husband. Rising from her seat, she stared at Ben Jacoway for a moment to show her indignation and then strode from the building.

Five blocks away Colonel Howard was arguing a case in circuit court when a friend rushed in and whispered an urgent message in his ear. He in turn whispered to Judge J. A. Bilbro, who immediately adjourned court, and Colonel Howard hurried out to find his wife. He intercepted her walking rapidly from the direction of their home toward the Opera House. After a heated conversation Sally surrendered a pistol she was holding beneath her cape, but continued determinedly on her way back to the Opera House where Professor S. L. Russell had just dismissed the school. Upon finding Edgar, she beseeched him to whip Ben, which he readily agreed to do. As the two boys struggled in the street, flailing at each other wildly and rolling in the dirt, the near-hysterical Sally gave Ben two frenzied kicks in the stomach with her number three shoe.

Friends of Ben's father, Postmaster Thomas R. Jacoway, rushed up to intercede and were met by jeers from a group of Howard rooters. Soon the gathering crowd became a shouting, jostling mob and the threat of a general riot hovered over the town. But the noise quickly subsided as an armed posse of some 25 men came charging down Gault Avenue on galloping horses, dispatched by the circuit judge to quell the disturbance.

Ben Jacoway was encouraged by his father to swear out warrants against Sally and Edgar, who were ordered to appear at the mayor's court on Saturday morning. Colonel Howard attempted to persuade Dr. W. E. Quin, mayor of Fort Payne, to permit his wife and brother to send an attorney to enter guilty pleas for them. Dr. Quin refused to consent to this arrangement, but did allow Colonel Howard to appear in his wife's place to enter her guilty plea.

Fearing there might be further trouble on Saturday, Colonel Howard and Edgar were accompanied by Dr. John B. Harris as they climbed the stairway to Dr. Quin's office. Fines of $10 each were paid for Edgar and Sally and the three started back downstairs when Thomas Jacoway suddenly bounded up the stairs and struck Edgar with his fist. While his brother engaged in his second fight in two days, choking and beating the postmaster, Colonel Howard kept watch over a group of men who stood by threateningly with drawn pistols. When one yelled, "Let's get rid of the Howards!" Colonel Howard drew his own pistol and held the men at bay until he could get Edgar to his feet and lead him away, with Dr. Harris following closely behind. Several pistols and one Winchester rifle were pointed at them but no one fired.

An angry Judge Bilbro, upon learning of the incident, had all the men involved brought into court and exacted a promise from each that there would be no further trouble or fighting. The Howards were indicted for assault and carrying concealed weapons. No one else was brought before the grand jury. Meanwhile, Edgar was expelled from school, but Ben Jacoway was exonerated of blame for the fighting incident.

About four weeks later the anger and resentment aroused by the Howards were expressed against an innocent victim, W. N. Ewing, Colonel Howard's law partner. Ewing, a quiet and inhibited intellectual, had taken no part in his partner's politics except to vote for him and to clear his name of the cotton-stealing charge. But he was waylaid and unmercifully beaten, apparently because of his association with Milford Howard. Left unconscious and bleeding by repeated blows to the head with rocks or knucks, the dignified gentleman never fully recovered and died several years later. His attackers were identified by witnesses and indicted for the crime. The following August the case against one was *nol prossed;* the other two pleaded guilty, with the solicitor agreeing to a fine of $5.00 each.

Colonel Howard railed at such injustice. Through the columns of the Populist *Sand Mountain Signal*, he openly accused both Judge Bilbro and the circuit solicitor, John G. Winston, Jr., of helping to encourage political persecution by subjecting the Howards to fines on two occasions while practically condoning lawlessness by Colonel Howard's enemies.

Upon reading these public charges against him, the circuit judge took quick and decisive action, bringing them to the attention of a grand jury in Marshall County, where the newspaper was published. He demanded that the grand jury make a thorough investigation and either uncover evidence of corruption upon which impeachment proceedings might be based or disprove the charges and show them to constitute criminal libel.

A large number of witnesses were summoned from Fort

73

Payne and Howard's allegations were investigated intensively for a week. In the ensuing report the jurors found the investigation of the fight on February 23 to be "very imperfect." Although there had been several eyewitnesses, the only person questioned had been Thomas Jacoway, a participant. On his testimony alone, indictments had been returned against Milford and Edgar Howard. They concluded that the solicitor had been negligent in his handling of the case.

As to the assault upon Ewing, the grand jury again found the investigation "very imperfectly conducted" and the solicitor negligent. From the evidence, the grand jury felt constrained to report that the *nol prossed* suit was "ill advised and improper under the circumstances" and that a fine of $5.00 in the other cases was "wholly inadequate punishment." The solicitor was again found negligent in the disposition of the case. However, the grand jury acquitted the solicitor of having been activated by "any corrupt or partisan motives," thereby blocking any possible impeachment proceedings. It was also found that Judge Bilbro had been "wholly ignorant at the time this disposition was made of said cases, of the character of the offense that had been committed," and he was pronounced free from all blame. Finally the grand jury declared that it would not indict either E. A. McHan, editor of the *Signal*, or M. W. Howard, author of the article in question for any libel.

Thus Colonel Howard felt in October, 1895, that he had been at least partially exonerated for his part in the much publicized embroilments of the spring. But in the meantime he had stirred up another hornet's nest.

In late August Colonel Howard had filled some speaking engagements in New York, making two talks at Buffalo, where he was quoted in the Democratic *Express*. In a long excerpt, which he claimed to be a misquote, very strong anti-southern and anti-white statements were attributed to him. Coming only 30 years after the Civil War, such sentiments were certain to cause quite an uproar in the rural south.

The white men of the south are themselves responsible for the so-called negro outrages, for which they lynch their fellowmen. They have stolen the negro's vote, then they have stolen the virtue of his wife, his mother and his daughter. When the negro sees these things, what can you expect of him but he will lose all respect for human nature? Why should he consider the virtue of white women any more sacred than that of his own race?

I do not say that there are not many occasions where horrible crimes are committed by the negroes, but I do say that the responsibility for these crimes rests on the whites. I am willing to go on record as having said that, and I am willing to repeat it wherever I raise my voice.

The Democratic papers reprinted the *Express* article with righteous indignation, the Populist with regretful consternation. Colonel Howard denied that he had made such statements and declared that a *verbatim* quotation of what he actually said was as follows:

The ballot box stuffers in the negro counties have robbed the negro of his vote, and these same men who are so base as to steal votes, have, in many instances, deprived their sisters and daughters of their virtue, and thus teaching them to disregard both honesty and purity, and having done this they become in a measure responsible for the spirit of lawlessness manifested on the part of the negroes, and are themselves to blame for having sown the seeds of dishonesty and corruption in ignorant soil where they have sprung up and borne such an abundant harvest.

But the damage had already been done; the hate of his enemies intensified; and in Fort Payne they grew in number. To an increasing majority Colonel Howard was a turncoat who had betrayed the Democratic Party and the whole south. He was the anarchist, the libertine and slanderer of the political essay. He was an immoral author of an immoral book. He was a troublemaker, from a family of troublemakers. The name HOWARD was despicable, contemptible, a word to be uttered or spat out with an oath.

There were rumors of impending violence, of plots to kill Colonel Howard and of schemes to burn his home. For many nights friends and Populist farmers from Cherokee County came to protect him, standing in vigilance from dusk until dawn around his home. During the day his sons, eleven and seven years of age, were tormented by youngsters who called their father names. Clyde, the older, often returned home with a torn shirt and a bloody nose.

But not all of 1895 was filled with bad news and conflict. If his enemies hated him, his friends loved him, in Fort Payne as well as the rest of the district. The more vocal his opponents became, the louder his Populist constituents shouted their approval. During the summer he had canvassed the district in the interest of strengthening his party and had been warmly received wherever he spoke. Even in Fort Payne he had drawn a large crowd. At Cedar Bluff, a crowd estimated at over 2,000 had listened attentively for almost two hours and had responded with a novel ovation Colonel Howard would never forget. A man on the grandstand had spoken to the large number of women in the crowd. All who pledged to stand by Colonel Howard with their sympathy and prayers while he battled for their cause in congress were to raise their hats and handkerchiefs in the air three times. When the signal was given the sea of fluttering hats and handkerchiefs thrilled Colonel Howard and rekindled his optimism.

During his speeches to such receptive audiences, Colonel Howard coined phrases and propounded theories on Populism, refining his arguments and his presentation, stressing the ideas most enthusiastically received. His thesis was always the need of the masses of the United States to support a party which represented their interests against those of the excessively rich people who formed the upper class or plutocracy. He began to formulate plans for incorporating his Populist beliefs into a book and announced in August that he was writing *The American Plutocracy*. Completed at the end of the year, it was published the following January.

Shortly before its publication, he began his brief career as a Populist congressman in the fifty-fourth congress, which opened on December 2, 1895. Joining Joseph Wheeler, John H. Bankhead, Oscar W. Underwood, and the other members of the Alabama delegation, he was the lone Populist, although T. H. Aldridge was to win the contested fifth district later. Shunned by many, Colonel Howard would never forget the warm greeting of Underwood, a young man exactly his own age. Though he would have preferred a Democrat from the seventh district, he told Colonel Howard, he clasped his hand and promised, "You can count on me as your friend."

News stories hinted and Washington rumors abounded that Colonel Howard would never be allowed to take his seat in congress, that he would not be assigned to any committees, that he would be socially ostracized, and even that he would be in physical danger because of the number of irate gentlemen who had recognized themselves in his famous book. However, the renewed publicity of *If Christ Came To Congress* also produced a few editors and ministers who commended it as a timely exposé of the corruption in the capital.

At any rate, he did arrive in Washington a marked man, pointed at by many and befriended by few. A member of a small minority party despised by the Democrats of the south and the Republicans of the west, from whose ranks its members had been drawn, he could command little respect and could wield little power. Lacking both social and political prestige, he felt like an outcast in the midst of the bustling Washington scene. His days inside the capital were unhappy and frustrating. They were also few.

Colonel Howard was an absentee congressman, voting or answering quorum calls approximately 14 per cent of the time during the 1895-96 session. Most of his voting occurred during the last two weeks of May after a dramatic return to the house following an extended absence because of illness.

The oratory of Colonel Howard was first exhibited upon the floor of the House of Representatives on February 10, when he spoke in favor of the bill to coin silver at the rate of sixteen to one. Four days later, when the bill was defeated by a vote of 290 to 90, with 50 abstaining, he was not present, though a fellow Alabama congressman, Gaston Robbins, announced he had planned to vote for the bill but was ill. The St. Louis *Republic* had a different explanation, claiming that Colonel Howard appeared on the floor drunk that day and had to be carried from the chambers by two porters.

On May 13, Colonel Howard arose to a question of personal privilege and defended himself in the halls of congress against the "cruel, baseless attack by the press of the country" three months previously. He explained that he had come to the house on February 14 to vote for the silver bill, coming against the advice of his physician and accompanied by his wife and Representative William Strowd, of North Carolina. The members around him, including Representative James McLachlan of California, had realized that he was desperately ill and had insisted that he leave. He protested the abuse he and his family had suffered because of his being a Populist and closed with the triumphant assertion:

> But whatever may be thought of the party to which I belong, I am a member of this house, and I am entitled to its protection against these assaults.

His speech of vindication received a loud round of applause from his fellow congressman.

He did not explain why his absence had lasted so long, that an initial illness, combined with the continued harassment of his political enemies, had brought on the first of four nervous breakdowns he was to suffer during his lifetime. He expressed his feelings during this time in a column entitled "The Murmurer," which he wrote for a Fort Payne newspaper.

> I have been ill, so ill in fact I felt the solid ground slipping from beneath my feet, and I was falling through space an interminable distance until I grew dizzy. Yes, sick in body and mind, so sick that I did not care if I never stopped falling . . . .
> And so I am convalescent; indeed I am well. For when my soul tells me all is well, my body quickly responds.

The turmoil of the previous year had taken its toll on his family. He would later describe this period of political involvement as the most miserable time of his life. A few months later, after their return from Washington, Sally was to spend several weeks resting at the Alabama White Sulphur Springs resort. In the fall Clyde would be sent out of town to a Bessemer school.

Colonel Howard was present and voting in congress for the last two weeks of May but there was little else for him to do in an official capacity. He had been appointed to two unimportant committees, the committee on the election of the president and vice-president and representatives to congress and the committee on expenditures in the post office department. He had introduced a number of bills, mostly private ones to provide relief for individuals, and several resolutions, including house resolution number 109, introduced in January. He had fulfilled a promise by offering this resolution which called on President Cleveland for "information regarding the distribution of patronage to induce members of Congress to vote for the repeal of the purchasing clause in the Sherman Law." The resolution was referred to the committee on coinage, weights, and measures and was never reported out.

Colonel Howard had supported the silver bill, defended his personal character, and attempted to investigate the means by which the silver-purchasing clause had been repealed. He had only one more important thing to do at the capitol. On Saturday, May 23, 1896, he attempted to start impeachment proceedings against Grover Cleveland.

Following the reading of the *Journal*, Colonel Howard rose to a question of privilege, which the speaker of the house, Thomas Reed, of Maine, asked him to present. His statement was sent to the clerk, who began reading this preamble:

I do impeach Grover Cleveland, President of the United States, of high crimes and misdemeanors on the following grounds:

The clerk was interrupted by Nelson Dingley, Jr., of Maine, who objected that the material was not privileged. But the speaker instructed the clerk to continue reading.

1. That he has sold or directed the sale of bonds without authority of law.
2. That he sold or aided in the sale of bonds at less than their market value.
3. That he directed the misappropriation of the proceeds of said bond sales.
4. That he directed the Secretary of the Treasury to disregard the law which makes United States notes redeemable in coin.
5. That he has ignored and refused to have enforced

the "anti-trust law."

6. That he has sent United States troops into the State of Illinios without authority of law and in violation of the Constitution.

7. That he has corrupted politics through the interference of Federal officeholders.

8. That he has used the appointing power to influence legislation detrimental to the welfare of the people: Therefore,

Be it resolved by the House of Representatives, That the Committee on the Judiciary be directed to ascertain whether these charges are true, and if so to report to the House such action by the impeachment or otherwise as shall be proper in the premises. And said committee shall have authority to send for persons and papers.

Representative Dingley raised the question of consideration and the house failed to consider the impeachment of the president. Colonel Howard, fully expecting such a rebuff, returned to his seat with a smile.

So much for the fifty-fourth congress. He would return to Alabama to test the political waters and decide whether or not to plunge into another political battle in the fall. Upon his return Colonel Howard traveled about his own district and other counties in the state as well. He then decided that the Populists had a good chance in Alabama if the national party would only stay independent, instead of joining the "Bryanized Democrats," as he called them. But the Populist Party was in a baffling and complicated predicament.

The Populists repeated their 1892 strategy of scheduling their national convention after that of both the Democrats and Republicans, hoping to attract the free-silver dissidents from both. However, after the Republicans nominated McKinley and came out for the gold standard, the Democrats nominated William Jennings Bryan and adopted a free-silver platform, leaving the Populists without a major issue. While it suited many of the western Populists to endorse the Democratic nominee, most southern members, more experienced in fusion with the Republicans, were aghast at the prospect. Colonel Howard, in a July speech at Scottsboro, predicted that the Populists would never endorse Bryan and made plans to fight such action at St. Louis later that month.

At the convention, the fifty-four member Alabama delegation elected Reuben Kolb, long considered the head of the state organization, as chairman over Colonel Howard but the majority approved Howard's opposition to a Bryan endorsement. Early voting on organizational matters revealed that pro-Bryan forces were in control, though some members thought the party could best retain its separate identity if it nominated Bryan instead of endorsing him. Colonel Howard, who didn't favor either action, saw that his faction was outnumbered but held out hope that Bryan's Democratic running mate, Arthur Sewall, a wealthy Maine banker and shipbuilder, would not be nominated by the Populists.

Colonel Howard arranged for a minority report to come out of the rules committee providing for a reversal of the usual order whereby the vice-presidential candidate would be nominated first. As this procedure would make it easier to nominate a Populist for this office, a fusion delegate moved to table the report. Colonel Howard demanded to be heard on the motion to table and obtained the floor of the convention. After his forceful and persuasive plea that the vice-president be nominated first in order to promote party harmony, the convention adopted the minority report.

Some Democrats who were in St. Louis to help promote Bryan's endorsement rushed out to telegraph their nominee of this strange turn of events. Bryan wired the convention chairman that he would not accept the Populist nomination unless Sewall were nominated also. However, if the chairman ever received the telegram, he failed to make it known to the convention.

In addition to Sewall, five other men were nominated for vice-president. They included Thomas E. Watson, former Georgia congressman who had been one of the first elected officials to join the new party. His name was placed in nomination by Colonel Howard, who referred to the sacrifices Watson had made for the Populist cause and exhorted, "A man who has borne the cross should wear the crown!"

Although Watson was not at the convention, those who knew him well had reason to believe that he would never withdraw from the race if nominated. On the other hand, many who favored fusion with the Democratic Party wanted someone who would later withdraw, leaving Bryan and Sewall as the candidates for both parties. Those delegates supported Harry Skinner, of North Carolina, whose name was placed in nomination by Peyton G. Bowman, of Alabama. Watson won on the first ballot and Colonel Howard felt he would be justified in again seeking election as a Populist.

Upon his return to Alabama, he spoke in Gadsden on behalf of Albert Goodwyn, the Populist candidate for governor on a Republican-Populist fusion ticket. His only reference to the Populist convention, however, was a brief comment offering congratulations to the Democrats for having nominated a Populist at the head of their ticket.

Goodwyn's race was not even close. Joseph F. Johnston, the free-silver Democrat, defeated him in the August election by carrying every district except Howard's seventh. Attention was then focused on the congressional races.

It looked as though Colonel Howard might have trouble in his district. Many influential Populists in Alabama opposed him and the national chairman was said to be in favor of replacing him. Among those mentioned as possible candidates was E. A. McHan, of Etowah County, who had announced that he was seeking the nomination. McHan was editor of the Gadsden *Tribune* and had formerly edited newspapers in Chattanooga, Fort Payne, Guntersville, and Boaz. Others included W. S. Foreman and J. S. E. Robinson, both of St. Clair County. George F. Gaither, of Walnut Grove, in Etowah County declared he would be a candidate if all the pro-Bryan forces would support him.

Of these men, the Gadsden *Times-News* chose Howard as being the most capable but made sure he didn't take this as a big compliment.

... He is decidedly the ablest man in the lot and that is not saying much for him. Howard is an orator of considerable ability, yet he does not impress one as being possessed of a great amount of intelligence.

The convention for the seventh district was held in Birmingham on September 3, at the Hood Building. In sharp contrast to the heated meetings of 1894, it was a quiet affair. Some Populists, apparently discouraged by the large Democratic vote in the governor's race, were losing confidence and interest in their party. DeKalb and Franklin Counties failed to send their alloted number of delegates and Franklin was not even represented. I. L. Brock, of Cherokee, placed Colonel Howard's name in nomination, declaring he was the only man who could be elected. He was seconded by M. W. McNutt, of DeKalb. Then E. A. McHan was nominated by the Marshall delegation and seconded by Dr. W. F. Coggin, of Etowah. No others were nominated and Colonel Howard won on the first ballot. The Populist candidate was the first in the field and anxious to see who would run against him.

The Republican district convention met two days later in Cullman, with two main contenders, Major C. O. Godfrey of DeKalb, and S. T. Fowler of St. Clair. For 80 ballots these two blocked each other from the nomination and the convention finally chose a 25 year old dark horse, James J. Curtis, of Winston County.

One week after the Republicans met, the Democratic convention was held in Gadsden and four names were placed in nomination. They were: L. L. Cochran, of DeKalb; W. T. L. Cofer, of Cullman; John G. Winston, Jr., of Marshall; and P. H. Newman, of Marshall. With even more obstinacy than the Republican delegates had shown, the Democratic delegates voted 139 times before settling on W. I. Bullock, of Winston County, as their compromise nominee.

A fourth candidate was George H. Parker, of Cullman, chosen by the Gold Democrats at their district convention in Cullman, on September 29. By taking votes from the regular Democratic nominee, Parker was to make the other three parties more nearly equal in strength.

The congressional campaign of 1896 bore little resemblance to the '94 race. When Denson had challenged him to public debate, Colonel Howard had declined on the grounds that there might be physical violence, logical reasoning in view of their encounter at the Populist convention. But in mid-September, 1896, when Colonel Howard challenged both Bullock and Curtis, the Democratic nominee accepted. Colonel Howard and Bullock were to travel together over the district

83

engaging in joint debates, with each making hour-long speeches and having 15 minute rebuttals. Whereas Colonel Howard and Denson had come dangerously close to killing each other two years earlier, he and Bullock traveled in the same buggy, ate at the same table, and sometimes even slept in the same bed. Although they were political opponents, they came out of the campaign the best of friends.

Their first joint debate took place before a large crowd at Centre on September 19. Bullock spoke first, delivering a carefully prepared talk in the polite and formal old oratorical style. After he had been loudly applauded, Colonel Howard complimented him on his beautiful address, but offered the opinion that it did not fit in with the political situation at that time. He spoke in flattering terms of his opponent's character and accomplishments, but expressed his regrets that Bullock was being used as an offering for the sins of the Democratic Party. He then proceeded to discuss some of those "sins," charging election frauds and citing three congressional elections in 1894 where the declared Democratic victors had lost their contested seats. He charged that the frauds committed in those elections involved carrying the names of bird dogs on the polling lists and claimed that scores of men who had long been dead continued to vote the Democratic ticket at every election. The Negroes in the black belt were allowed to vote as they pleased, he said, but their votes were counted for the Democratic ticket no matter which way they voted. At the conclusion he pointed out the advantages of the tariff and promised to support it.

As Colonel Howard saw it, his fight was against the Democratic Party. And that party was growing stronger and welcoming back many of those who had recently strayed. Even R. F. Kolb, who had twice run for governor on the Populist ticket, campaigned hard for Bullock, circulating thousands of copies of the paper he edited, the *People's Tribune*, throughout the district. Others who rejoined the enemy included Peyton G. Bowman and George Gaither, who both actively campaigned for Bullock.

Colonel Howard knew one *real* Populist who might help him. After he had made arrangements for Tom Watson to speak on his behalf in Gadsden during the month of October, the *Times-News* quipped, "No one but Howard would have thought of getting the biggest man in the whole party to help him out."

The Gadsden paper noted that his city had never been visited by a vice-presidential candidate before. But it was difficult to tell just how impressed the editor was by Watson's scheduled visit.

Gadsden is to have the pleasure of entertaining a very distinguished gentleman sometime during the month, probably near the 15th instant. He is one of the most talked of persons in the country today, and is no other than the brilliant but erratic Hon. Thomas E. Watson, of Georgia, candidate for vice-president of these United States, on the people's party ticket.

He will make a speech here for the ticket on which he has the honor of occupying the tail end.

Speaking in Gadsden on October 22, Watson endorsed Colonel Howard's candidacy and promised that he would never withdraw from his own race until he reached either victory or defeat.

With his wife capably in charge of his campaign headquarters at Cullman, Colonel Howard continued his speaking tours. While he lashed out repeatedly at the Democrats, who seemed confident of victory, he probably peered anxiously over his shoulder at the Republican activity also. Their candidate was young and was not well known but they were running a well-financed campaign and expected a heavy vote during this presidential election year.

On November 3, the election was held and the suspense should have ended. However, the election was close and some ballots with write-in votes for presidential electors were thrown out. Two days after the election one newspaper reported that Howard was probably the winner by less than 200 votes and another predicted that Bullock had won by about the same number. Two weeks after the election both Howard and Bullock were claiming victory. The official vote finally showed Howard the winner with 6,168 votes. Bullock had 5,628; Curtis received 4,982; and Parker had 454.

Colonel Howard had run well ahead of the Bryan-Watson ticket and only slightly behind Bryan and Sewall. Over all, he had run well, except in DeKalb County, where he had fared badly. The vote from his own county was: Curtis 1,390; Bullock 1,236; Howard 305; and Parker 18.

Even if Colonel Howard had lost the election, he would have gone back to Washington for the "lame-duck" session of the fifty-fourth congress which began on December 7, 1896. The country was by then caught up in debate over the best policy to adopt in regard to the trouble between Spain and Cuba, with President Cleveland taking a decidedly "dovish" position. One week after congress convened Colonel Howard introduced a resolution providing for our recognition of Cuba's independence. It was sent to the committee on foreign affairs and never reported out.

In February he presented two bills embodying Populistic principles. One would have provided the government's issuing of larger quantities of paper money and one would have placed more restrictions on national banks. He also introduced a type of "right-to-work" bill which would have prohibited workers from being coerced either to join unions or not to join them. These bills were also buried in the committees to which they were assigned. At the end of the term, Colonel Howard voted to override Cleveland's veto of a bill which would have restricted immigration to this country by literacy qualifications.

As soon as McKinley took office he called congress into session to revise the tariff along lines which had been prepared by Nelson Dingley. Colonel Howard, who had long promised to support higher tariffs, made a congressional speech on March 23, 1897, in support of the Dingley bill. While he had the floor, he got in a few words on some unrelated subjects, urging proper financial legislation, destruction of the trusts and monopolies, and a curb on railroads.

The Democratic press was critical of Colonel Howard's support of the tariff. The Fort Payne *Journal* noted:

> One Populist, our own Howard, and five Democrats, three from Louisiana caught by the sugar schedule, and two from Texas who doubtless own a few sheep, voted for the Dingley bill in the House.

The Eufaula *Times* mused sarcastically that perhaps

Howard thought this bill would keep out dirty books and give his own somewhat of a monopoly.

Colonel Howard had moved from Fort Payne to Cullman early in 1897 so that his family might be in a more friendly atmosphere, especially while he was away from home. After congress adjourned he was still gone much of the time on speaking engagements. Much of the summer was spent helping Populists campaign in Louisiana and Kentucky.

During the year there was more and more talk throughout Alabama about the possibility that Colonel Howard would run for governor on the Populist ticket. When questioned by reporters, however, he skillfully avoided giving any definite plans for the future.

He did give some indication that he was tiring of politics, though. For one thing, he had found that congressmen didn't really have such a good life after all. "Unless a poor man wants to be a scalawag," he told a reporter, "politics don't pay for a man who is not rich."

He elaborated further in a Birmingham interview:

No, politics doesn't pay. On the $5,000 salary I could not save anything and live decently like a Congressman. I do not care to remain in politics much longer. I once made $100,000, but lost it, and if I keep in politics I will leave nothing for my family in case I should die.

He also revealed that he had been writing short stories and might drop out of politics sometime to pursue a writing career.

Speculation continued as to whether or not Colonel Howard would accept the Populist nomination for governor. During an interview in Birmingham in November, both Colonel Howard and A. T. Goodwyn, the candidate in the previous election, assured a reporter that their party would have a candidate who could win over the Democrats. When asked if he would run, Colonel Howard replied that the honor should go to someone else, but did not make a flat denial that he would run. It was generally agreed by the year's end that Colonel Howard was the leading contender for the Populist nomination for governor of Alabama.

With his political future unsettled, he returned to Washington in December for the second session of the fifty-fifth congress. He voted with the majority of representatives to give President McKinley power to intervene in Cuba, if necessary to assure peace, and remained on the side of the hawks through the period leading up to the Spanish-American War.

The only time Colonel Howard made any headlines himself during this session was in January, 1898, when he introduced a bill to change the currency and to increase its volume. It provided that all United States money would be paper units, starting with mills and ascending to cents, dimes, dollars, eagles, condors, and talents. A condor would equal ten eagles or $100 and a talent would be worth ten condors or $1,000. The government was to distribute $40 per capita annually to states, counties, and municipalities and every citizen would, upon application, be eligible to receive $1,000 each year. Needless to say, this bill met the same fate all his others did.

Meanwhile, in Alabama the Populist executive committee had decided to put out a straight ticket rather than fuse with either of the old parties. Colonel Howard feared their chances would be slim if they had no help from the Republicans and he shied away from the governor's race. At their convention in May, the Populists nominated G. B. Deans for governor and selected ten men, including Colonel Howard, to attend the national convention if one were held.

Colonel Howard had still not made a definite stand on whether or not he would run again for congress but had received confidential assurances that the Republicans would support him even without a fusion of the parties in other races. At their convention only one man, F. H. Lathrop of Saint Clair, announced as a candidate. Even though there was some opposition, he was nominated and Colonel Howard knew there would be a three-way contest for his seat in the house. He began immediately to investigate some business ventures.

The Democrats were so certain of victory this time that seven candidates sought the nomination for congressman. However, another dark horse, John L. Burnett, finished as the winner. The Populists waited until after the state election in August to schedule their convention and choose their candidate.

Colonel Howard campaigned for the Populist gubernatorial candidate, G. B. Deans, who was attempting to unseat the incumbent, Joseph Johnston. In July he debated Burnett at Centre and Congressman John Bankhead at Russellville. However, Johnston won easily, carrying 57 of the state's 66 counties. Colonel Howard was feeling less like a candidate every day.

Between the state election and the Populist district convention, Colonel Howard announced his decision, stating emphatically that he would not be a candidate for congress. He announced that he had bought a home in Fort Payne and would devote his time and efforts in the future to the upbuilding of his former hometown and county.

When the Populists met at Albertville on August 17, Colonel Howard's name was placed in nomination, even though he was there insisting that he would not run. A motion to nominate him by acclamation was stopped only by his rising to oppose it. The convention, disappointed at losing its chief standard bearer, nominated Oliver D. Street, of Marshall County.

Having voluntarily retired from congress, Colonel Howard registered his family at the DeKalb Hotel in Fort Payne and made arrangements to enter once again into the business world.

Part II

An Interlude

It was some time in 1896 when he saw her and was captivated by her striking appearance, by her ruby-red hair and sapphire-blue eyes. Her complexion was like that of Ireland's maidens, her body perfect and graceful, her manner subtle and comely. Her personality was effervescent, her intelligence astonishing for one so young.

She was only 17 and she listened breathlessly as the big congressman in his early 30's spoke to her about her treasured books. She trembled in awe as he placed a hand on her shoulder and complimented her literary taste.

It was a brief and innocent encounter of two people who were much alike, and each lonely in a strange melancholy way, each seeking expression through solitary journeys into the land of books and dreams.

He had been lecturing in Rome, where he had spoken at

Shorter College. During his stay in Georgia he was the house-guest of a cousin, Thomas A. Lloyd. It was Thomas' daughter, Stella Vivian Lloyd, whom he saw for the first time.

He had visited her study and had been amazed at the array of books she exhibited so proudly. There were books of poetry, Burns, Byron, Shelley, Keats, Longfellow, Whittier, and many others. She owned the works of Shakespeare and shelves of Emerson, Carlyle, Ruskin, Huxley, Darwin, Paine, Poe, Dickens, Scott, Hugo, Bulwer, and the standard books of philosophy, fiction, and great literature. She had read every one of them and could discuss with enthusiasm any subject he chose as he read the authors and titles of many old favorites.

A few golden days in the spring of life, a brief communion of kindred spirits, and then they went their separate ways. But her memory would linger on in a secret corner of his mind. And one day—many, many years later—she would become his wife. She would be his "Lady Vivian."

Part III

The American Plutocracy

Colonel Howard's Populist treatise, covering 246 pages in a small, five by seven inch book, is a belligerent presentation of his three basic positions on economic policy:

1. The United States was definitely ruled by the wealthy class, whose power had been firmly established by the contraction of currency caused by the gold standard.
2. The ever-widening gulf between the abject poor and the excessively rich made it necessary for the great masses to labor and toil to enable the plutocrats to lead lives of idleness and luxury.
3. The rapid concentration of wealth in the hands of a few was the most alarming sign of the times and could lead to revolution and disaster.

Colonel Howard claimed that both the Republican and Democratic Parties were financed and controlled by plutocrats. In discussing plutocracy versus democracy, he explained, "I do not mean the Democracy of Grover Cleveland, for it is only plutocracy masquerading in a stolen costume."

90

The plutocrats collectively constituted the despised "money power" which had complete control of the country and its resources and was the enemy of all working men and women. According to the author, nearly all the money was controlled by the trusts, the wealthy corporations, and the plutocrats. All the commodities were controlled by trusts, which squeezed money from the poor and emptied it into the pockets of the plutocrats; every raise in price constituted robbery. Plutocracy was portrayed as the modern highwayman, who was feted and honored by the state instead of being punished. Andrew Jackson and Abraham Lincoln are quoted extensively as having warned Americans about the potential dangers of the money power.

Nearly all the newspapers of the country were said to represent the voice of this monstrous money power, and continuously taught false economic and political doctrines. Even the military was against the working class. Its forces had been called upon to compel laborers to submit to capital but had never been employed to make greedy plutocracy do its duty. The system of lobbying further perpetuated the rule of the money power. For in actual practice, lobbyists participated in large-scale bribery, with huge sums of money furnished by trusts, combines and rich corporations.

Of course his main target as a basic cause of what Colonel Howard deemed to be "rule by plutocracy" was the gold standard. It was, he asserted, "the stronghold of plutocracy, the powerful bulwark behind which it is entrenched." He used historical references to the Roman and British Empires to prove that panic and poverty resulted from tight money, or contraction of value. The banner of free silver is raised as the panacea for the nation's monetary problems:

Contraction means misery, hunger, ruin.
Expansion of the currency means prosperity,
  happiness and joy.
Which shall it be?
The voters of America must decide.

The poor "wage slave" class was growing larger, while the once great middle class was shrinking, Colonel Howard declared.

Soon the middle class would entirely disappear and the pluto-crat class, though small in number, would become more mighty in power. Quite adroit at portraying vividly the tragedy and pathos of poverty, he repeated the practice used in his earlier book of quoting actual newspaper accounts of starvation and suicide cases. Each was presented, not as an isolated case in a large city, but as a typical example of the fate of the working class.

The lives of paupers and princes were compared, with 28 pages devoted to the famous Paget-Whitney wedding, where the flowers alone were said to have cost $60,000. The multi-millionaires, John D. Rockefeller, William Astor, Jay Gould, Russell Sage, and Cornelius Vanderbilt had gained their vast fortunes, not by their own labors, he claimed, but by legalized methods of robbery by which they stole what others earned. These men were leaders of the organized plutocrats who had gained control of all legislation and possession of every avenue of commerce and trade while eliminating all competition and opposition.

Impressive charts and figures were clearly aimed at the less affluent people of the nation. They revealed, for example, that the *per capita* value of 30,000 people was $285,628. And, to earn the amount of William Waldorf Astor's income for one day would require 81 years for a man working at $1.00 a day for 300 days a year.

Interspersed among the pages of Populist doctrine and Howard theory were pictures of "twelve apostles of wealth" who had a net worth of $1,000,000,000, which they had alleg-edly gained without labor by robbing the poor. These pluto-crats, who had been protected, along with their "stolen booty," by laws passed by "perjured lawmakers," were the following eleven men and one woman: George M. Pullman, Andrew Carnegie, Hetty Green, John Jacob Astor, Russell Sage, William C. Whitney, John D. Rockefeller, C. S. Brice, Collis P. Hunting-ton, W. K. Vanderbilt, George Gould, and J. Pierpont Morgan.

Colonel Howard warned repeatedly that the concentration of wealth in the hands of a small minority was a danger to democracy and could cause revolution.

If they will not consent to give back to the people

some of their earnings of which they have been robbed, the time will come when the people, lashed to fury, will rise up in anger, and take back, not a portion, but all.

His arguments were often eloquent:

... liberty is a tender plant and requires constant watching and careful culture.
Plutocracy is on trial before the American people and Liberty looks on in breathless suspense.

They were usually dogmatic:

Labor created capital; therefore labor is the rightful master, and capital should be the obedient one.

To prevent revolution and chaos the currency would have to be expanded and a limit placed upon the amount of capital which individuals could possess. To achieve the latter goal, Colonel Howard proposed a constitutional amendment "precluding private property rights carried to absurd infinitude" which would prohibit any citizen or resident of the United States from possessing over $1,000,000 in property or money.

It was a radical young man who wrote *The American Plutocracy*, a man who had briefly experienced some of the pleasure and power of money and prosperity before rejoining the struggling "have nots" of the country. Blinded by bitterness and envy, he presented a one-sided, distorted view more notable for exaggerations and omissions than for clarity or fairness.

Men who had been leaders during the industrial era were all described as parasites or thieves. They were given no credit for their knowledge or genius. No mention was made of the number of jobs they had created, of the industrial progress they promoted, the colleges they endowed and other philanthropic endeavors they pursued.

The book is a stinging attack upon the capitalistic system and all who were financially successful, penned by a disillusioned business failure passing through one of many metamorphic stages of his political philosophy. But his literary skill often eclipsed his shallow reasoning. For, no matter what he said in this book, he usually said it well.

93

His Last Hurrah

Though he had served in Congress for four years and had maintained a home in Cullman for almost half of that period, Colonel Howard had never lost interest in the town of Fort Payne. It was there that he had begun to practice law, had courted and married his ever-faithful Sally and had buried their infant son, Clarence. He had followed the town's struggle for survival following the collapse of the boom and through the nation-wide depression which followed the panic of 1893.

The holdings of the Fort Payne Iron and Coal Company, which included various buildings and industrial sites, as well as some 30,000 acres of mineral and farm lands, had been placed in receivership in 1892. This property, representing over $1,000,000 in investments, had been sold at public auction in February, 1894 to E. N. Cullen, a Birmingham businessman, for $60,000. Cullen was representing a syndicate of ten men, mostly Massachusetts and New Hampshire investors, and it was hoped that their new DeKalb Company would furnish capital to create some factory and mining activity. All Fort Payne industry, except the lime works, operated by B. A. Rodgers, and the Standard Basket Company, run by D. R. Saunders and W. T. Folsom, had long since ceased operations.

Unfortunately, little was accomplished by the new company, other than the reopening of the coal mine at Beeson Gap, with E. A. Stinson in charge. Two years later the steel mill, which had been run only 30 days during the boom, was started up briefly for a few trial runs. Most of the company property was either stripped of whatever might be salable or merely left in a state of disrepair to deteriorate further. Kilns at the fire-brick plant which had cost about $2,500 were dismantled and the iron bands sold for a trifling sum as scrap iron, leaving the remains a mass of rubble. Indignant observers were prompted to comment that the company would be better advised to give such property away to interested people who would at least help preserve it; then the DeKalb Company's adjoining proper-ties would have a much higher value.

No further industrial progress was made, however, until direction and leadership came from an unexpected source. Major Godfrey returned. The hustling Massachusetts promoter, who had lived in St. Louis since the Fort Payne boom had fizzled, returned in 1894, purchasing the beautiful Rice home on Forest Avenue as his permanent residence. Though he was at the time manager of Granite City, Illinois, and would become receiver for various land companies and a railroad, he was to call Fort Payne home until his death six years later. In addition to his own varied and extensive business interests throughout the period, he was to be continuously searching for prospective investors and industry for Fort Payne.

Dr. A. B. Green bought the basket factory and Saunders and Folsom then purchased the Fort Payne Stove Works and began manufacturing hundreds of Southland Stoves, which were shipped out to various distant cities each week. With three com-panies in operation, Major Godfrey vowed that he would not rest until Fort Payne had at least 12.

Several well-laid plans failed to materialize, however, and little headway was made until 1897. In June of that year, Major Godfrey called a meeting of leading businessmen and civic leaders at the courthouse, advising them to organize as a group to concentrate upon securing one industry at a time. Later in the year, largely through the Major's efforts, eastern buyers were found for the Kaolin Mines, north of Valley Head, and for the clay plant at Fort Payne. Two mines were developed, with the little community which sprang up being first called Kaolin, then Eureka, and eventually, after it obtained a post office in 1899, Metcalf. New and improved machinery, costing $12,000, was bought for the fire-brick plant. A pottery company was also organized in Fort Payne and it appeared that a modest boom had been launched in 1897. Colonel Howard watched closely and began to consider returning to Fort Payne.

He also had reason to expect that his reception in that town would be more friendly at this time. For one thing, there had been a change in the city government. Evidently, Colonel Howard's political bouts with the Democrats had been the major cause of the dissension which led him to move away. But in the city election of 1897, the Democratic candidate for mayor, W. T. Folsom, was defeated by the Republican, S. C. Adams, in a disputed election which had to be settled finally by the Alabama Supreme Court. Thus, with a Republican mayor in office for the term of 1898-99, with McKinley as president, and with Captain Joe J. Nix taking over Thomas Jacoway's job as postmaster, Colonel Howard may have felt his position as a Populist would not be as untenable in Fort Payne at this time.

Thus Colonel Howard again joined Major Godfrey in an attempt to industrialize the Fort Payne area. First, he promoted the organization of the Fort Payne Land and Industrial Company, incorporated in September, 1898, with the backing of both eastern financiers and Alabama investors. It was hoped that the group could purchase the vast holdings of the DeKalb Company and put its properties to better use. The two companies could not come to terms, however, and the latter did not sell until five years later.

Colonel Howard's next project was that of establishing a new business in which he could invest in an effort to rebuild his own fortune. As a large amount of wheat was raised in DeKalb County at the time, he reasoned that a good flour mill would be successful. Rounding up other local investors, he organized the Fort Payne Milling Company, which was incorporated in September with a capital of $10,000.

Busily pursuing his new business interests, Colonel Howard took little part in the congressional campaign. Burnett, to no one's surprise, recaptured the seat for the Democrats with 7,035 votes. Street trailed with 5,066 Populist votes and the Republican candidate, Lathrop, received 3,636 votes. Had the Populists and the Republicans backed the same man, they could have won; but by placing separate nominees in the field, they had practically assured the Democratic victory which Colonel Howard had foreseen.

For the moment, Colonel Howard's attention was not focused upon either party politics, which he had shunned, or upon the work of a congressman, the position he still held. He had moved his family back to Fort Payne in December, 1898, and was totally absorbed with the interests there. Although he spent some time in Washington during the last session of the fifty-fifth congress, he was involved most of the time in searching for capital to finance Fort Payne industries.

Among the things he had learned in Washington was the fact that congressmen were able to save little of the salary he had once considered more than adequate. His own savings at the time amounted to less than $1,000 and he could furnish little more than ideas and leadership toward realizing his dream of rebuilding an industrial city.

In April, 1899, Colonel Howard served on a committee with A. L. Campbell and S. E. Dobbs to plan a mass meeting with its purpose being to form a permanent organization to promote industry. A large crowd attending the meeting at the courthouse on April 19 was entertained with music by the Fort Payne Band and speeches by Colonel Howard and W. W. Haralson. The Settlers' and Manufacturers' Aid Society of North Alabama was organized, with Colonel Howard elected president. Other officers included L. L. Cochran, vice-president; Earl Cochran, secretary; C. M. T. Sawyer, treasurer; A. L. Campbell, trustee; W. W. Haralson, attorney; and L. Scott Allen, general manager. The purpose of the organization was to aid in "reviewing our languishing industries, colonizing our agricultural lands, and developing our wonderful resources." According to the *Journal*, it was strictly a conservative business organization and was "opposed to booms and clap-trap." Allen, the general manager, had formerly managed the Southern Railway's advertising bureau in Boston and was expected to make a good area booster. Colonel Howard did his part in providing publicity for the industrial movement through speaking engagements and by means of interviews he arranged with reporters in various large cities.

Meanwhile, he and his family were enjoying living in the beautiful Pierce home, a large boom day residence on Elm Street, which he had purchased for a fraction of its original cost. In May a wedding took place there when Colonel

Howard's sister Octie married Forney Stephens, editor of the Oneonta *Democrat*.

The Howards also purchased a farm just north of Fort Payne where Willstown Mission had been established by the American Board of Foreign Missions in 1824. The large two-story log structure, built by the Indians and missionaries, along with the smoke house and the spring house, was still there, the oldest building in DeKalb County. Though Colonel Howard continued living in town, he supervised the planting of an orchard, the purchase of livestock, and the gardening.

In June, 1899, Colonel Howard called a meeting of the Settlers' and Manufacturers' Aid Society at their office in the opera block, urging that a great celebration be planned for what was mistakenly looked upon as the county's last Fourth of July observance of the nineteenth century. The assembled leaders decided to work toward making this a day of "friendly reunion, a red-letter day of harmony and accord" for all the people of DeKalb County and for citizens of adjoining counties as well.

On a bright and clear Tuesday morning people began arriving early for the holiday festivities. They came in buggies, in wagons and carts; some rode horses or mules and some walked. The morning trains brought many more and by 9 o'clock the streets were more crowded than they had ever been during the boom. A giant procession formed near the court house at 10 o'clock and marched northward behind the band to a shady grove where temporary seats had been constructed. With less than a third of the huge crowd able to be seated, the others gathered as near as possible to the crude grandstand where Colonel Howard served as master of ceremonies and delivered the main address, a stirring and emotional old-fashioned speech. At noon, an estimated 3,000 persons gathered twenty deep around the long tables where the ladies had spread basket lunches of fried chicken, pies, cakes, and many other appetizing and aromatic foods.

It was truly a time of harmony and accord, with Colonel Howard the driving force and the center of attention. But it was Milford Howard, the businessman-farmer, the civic leader and renowned speaker, who was accepted with such respect and affection, not Howard the politician.

He even returned to the scene of the Howard-Jacoway

fight and delivered a speech at the crowded lecture hall of the Opera House for the opening exercises of the North Alabama College in October. And that highly esteemed institution joined the rest of Fort Payne in showing its full acceptance of Colonel Howard by making him a director.

His speaking engagements were not limited to Fort Payne. Colonel Howard's fame as a lecturer had spread throughout the nation during his congressional terms and he could always turn to the lecture circuit as a source of additional income. In need of money in the fall of 1899, he left on another tour, spending several weeks speaking in Kentucky, where he also gave support to the Populist organization in that state.

With the year 1900 looming ahead as a big political year, with voters preparing to choose a president, a governor, and congressmen, the Populist party of Alabama looked toward their best known member to seek some office. There was talk of Colonel Howard's being nominated for governor and many believed he would seek the office of United States senator, even though he would stand little chance of being chosen by a Democratic state legislature. His main political concern at this time, however, was the prevention of a Populist fusion with the Democrats.

The national Populist Party had become irreparably split over Bryan's nomination in 1896 and the fusionists and "midroaders" held separate conventions in 1900. At the Alabama convention on May 2, Colonel Howard was elected as one of the delegates to the national convention of the anti-fusionist or middle-of-the-road Populist Party faction, which convened in Cincinnati shortly afterward.

When he arrived at the Ohio meeting, Colonel Howard was pleasantly surprised at both the number and enthusiasm of the delegates who wanted to keep the Populist Party active in American politics—even though the older parties had adopted most of its policies. The 400 delegates organized and chose Colonel Howard as temporary chairman. In his ringing keynote address he proclaimed that moment as a time of crisis in the history of the People's Party, and he utilized his dramatic oratory to rally the troops to battle one more time.

Deafening cheers and applause resounded through the auditorium and Colonel Howard instantly became the favorite spokesman of a majority of the assembled party loyalists. He appeared to be their best possible nominee for president of the United States and his name was quickly placed in nomination. But another man had been actively seeking this honor and when Whorton Barker, a Philadelphia newspaperman, was also nominated, his supporters threatened to bolt the already fragmented organization if Colonel Howard were chosen. Sensing a political disaster, the former Alabama congressman requested permission, before the balloting began, to address the convention for a few minutes to plead for unity.

Before the hushed crowd he declared, "It would be a frightful mistake, Mr. Chairman, for us to commit a blunder today that would cause another split in the People's Party." In an emotional speech, interrupted several times by loud and prolonged applause, he vowed that he could not accept the nomination of the convention. After this statement, there arose cries of "Yes, you will!" prompting this conclusion:

> I came here to do what I believed was right. I never dreamed that this nomination would be offered me. I realize today, my friends, that you are in the majority in the convention. I appreciate the loyal support you have tendered me, but for the good of the party, for the good of Populism, which I place above Howard and Howard's ambition, I desire today to offer myself as a sacrifice upon the burning altar of Populism and Liberty, and withdraw my name from before this convention.

The delegates stood and cheered as Colonel Howard returned to his seat. In the voting which followed, many cast their votes for him anyway, as a first ballot courtesy. On the second ballot Barker was chosen as the presidential candidate and Ignatius Donnelly, a Minnesota author and former Republican congressman, was nominated for vice-president.

The next order of business being the election of a chairman of the national executive committee, Milton Park, a Texas delegate who was a native of Alabama, was nominated first. Then Colonel Howard arose once more, to nominate J.A. Parker, of Kentucky, and the convention—at least partially out of respect for Colonel Howard—elected Parker. Then the final

100

motion, the customary expression of appreciation to the mayor and the citizens of Cincinnati, also offered by Colonel Howard, was adopted and this convention—in which the big Alabamian had played a major role—adjourned on the afternoon of May 10, 1900.

In a heroic effort to help the Populist cause, Colonel Howard hit the campaign trail later that month, beginning in Kentucky and covering Nebraska, Oregon, and Ohio, as well as Georgia and several other southern states. His speeches consisted mainly of impassioned attacks on the Democratic Party, often referred to at the time simply as "Democracy."

Democracy in the west is a vague reaching out for something in the nature of a reform. Democracy in the east is an organized appetite for office, and Democracy in the south is a thing opposed to everything, something that never learns and never forgets; it is bourbonism.

In the western states, he exhorted his listeners to oppose fusion with the Democrats, insisting there was not a single basis for fusion between Populists and Democrats. Kansas, Oregon, and California had been lost to the Republicans, he claimed, because the combined votes of the two more liberal parties had decreased after fusion.

His most bitter and dramatic charge was that of Democratic frauds in the south. He claimed that the specter of Negro domination was constantly flaunted before the voters, when it was actually by means of the frightful frauds in the Negro counties that the Democrats of the south had stayed in power.

While walking alone down Market Street in Chattanooga one hot day in July, Colonel Howard was suddenly attacked and bitten by a vicious dog, which escaped before surprised bystanders could catch it. Although he had received an ugly wound, he continued on his way to Georgia for a week's campaign there. Most of his trips were made alone or in the company of other Populist speakers. But he was occasionally joined by his wife, who spent two weeks with him in Nebraska in September.

He spoke to large crowds of curious listeners and to small groups of attentive party members, heard flattering, laudatory introductions and loud rounds of applause, read favorable, even highly complimentary newspaper accounts of his speeches. But in his heart he knew he was laboring in vain. His campaign speeches were only parting shots in a lost cause. For the greatest strength of the Populist Party, its impact and influence on the policies of the two major parties, had proved to be the cause of its weakness; with most of its platform having been adopted by the Democrats and Republicans, a small minor party offered little attraction for most voters.

His own fortunes were also declining. While Colonel Howard fought valiantly for the Populist Party he again incensed former political enemies and also made new ones. By further estranging himself from the party of his youth, he was eliminating any possibility of again being accepted by the Democratic Party, as most of his fellow Populists soon would be. Nor were his long absences helping his business interests which suffered increasing losses. In December he finally faced the inevitable fact that he must concentrate upon earning an income. Returning to the profession at which he had been most successful, he bought the law library of L. L. Cochran, who was retiring, and opened an office. His return to the practice of law came too late, however, for him to settle his accumulated debts. On Saturday, March 9, 1901, Colonel Howard filed a bankruptcy petition in the federal court in Birmingham. His liabilities were given as $10,027.36 and his assets were $796.

For a while it appeared that Colonel Howard had learned that he fared much better away from the center of politics. On March 13, 1901, a Populist-Republican mass meeting was held at the court house for the purpose of endorsing a delegate who would oppose the proposed state constitutional convention. The opening was delayed for some time, due to the absence of the chairman of the Populist executive committee, but a messenger who was dispatched to find him returned with the information that Colonel Howard had gone to his farm.

In the absence of the Populist leader, his party and the Republicans held their meeting anyway. Led by Dr. E. H. Killian, J. B. Franklin, and John J. Durham, they endorsed a mysterious Democrat, whom they refused to name for publication, to oppose a constitutional convention which was expected to provide for literacy tests for voters. The unnamed candidate endorsed by the group proved to be Davey Crockett Case of Lebanon, who consequently defeated R. H. Smith, of Collinsville.

Colonel Howard continued to keep his speeches and other activities nonpolitical during 1901. In June, he helped plan a festive barbecue to be held in the grove north of town on the Fourth of July, and agreed to serve as master of ceremonies. Later in July, he spoke to the diminishing remnant of the Third Confederate Cavalry during its three-day reunion at the old soldiers' camp in the grove.

He also applied himself to the practice of law, where he especially excelled in criminal law. By August he was doing well enough financially for Sally and her aunt to spend a month at Sally's favorite retreat, Alabama White Sulphur Springs. At about this time, Colonel Howard and John B. Isbell, who had just received his law degree from George Washington University, formed a partnership which also extended to some joint investments in real estate.

Colonel Howard continued his interest in community activities. He served during this period, along with J. H. E. Guest, S. B. Slone, W. M. T. Wear, Dr. W. S. Duff, A. L. Campbell, and J. A. Lankford, on the committee in charge of the "Old Cemetery" which was later named Glenwood. They had general superintendency of the cemetery and planned programs for the annual decoration in May. Colonel Howard also remained the most popular speaker in the county, appearing before veterans' organizations, farmers' unions, Woodmen of the World, Odd Fellows, family reunions, and other groups. Each Fourth of July found him as the featured speaker at one or more communities.

Meanwhile, his law practice continued to prosper and he was often engaged in cases in nearby cities, especially when prominent criminal cases were tried. The firm of Howard and Isbell was dissolved and Colonel Howard formed a partnership with Luke P. Hunt in 1904.

The Howards were active members of the Fort Payne First Baptist Church, where Colonel Howard taught a large Sunday School class and sometimes expressed views and interpretations of the Bible which were considered extremely liberal by some. They were entirely too liberal for a young pastor who had graduated not long before from the Baptist Theological Seminary at Louisville. The minister became quite furious with Colonel Howard after visiting his class and observing some of his unorthodox teaching. Colonel Howard was informed that he was surely on "the swift road to hell." His pastor was told that *he* was already there and didn't know it. A committee was appointed and given an ultimatum by the minister: either Colonel Howard would be expelled from the Baptist Church or its pastor would resign. The committee, however, reached the conclusion that Colonel Howard had not committed any wrongs which would justify his expulsion. In fact, some of the members had shared most of his views. This controversy—provoked by a master of controversy—ended with the resignation of the pastor and also of the Sunday School teacher. Embarrassed by the episode, in spite of the support shown him by fellow church members, Colonel Howard stopped attending church for a while, becoming more deeply entangled in a confused philosophy which combined traces of mysticism, fatalism, and agnosticism, mixed with his own progressive interpretation of Christianity.

The father of sons only, Colonel Howard gained his first daughter-in-law in 1903. The previous summer, the Reverend J. R. McMullen, the father of three daughters, moved to Fort Payne to serve as pastor of the Cumberland Presbyterian Church. The eldest daughter, Perle, and Clyde Howard were married at the bride's home by her father on December 2, 1903.

For four years, Colonel Howard had concentrated on his family and profession, but in the fall of 1904 he consented to make several Populist speeches for the small following which remained active. He returned to the political stump in order to campaign for Thomas E. Watson, the presidential nominee and on one occasion they spoke from the same platform in Kentucky. Little did Colonel Howard suspect at that time that their next encounter would be as bitter opponents.

The early 1900's were comparatively happy and prosperous years for the Howards. This period provided a respite of tranquillity, with few major disappointments or mishaps. Perhaps the most serious misfortune was an accident to Claude, who had two fingers cut off at Auburn, where he was attending school, in April, 1905. That same month, Sally may have narrowly avoided disaster by leaving San Francisco, where she was visiting, just before a major earthquake caused great destruction and 700 deaths.

Colonel Howard remained a popular speaker and lecturer and also frequently enjoyed opportunities to reveal his versatility as an entertainer. Such was the case in April, 1905, when he appeared before the Robert E. Lee Literary Society at the North Alabama Conference College in Birmingham. Introduced as "the greatest platform speaker on the American continent," he spoke on the subject, "Dr. Jekyll and Mr. Hyde." Departing from his serious lecture on the objective and the subjective in human nature, he gave impersonations of Jekyll and Hyde which thrilled and astounded his audience and was interrupted frequently by furious bursts of applause. He quickly moved from tragedy to Negro dialect and went on to "surpassing flights of poetic prose" before the delighted listeners. The society booked him for a return engagement before he ever left the hall.

In September the Howards moved to their country home, formerly known as the McSpadden farm, and made their home in the historic old mission. It was also to serve as home for Clyde and Claude and their families.

On January 30, 1908, Claude and Jennie Norris, of Tuscaloosa, were married at her home. Jennie, a highly intelligent and sensitive young high school girl, had been swept off her feet by the dashing and handsome Claude, whom she had met while vacationing at Mentone with her parents, Mr. and Mrs. Charles Norris and her brothers, Kenneth and Charles Jr. The wedding came as a surprise to friends who had expected 17 year old Jennie to complete the education her father had planned for her.

But her young suitor had journeyed to Tuscaloosa, to the beautiful two-story ante-bellum Norris home on University Avenue. In this carpeted house, filled with large gold-framed oil portraits—on the large airy porch with its big comfortable rockers—and in the spacious court yard, still lined with one-room log slave cabins, he had pleaded with Jennie to become his wife. The young couple was married and returned to Fort Payne on the day of the wedding to live on the Howard farm.

Though Colonel Howard was fast becoming the patriarch

of a large family which looked to him for leadership and financial support, it was the addition of Jennie which would mean most to him. His younger son would one day desert this child bride, but Colonel Howard would always cherish her steadfast character and loyalty. Upon his death many years later, Colonel Howard would leave all his worldly possessions, not to either son, but to his former daughter-in-law, Jennie.

During these years on his farm, Colonel Howard remained active in the civic affairs of Fort Payne and played a significant role in the history of the first high school. When efforts were first begun, in 1907, to build the school, Colonel Howard was named to head the committee to secure a five-acre site. Serving with him were John A. Davis, W. E. Dobbs, T. J. Cook, and A. B. Green. When the laying of the cornerstone ceremony was held, on a rainy Fourth of July, 1908, Colonel Howard delivered the main address. After dinner on the ground and a Masonic cornerstone ceremony, additional speeches were made at the Opera House when threatening skies turned into torrents of rain. In June, when the first graduation exercises were held at the new high school, Colonel Howard delivered the commencement address. The following night he was featured in a community play at the school, appearing in the appropriate role of a land speculator, while Claude took the role of a Mexican renegade.

Another forerunner of the chamber of commerce, the Fort Payne Progressive League, was organized in March, 1909, with Colonel Howard elected president. Its purpose was to make efforts to attract a number of small industries to Fort Payne. It would also cooperate with E. C. Drew, a Louisiana businessman, who wanted local investors to purchase the Fort Payne Company holdings, especially the coal mines. Colonel Howard and Drew left immediately on another quest for Boston capital to start new industry. The Montgomery *Journal* took notice of Colonel Howard's renewed activities in his city's behalf.

M. W. Howard, former member of congress, author of a sensational book about the bad habits of congressmen and Populist of the flowing locks type, has been restored to a good business status and is engaged in telling what a wonderful place is Fort Payne, Alabama, his home town.

106

He is on far more substantial ground now than at any time in his public career, for Fort Payne really has a vast wealth in natural resources.

Once scorned by Fort Payne society, the Howards were again accepted and active in local social circles. Sally, Perle, and Jennie were all members of the exclusive Cloverleaf Club, which met for bridge every Thursday, and the two daughters-in-law also belonged to the Wednesday Embroidery Club.

During the summer of 1910 Claude and Jennie took rooms at the DeKalb Hotel and enjoyed entertaining friends with bridge parties held in the newly decorated parlor. On Friday, August 19, they held a dance there in honor of Jennie's guest, Miss Virginia Mitchell of Bessemer. It evidently turned into a lively affair as George H. Edwards, the hotel manager, was willing to take drastic steps to prevent a recurrence. A notice in the next issue of the *Journal* declared there would be no more dances at the hotel and that no roomers, other than business-men, would be accepted. The editor, however, suggested that this action be reconsidered, which was done, and a Gadsden band furnished music for a dance at the DeKalb the next Friday night after the Howard entertainment.

Meanwhile, the lure of political involvement remained a temptation, in spite of Colonel Howard's resolve to stay away from it. However, he knew there was no place for him in the Democratic Party, which dominated Alabama politics. It was while in the state of being a man without a party that Colonel Howard became involved in a brief encounter with a little-known third party in 1908.

The Independence League was formed in 1904 by William Randolph Hearst, of "yellow journalism" fame, who was cham-pioning liberal causes in his newspapers. Its purpose, at first, was to prevent the Democratic nomination of Alton B. Parker, a conservative New York judge, for president. It appeared that the party whose candidate, William Jennings Bryan, had lost the last two elections, was about to choose a man who would be Bryan's exact opposite. Hearst, who served as a New York con-gressman from 1903 until 1907, wanted a political liberal—such as himself—nominated instead. Although Parker did receive the nomination, Hearst's organization furnished his most effective opposition and showed surprising strength.

In 1908, the Independence League was organized as a political party and fielded candidates chosen by its founder. One of its main attractions for Colonel Howard was probably the suggestion by some of its members that he might be nominated for president. In July, he and Clyde went to Chicago to attend the convention. Colonel Howard was not Randolph Hearst's choice as the presidential nominee, but the long trip was not a total loss. He and Clarence Darrow, legal advisor to Hearst at the time, spoke on opposite sides of an issue and Colonel Howard had the satisfaction of determining, in his own mind, at least, that he was the better of the two debaters. During the fall he made a few speeches for the Independence League, an almost ignored organization and a one-election third party.

The next political activity in which Colonel Howard participated was on the state level. In 1909, Governor Braxton Bragg Comer, a dramatic and colorful Theodore Roosevelt type politician elected in 1906 on a reform platform, supported the incorporation of a prohibition amendment to the state constitution. The issue became a very heated one, with supporters and opponents often caring more about Comer's future than that of prohibition itself. Colonel Howard was persuaded to speak against the amendment at several different cities, including Birmingham, where his audience was said to have been the largest ever assembled in Alabama up to that time.

Also opposing the prohibition effort were many other prominent speakers of the state, including the two United States senators and a majority of the congressmen, as well as most newspapers. Supporting the amendment and Governor Comer were the Anti-Saloon League, the Women's Christian Temperance Union, prominent churchmen and ministers, the latter referred to in the press as "the political parsons." The opponents apparently convinced a majority of the voters of Alabama that the amendment would have provided for unnecessary additional police regulations and it was defeated by some 25,000 votes, losing in 60 counties. Milford W. Howard had once more emerged on the victorious side of a political issue. The instincts of the campaigner had been aroused and he became susceptible to overtures from Republicans to make one more political race.

Colonel Howard's last political adventure started with a disputed nomination, turned into a disappointingly one-sided campaign, and ended in an extremely close election, the results of which he never accepted or truly believed. It began on March 19, 1910, at a Republican meeting at the DeKalb County Court-house, called for the purpose of nominating candidates for county offices. Some, who wanted Colonel Howard to run in the congressional race, thought he would have a better chance of winning if no local ticket were put out. But the county's "true-blue," hard-line Republicans did not want Colonel Howard as their candidate and held out for party regulars. The group finally approved a resolution by L. A. Durham adjourning the meeting until some future date when a citizens' meeting would be called.

At that meeting, held on May 14, G. L. Malone, chairman of the county Republican executive committee, opposed the plan to endorse Colonel Howard for the congressional race. Howard backers then decided to choose a new executive committee, which was done immediately, with J. J. Durham being elected chairman. The meeting proceeded to endorse Colonel Howard and he was asked to address the gathering. Urging the party to make the fight along the amendment lines, he predicted that many Democrats would support him. He also advised the Republicans not to put a candidate in the race for representative to the state legislature, as the Democrat opposed prohibition, but requested that they run a candidate for state senator against the Democratic nominee who was an amendment supporter.

Although the pro-Howard Republicans had succeeded in giving him the county organization's endorsement for the district's congressional nomination, they failed to unite the factions of their party behind him. Malone steadfastly maintained that he was still the chairman, and bitterly denounced the group which had elected Durham. Charging that the crowd had contained a number of Democrats, he declared that Durham might as well claim to be chairman of the Democratic executive committee. He called on Republicans to support the Republican platform and a full Republican ticket and urged members of his party not to surrender to the "whiskey ring" of the Democratic

Party. Now both factions of the Republican Party had a chairman. But Durham was recognized by the state chairman and Colonel Howard was nominated as the Republican congressional candidate at the district convention at Cullman.

However, the state Republican organization chose to ignore his candidacy and gave him no support of any kind. No speakers were sent into the seventh district to help Colonel Howard in what became a lonely but determined campaign. All the newspapers in the district, except one, supported John L. Burnett, the Democrat who had been elected in 1898 to replace Colonel Howard. Governor Comer, both United States senators, and the entire Alabama congressional delegation campaigned against Colonel Howard. Not one speech was made in his behalf except those he made himself. It was one man against the entire field. Even Thomas Watson of Georgia, who had returned to the Democratic Party, opposed him and sent free copies of the Georgia newspaper he edited into the district. This flooding of the district with Watson's editorial endorsement of Burnett was estimated by Colonel Howard to have cost him at least 1,000 votes.

The Democratic whip lashed all the prominent Democrats who had promised to support Colonel Howard back into the party fold except R. B. Kyle, of Gadsden, who opened Howard headquarters there and financed its operation. Most Democratic leaders waged a vigorous fight against the lone man running as a Republican in a district which had twice elected him as a Populist.

The Mobile *Register* printed the following comments from its Montgomery correspondent in September:

Burnett in No Danger

Reports from the bloody seventh district, where M. W. Howard, author of "If Christ Came to Congress," is trying to beat the Democratic nominee, John Burnett, for congress, are encouraging for Mr. Burnett. N. M. Gallant, tax collector of Etowah County, who was in Montgomery this week, stated that there need be no fear. "We are all right," he stated. "He has made us a good man and there is no likelihood that Howard will be able to hurt him much."

The Gadsden *Times-News* made no attempt to conceal its glee at the lack of visible support for Colonel Howard.

Howard's Boom Has Collapsed

From every county in the district the report comes that the Howard boom is about to go to pieces and that the republican candidate now sees the handwriting on the wall. He has had frost after frost in every county notwithstanding the loud claims of his handful of supporters in Gadsden. The reports of enormous crowds going out to hear him have proven false whenever investigated and the lack of enthusiasm for him is weighing heavily on Mr. Howard according to report. He is coming to Gadsden October 29th and will make several speeches in the county after that date as a last grandstand play. He is then expected to enthuse the local crowd with highly colored reports of his campaign, but it will be too late. From every corner of the district the news comes that the Howard boom died aborning.

The Fort Payne *Journal* made little mention of the Howard campaign, other than the brief write-ups of speeches by candidates. Some local citizen, who wished to use his first book against him in the campaign, ran the following want ad each week:

Wanted—copy of book "If Christ Came to Congress." Will pay good price for same. Address G. H., care Journal office.

The election was held on a beautiful, clear November day, but the vote was much lighter than expected. In DeKalb County, where interest was centered on the congressional race and the contest between John B. Isbell and C. C. Appleton for the office of circuit solicitor, less than half the registered voters turned out to give Burnett a very narrow lead over Colonel Howard. Isbell, the only Republican running ahead of his opponent, had a larger lead over Appleton. However, Cherokee County gave Appleton a large vote and both Colonel Howard, who carried only Winston County, and his former law partner were defeated. But the forecasters had missed their mark in predicting that Colonel Howard would be literally swamped by all the opposition which had organized against him. The official count was 9,496 votes for Burnett and 8,977—only 519 fewer—for Colonel Howard.

The old campaigner had really believed he would win, in spite of the many handicaps he faced. Even after the final returns were in, he refused to accept the results as an honest count, claiming that the Democrats had "stolen another election" and that his majority should have been 2,500. In anger and frustration, he startled a number of acquaintances by filing suit to have $320 returned to him by a businessman acting as stake holder for an election bet.

This time M. W. Howard was *really* finished with politics.

A Frantic Search
For Fortune

Almost thirty years after passing his bar exam, Colonel Howard reassessed his career and accomplishments. He was approaching the age of fifty without having ever attained any great achievement for which he would be remembered, without accumulating the fortune he had confidently sought. Surely the poor farm boy of the Georgia hills had developed enough ambition. But where were the fame, the glory, the wealth, the outstanding public service of his dreams? They must come yet. But time was running out.

Members of his family had long believed that a man of Colonel Howard's ability could achieve great success practicing law in a big city. With their encouragement, he left Fort Payne soon after his political defeat to seek his fortune in Birmingham. Early in 1911, he formed a partnership with Oscar R. Hundley and helped persuade his former partner, Luke Hunt, to join them. In February the firm of Hundley, Howard and Hunt was formed and the junior partner moved to Birmingham. Colonel Howard continued to maintain his home at the farm until the fall of the year, when he engaged W. H. Wilbanks to oversee the farm and livestock. His sons, Clyde and Claude, who had enjoyed life as "gentlemen farmers" while engaging occasionally in real estate transactions, moved to Birmingham soon afterward.

The women of the family regretfully left their many Fort Payne friends. Sally Howard entertained the Cloverleaf Club for the last time late in September. Two months later the group of ladies met one Saturday night at Haralson's Drug Store before going to the home of Mrs. L. A. Dobbs to hold a surprise party for Perle before her departure for Birmingham.

With the whole family in the city, where expenses were greater, Colonel Howard slaved at his legal work in order to pay seemingly endless bills, and to secure funds for investment. Always looking for the end of a rainbow, a lucky break, a good "tip," he was drawn into wild channels of speculation. Such gambles were frantic, desperate, and inevitably unwise.

Stock in a Mexican mine became worthless after the Madero Revolution. Even after losing on a Louisiana oil well Colonel Howard went to Mineral Wells, Texas, and became excited over prospects there. Next, he turned in desperation to Alaska and spent two summers there installing a hydraulic plant for washing gold and also constructed a factory to can salmon. But all these investments were failures.

These were years of physical fatigue, continuous anxiety and mental stress. During this period more of Colonel Howard's close relatives were taken by death. First, his brother Wallace died in Texas in February, 1912. Then Wallace's wife, Eula Lea, died soon afterward, leaving six children as orphans to be cared for by relatives. Colonel Howard took his namesake, thirteen year old Milford Rice Howard, to live with him. However, both the young teenager and his harried uncle were apparently greatly affected by tragedy and tension at this time and they did not get along very well. Rice ran away from home and went to live with his Aunt Octie Stephens in Oneonta.[1] In June, 1916, Colonel Howard received word that Octie had died. He had now lost two of his three brothers, both sisters and his mother in addition to his own infant son. Weakened by grief and exhaustion, facing the crushing humiliation of a series of business failures, and worrying about Claude, who was helping fight World War I in France, Colonel Howard became a tragic, broken man and was forced to seek medical aid when he suffered a nervous breakdown.

Soon thereafter, Colonel Howard made what would be a permanent withdrawal from the practice of law and returned to

---

[1] In 1939, when his uncle Forney Stephens died, Rice became editor of the Oneonta Democrat.

114

his Fort Payne farm. At the age of 56, he gave up the profession which he had struggled so valiantly and persistently to enter and returned to the life of a farmer which he had succeeded in leaving as a youth. Welcoming the opportunity for physical activity, he turned land, planted, tended crops and harvested, performing as much work as any of his hired men or tenants. With the mental relaxation, the invigorating fresh air and sunshine, and the unhurried pace of life on the farm, he regained his strength and some of his zest for life.

His great concern for the safety of his younger son was also eased. After serving in France as a first lieutenant of field artillery, Claude was promoted to captain and sent back to the United States to serve as a military instructor. In May, 1919, he returned to Fort Payne, stunningly handsome in his officer's uniform, to spend a week with his family at the farm. In August his mother visited him at Louisville, Kentucky, and brought her grandson, Morris, back to Fort Payne. Claude and Jennie came two weeks later for a short visit before returning to Kentucky with their young son.

Clyde and his family spent the year on the farm, also. Sally and Perle rejoined the Cloverleaf Club, giving teas and luncheons for ladies who "motored" out in their new automobiles. Picnics were served on the lawn under the spreading branches of the famous old Cherokee Council Tree.

At the end of each day Colonel Howard patiently coached his grandson, Milford, in his lessons for the next school day. Then he studied his own correspondence courses in short story writing from an eastern school and read instructions in photoplay writing from a Los Angeles institution. He also pondered his future.

They still had enough money and property for him to retire to a leisurely life on the farm. He would have his flowers and his books. He could watch the growing things around him and cultivate his mind and soul.

But still his dreaming could not be stifled; his restless longings could not be stilled. His great accomplishments were yet unattained, his self-promises unfulfilled, his life still incomplete. After all his efforts and struggles there had been no significant moment when he could say, "This is the time I have waited for." There had been no special reward or achievement

115

for which he might proclaim, "This is what I have sought." On solitary walks through forest lanes, on quiet nights under a bright Lookout Mountain moon, at times of deep meditation, he raised his head skyward to pose a silent question, "Is this all there is?"

Then that surging drive within him would fashion its own answer, with a resounding, "No!" He would redeem himself for being a failure. He would act out the part of success before he passed from the stage of action. Somehow, somewhere, he would leave something behind by which Milford W. Howard would be remembered after he had left the scene.

The Los Angeles correspondence school persuaded Colonel Howard that a ready market was available for all the good scenarios which could be turned out. Perhaps he would find success in California as a script writer for the movies. He discussed the idea with Sally, who had been favorably impressed with the west coast on two visits there. As usual she encouraged her husband to make any move he wished. So, shortly after Thanksgiving they left the Fort Payne depot with their baggage and high hopes, headed for the "Golden West." For the first time, except during Claude's army service, the three families were being separated. Both Colonel Howard and Sally fought back tears as they bade farewell to their sons and four grandchildren.

Their California home was a small bungalow on a lush ten-acre plot which Colonel Howard referred to as "the ranch." There was also a small orchard to help supplement their income, which he expected to be receiving soon from nearby Hollywood.

Back in Fort Payne, Perle began urging Clyde to move to California, too, and they were soon making plans to do so. One Saturday night in December, 1919, their friends honored them with a pound supper at the farm. On the following Monday an auction was held for the sale of all the farm equipment and furniture. Near the old Council Oak, the auctioneer took bids on the following items: disc plows, cultivators, turning plows, scratchers, harrows, corn planters, two buggies with harnesses, one buggy horse, two mares, two cows, pigs, hay, and cotton seed. The Howards had gone out of the farming business. But instead of selling the farm, Colonel Howard mortgaged it, hoping it would bring a higher price the next year. Then, against his wife's advice, he gave Claude the money to invest in a lumber business.

Meanwhile, Colonel Howard had completed several scenarios for submission to his photoplay school. They were pronounced excellent and he was accorded the supposedly rare privilege of meeting the president, who promised to help promote the scenarios himself. But after a long, impatient wait, Colonel Howard returned to see the school executive, only to find that he had forgotten all about the personal attention this work was to have received. The disappointed Hollywood hopeful then demanded that his scripts be returned to him and he began a round of all the studios himself. Rejected by all, the old familiar disillusionment once more engulfed him and he bitterly concluded that the only reason the studios maintained reading staffs was to obtain ideas to pass along to their own writers and directors. One more plan had gone awry.

Nor were the other Howards finding happiness in their new location. Sally longed for her "baby boy" and for Morris, his son with the golden hair, brown eyes, and freckles of his grandmother. In vain she waited and looked forward to a visit which was never made. Perle found the bungalow too cramped for all seven Howards and repeatedly expressed her wishes for a home of their own. Nobody's dreams came true that first year in California.

In the fall of 1920, Sally returned to Alabama alone to see Claude's family and to sell the farm. She sold the whole 101 acres to T. B. Scott on October 23, for $3,400 and returned with the money left after paying the mortgage.

The Howards then moved to a place between Los Angeles and Pasadena called Montrose. This was a town site which had been developed in the green coastal hills at the time of the outbreak of war and the promoter had lost a fortune when the real estate market declined. On a beautifully laid out development, there were only about ten homes, a real estate office, a gas station, and one vacant brick building.

Colonel Howard leased the building for use as a grocery store, made a second mortgage on his ranch, and invested in the business for Sally and Clyde. He also bought several lots and labored along with the hired carpenters to build two bungalows,

117

one for Clyde's family, and one for himself. The San Fernando Valley property was leased for a year and the Howard Grocery Store opened in Montrose. Clyde, who was to receive half the profits from the business, also opened a small store in a cheap building they erected on a lot his father gave him. Perle was to operate the little one and they were to keep all the profit.

Within a year the Howard Grocery was bankrupt. After the stock was sold, there was still an indebtedness of several hundred dollars in addition to the lost capital investment which had been obtained by mortgaging the ranch. However, real estate business began booming in Montrose and Clyde sold his lot for a good price, after which he entered the real estate business. As an agent, he proposed that his father sell his ranch to pay off their indebtedness. After finding a buyer, Clyde charged a $500 commission for the transaction.

Colonel Howard was left with two little bungalows, still in debt and still in broken health just as his faithful and beloved Sally began to fall victim to a malady which would prove to be fatal. She was able, however, to carry on a real estate business and earn an income while Colonel Howard again pursued a writing career.

This time he wrote a novel about mountaineers who lived at Buck's Pocket, in north Alabama. *Peggy Ware* was published in the fall of 1921 by J. F. Rowny, a Los Angeles printer, who had a very limited circulation and the number of sales was very disappointing. The book was read by Henry Otto, who had filmed *Dante's Inferno* for William Fox. He commented favorably on the novel and expressed a willingness to direct a movie based on *Peggy Ware*, but no steps were ever taken toward filming it.

A second novel about an escaped convict who poses as a bishop in the Ozark Mountains was soon underway. *Bishop of the Ozarks* was published in 1923, by the Times-Mirror Press in Los Angeles. Later in the year, Colonel Howard succeeded in his efforts to have the book made into a movie. Finis Fox directed the silent movie for the Cosmopolitan Film Company and agreed to permit the author to play the dual role of the convict-bishop.

In costume and wearing heavy makeup, Colonel Howard was coached in the slow-moving exaggerated expression method

118

of acting of the silent movies before each of his close-up scenes. At first his acting was done in an agony of self-consciousness. Stiff and awkward, with a dry mouth and perspiring forehead he was tempted to revert to the "yaller jacket" of yesteryear, to turn and run away. To help him overcome his camera shyness, his director changed to the outdoor scenes of the escaped convict being chased by bloodhounds. But even then his running was unnatural, his long legs feeling like weighted appendages moving in slow motion. These scenes were shot over and over while he gradually lost some of his fright and stiffness. Then, after several days in front of the camera he became quite a ham, enjoying the exciting activity and feeling as important as any "star" in Hollywood.

For eight glorious weeks Colonel Howard acted out the roles of the convict and the minister, relying upon his eyes, his posture, and his facial expressions to portray the contrasting characters. The *Bishop of the Ozarks* was filmed at the Fine Arts Studio in Hollywood, where D. W. Griffith had produced the great historical spectacle, *The Birth of a Nation*, and Colonel Howard was assigned the same dressing room Lillian Gish had used during the filming of the epic movie. Sally was present during all the filming and appeared momentarily in one of the mob scenes. Little Milford and his sisters, Virginia and Mary Ann, were also thrilled to be included in some small "bit" parts.

The modest salary Colonel Howard earned for his part in the movie was invested by Sally in Montrose real estate and they anxiously awaited the picture's release. Finally, the 77 prints of the six-reel movie were distributed in this country and in Canada and Colonel Howard was honored on a number of occasions by being asked to make personal appearances at theaters where his movie was being shown.

Thus encouraged, he began writing a third novel about the conflicting sentiments of wealthy slave holders and poor white southerners during the Civil War period. The manuscript of "Po' White Trash," subtitled, "By Milford W. Howard, One of 'Em," was completed in 1923, but before he made any arrangements for having it published he had found another interest.

Suddenly, on a sleepless, restless night, the idea came to him. He could make his whole life have meaning and purpose. He could redeem himself for all his past mistakes and shortcomings. He would be remembered long after his death and all his struggles would have been worthwhile. He would establish a great school to provide a free education for mountain children who were underprivileged, as he had been. It would be modeled after the successful institution established by Martha Berry near Rome, Georgia, in 1902. Perhaps at Buck's Pocket, where his fictional heroine, Peggy Ware, had founded such a school . . . .

He could hardly wait to get back to Alabama. He was sixty years old and anxious to begin this next great venture.

Part II

Peggy Ware

The locale for *Peggy Ware*, Buck's Pocket, the beautiful and rugged mountainous area near Scottsboro, is the most interesting feature about this novel by Colonel Howard. Many readers will recognize much of the scenery described in the book, but few will discover much about either the plot or the characters with which to identify.

All the characters are either extremely virtuous or totally despicable. Among the former, the old Negro, Simon, who tenderly cares for Peggy throughout the tale, provides the author with the opportunity to write in dialect, which he does in all his fiction. The heroine, Peggy Ware, is an unbelievably saintly person whose determination and faith never falter. The dialogue, written with a view toward being used in a photoplay, had Peggy making unnatural, stilted speeches from early childhood. Yet her mystical influence easily changes all evil forces into good ones. The most outstanding conversion is that of Cliff Anderson, a successful mountain bootlegger.

With Anderson's help, Peggy establishes a free school for mountain children, eliminates ignorance and disease from the area, starts 100 community centers and Sunday school classes and brings electricity to this section from power furnished by Sauty Creek. She thereby succeeds in spreading knowledge, morality, good health, prosperity, and patriotism in every direction.

In seeking to create dramatic scenes, the author presents

120

one crisis after another and sometimes comes close to achieving some degree of suspense and interest. However, the melodrama is overpowered by the author's lack of perception of realism and by his constant preoccupation with rhetoric and philosophy.

Part III

The Bishop of the Ozarks

In *The Bishop of the Ozarks*, the author presents a rather unskillful weaving of the forces of psychic phenomena, magic, and religion. He seems to be advancing several social and religious messages in his curious blend of the supernatural, but little comes across as truly convincing in what amounts to a long fairy tale.

Howard borrowed part of his plot, including a segment devoted to the effects of a talisman's powers upon a selfish and greedy man, from a novel by the French writer, Honoré de Balzac. Adding some of his own concepts of spiritualism and religion, he originally prepared a very brief photoplay, which he later developed into this 232 page novel.

This struggle between the dark forces of evil and the noble and good ones, a feature of most of Milford Howard's fiction, involves seven main characters. The two parts especially designed for—and played by Colonel Howard in the movie version—are Tom Sullivan, an escaped convict, and Roger Chapman, a demented minister. The convict forces the minister to change clothes with him in a mountain cabin. After the real Chapman is shot on sight by members of a posse, Sullivan takes his place in order to care for the minister's young orphaned daughter, Margy.

Old Simon is the faithful Negro who always helps look after Margy's welfare, just as he had for her mother. The Shepherd Woman, a mysterious holy person, dwells in the Ozarks with her sheep and reveals her true nature as a spiritualistic medium to the Bishop of the Ozarks only. Two young physicians, Earl Godfrey, and Percy Burroughs, personify evil and virtue. Godfrey, the materialist, seeks pleasure by trading his soul for magical powers, but finds misery and death. Burroughs

121

accomplishes medical miracles through the guidance of spirits, winning happiness and the beautiful Margy.

After the bishop transforms Devil's Den, in the Ozarks, into Happy Valley, he is persuaded to become pastor of Saint Paul's Episcopal Church in Birmingham. While there he reforms hundreds of convicts placed in his charge by a Brandon-type governor and becomes famous for massive faith-healing successes. He finally reveals his true identity, but is pardoned by the governor and is still loved by his followers.

This book was written for the purpose of being produced as a silent movie, rather than for its own intrinsic literary value. No doubt it was more successful in its original endeavor.

The Vagabonds in 1928.

Milford Howard at four differ-
ent ages, from inhibited and
unhappy youth to self-
confident lawyer.

Silas Andrew Howard.

Uncle Samuel Milford
Jemison Howard.

Wallace Warren Howard.

Ada Howard.

Stephen Oliver Howard, Milford's father.

Martha Ann Maddry Howard, Milford's mother.

The congressman's wife.

An older Sally.

Andrew, Milford's favorite brother.

Reverend Wallace Howard, Milford's younger brother who, like Andrew, died of tuberculosis.

Jennie Howard at work as assistant dean of women at University of Alabama during 1940's.

Colonel C. M. Howard (U. S. Army, retired), son of Claude and Jennie.

Milford and Sally are shown while visiting her brother, Jeff, about 1908. Sally's half sister, Mae Lankford, stands to the left of Sally and Milford. The others are Ethel Lankford, Sam Johnson (Sally's nephew), Myrtle Lankford, Helen Lankford Johnson, Emma Lankford Henderson, Jeff (holding his grandchild, Jeff Henderson), Ellen Garrett Lankford (Jeff's wife), Milford Lankford and Robert Lankford (holding calf).

Wee Kirk O' the Heather at Forest Lawn Cemetery, Glendale, California.

Sally A. Howard Memorial Chapel at Mentone.

Rear view of chapel soon after completion in 1937.

Colonel Howard playing the title role in Bishop of the Ozarks.

Small and lonely monument of Clarence, middle son of Milford and Sally, stands in old section of Glenwood Cemetery, Fort Payne.

One of his many namesakes, Milford Durham of Collinsville, is shown with Colonel Howard. In 1929 the former congressman wrote, "All over my old congressional district there are scores of grown men named Milford or Howard, and an occasional one with my full name, Milford Howard."

Including Aubrey Howard Gilchrist (1909-1964) maternal uncle of author E.

The author stands above Buck's Pocket, locale for Colonel Howard's Peggy Ware.

Cabin across road from Alpine Lodge, built for Lady Vivian and the Colonel by Frank Kirk of Mentone.

Joe Wheeler Dam, constructed for Colonel Howard near Alpine Lodge.

Side of McGee Building on First Street, Fort Payne, showing original boom-period brick of the city's first brick building, constructed by Colonel Howard.

Grace Crow, of Mentone, with the Colonel in 1925.

"The Cabin," where Colonel Howard lived after selling Alpine Lodge property.

The Colonel's grandson, Milford Howard, who died from tragic accident.

Joe Biddle, the Colonel's favorite craftsman.

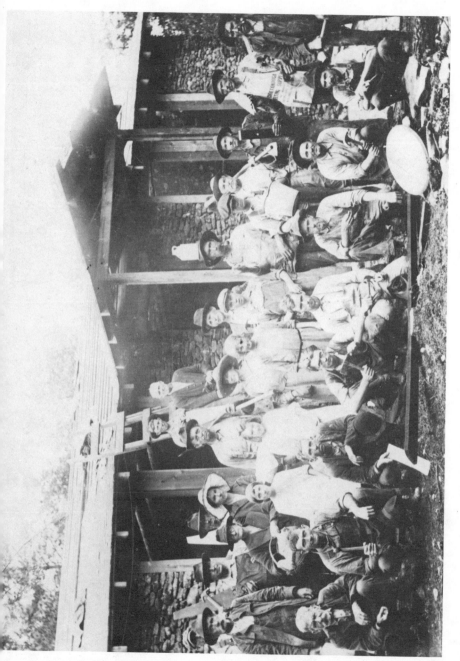

A "working" at Master School during summer of 1923.

Colonel Howard and Stella Vivian Harper stand before the almost-completed school.

Roofing Alpine Lodge: Joe Biddle's last job.

Master School founders, Colonel Howard and Stella Vivian Harper.

Program

Toastmaster—DR. FRANK WILLIS BARNETT.

Master of Ceremonies—MR. HOLLAND E. COX, Pres.

Song—"America"..All

Invocation..........................Dr. James A. Bryan

Purpose of Banquet.................Holland E. Cox

Response.................................Toastmaster

Vocal Solos—"One Fine Day," from Madame Butter-
fly—Tuccini, "The Nightengale"......Ward Stephens

Miss Marion Stavrovsky, accompanied by Miss Bonnie
Howard.

Violin Solo—"Ave Maria"..........Schubert-Wilhemj
Carl F. McCool accompanied by Miss Irene Prier.

Address.................Governor William W. Brandon

Lecture.................Hon. Milford W. Howard

Brief Remarks...............Some of our Guests

Benediction...............Dr. William M. Sentell

The Colonel's overshot wheel.

One of many programs which featured Colonel Howard as speaker.

Rear view of Alpine Lodge.

THE BANK OF VALLEY HEAD

CAPITAL $25,000.00

VALLEY HEAD, ALABAMA

ACTIVE OFFICERS
R. D. LOWRY, PRESIDENT
C. L. PORTER, CASHIER
G. L. THOMPSON, ASST. CASHIER

The State of Alabama }
DeKalb County } Whereas The Master Schools, Incorporated through its President Milford W. Howard executed a power of attorney on Sept. 22nd 1927 authorizing and empowering C. M. Howard or Island M. Howard to sell and make conveyance to lots in East River Park, on the town site of River Park, DeKalb County, Alabama, which instrument was recorded Jan. 3rd 1929 in the office of the probate judge of said County. This instrument is made by the Master Schools, I. said for purpose of revoking said power of attorney, and it is hereby revoked.

Signed, sealed and delivered this the 14th day of Feb. 1929.

The Master Schools, Inc. (Seal)

By Milford W. Howard
President

Witness:
Stella Vivian Howard.
Secretary

Colonel Howard's handwriting, as revealed on legal document in 1929.

ALABAMA VAGABOND INTERVIEWS IL DUCE

MILFORD W. HOWARD

BY MILFORD W. HOWARD
Former Seventh Congressional District, Alabama

Benito Mussolini in a characteristic pose—one of his favorite pictures, presented to Col. Milford W. Howard on the occasion of the interview printed on this page, which tells of the impressions of the Alabama vagabond as a result of his visit with the head of Italy's Fascist government.

Here Are Highlights Of Interview Of Alabama Vagabond With Il Duce

MUSSOLINI'S APPEARANCE—"He is of medium stature, stockily built, muscular, vigorous, athletic; in the full prime of manhood, being just in his forty-fourth year. His head and face are strangely like Napoleon's; his attitude and bearing very like that of the great emperor; Roman to the core in his ideals of discipline, duty and the glory of country."

HIS PERSONALITY—"Mussolini is as magnetic as was Roosevelt; as quick to act, going from one subject to another with lightning-like rapidity."

HIS PATRIOTISM—"His eyes burn like the eyes of Savonarola, the great religious reformer of his day."

HIS ESTIMATE OF FASCISM—"The Fascist State has arisen as the most complete juridical and administrative organism the world has seen since the days of antiquity."

HIS BEARING—Mussolini came into the Chamber looking neither to the right nor to the left; took his seat on a raised platform in front.

VIEWS ON GOVERNMENT—"Mussolini has no respect for parliamentary governments, and frankly says so. He says 'talking-parliamentary systems must be abolished and in their stead established pragmatic bodies with one purpose in view, to get at times and under all conditions, WORK.'"

HIS AIM—"It is my purpose as President of Italy, and a menace to the world's peace. He wants peace for Italy, but wants peace for all."

HOWARD'S ESTIMATE OF MUSSOLINI—"Mussolini is not a menace to the world's peace. He wants peace for Italy, but wants peace for all."

Cting To Some "Vices," Cut Out Other Things, Martin Advises For New Year

BY ABE MARTIN

McIntyre Finds Some Spice Of Life For Fourth Estate In Old Metropolis

Naval Reserve Expert Says Soul Is Really Human Wireless Tower

Colonel Howard's most sensational Vagabond article.

Faculty of the Summer School of Psychology, held at Alpine Lodge during July, 1929. At center, seated, is Dr. Henry Knight Miller, editor of Psychology Magazine.

Women at the psychology school included Lady Vivian (third from left, front row), Mrs. B. L. Noogin, Sr., of Gadsden (fifth on front row), Lucile Price (first on back row), and Dorothy Lloyd (fourth on back row).

Alpine Lodge.

Alone and ill, the elderly Colonel hoped Beatrice Crow would become his third wife.

At his death, the Colonel's billfold told the story of his life. Filled with newspaper clippings about his fascinating career, it held no money.

Colonel Howard as he appeared to an artist, Alfred J. Bowman, in 1934.

The Master School

A free school available to all mountain children—how he would have given ten years of his life for such an opportunity! To establish the school would be the biggest challenge, and hopefully the greatest achievement, of his life. His enthusiasm grew as he described his new vision, as he explained to Sally: the call had come and he must go.

She saw his brown eyes sparkle with new life and watched his animated gestures as he looked boldly into the future and told her what was there. But this time she could not see his dream. She saw the bright sunshine and felt the balmy breezes of the western coastland. The ties of a home and her work were there.

She wished neither to stop him from going, nor yet to send him blindly on his way. Cautiously she raised the question of how he would pay for his school.

"On faith," he answered, "the same as Peggy Ware did."

"Yes, but that was just in your imagination," she argued gently, "and doing this in reality will be quite different."

But Colonel Howard prevailed, as always, insisting that anything could be accomplished if a person had ability and faith. His own faith had been bolstered by the ecstatic praise he had received from his cousin, Stella Vivian Harper, to whom he had sent an autographed copy of *Peggy Ware*, along with some of the press reviews. She had congratulated him enthusiastically, not only for his literary accomplishment, but for the idea of the Peggy Ware School. She herself had dreamed of just such an institution for the past five years while engaged in welfare work in Brunswick, Georgia.

After deciding to establish a real school in Buck's Pocket, he wrote to Mrs. Harper, asking if she would help him. Without waiting to write, she wired him that she would be ready at any time.

On June 18, 1923, Colonel Howard kissed his wife good-by at the Los Angeles station and boarded the train to return to Alabama for the first time in four years. Sally smiled through her tears, believing her wanderlust husband would return by October 1, the expiration date on his round trip ticket. Later, as he watched the scenes race by his window while the train sped toward Salt Lake City, a strange feeling seemed to tell him that he would never call California home again.

After arriving in Fort Payne, Colonel Howard made his way to the Lookout Mountain home of Elijah and Lelia York. He told his old friends about his plans and explained that he needed to go to Buck's Pocket to look the area over. Frank Kirk, a 14 year old orphan who was living with the Yorks, made preparations for the trip. After loading a wagon with quilts and provisions, the youngster hitched up two mules, one red and one black, which he called "Red" and "Nig."

With Kirk and a neighbor, Mac McCurdy, in the wagon and Colonel Howard riding a horse, they left on the day-long trip from Mentone, on Lookout Mountain, to Buck's Pocket on Sand Mountain. At Rainsville, several of Colonel Howard's friends there joined them for the rest of the journey. At sunset, the group reached the brow of Sand Mountain and peered down into the deep "pocket" in the wilderness where Sauty Creek plunged down the cliff walls and flowed toward the Tennessee River.

After camping for the night, with Colonel Howard sleeping in the wagon, the men watched the summer sun rise and again looked over the wild beauty of the pocket area. After a final ride around the pocket, Colonel Howard reined his horse and said, "No, this is not the place."

On June 23, almost thirty years after their last meeting, Colonel Howard met Vivian Harper as she arrived on the afternoon train at Fort Payne. Time, struggle, and disappointment had taken its toll from both since the seventeen year old impressionable girl had looked in awe upon the handsome congressman. If she was surprised at his lined face and melancholy countenance she failed to show it as she burst upon the scene, a matronly but vibrant woman, filled with enthusiasm and confidence. Little about her appearance remained the same except her bright auburn hair and expressive blue eyes. Nor did she retain any of her former shyness as she chattered endlessly about the plans she had already formulated and expressed so many theories and expectations that Colonel Howard was quite startled at first, as visionary as he was.

He found her to be, as he had expected, a very unusual and talented person. A graduate of Shorter College, Vivian Harper was an expert stenographer and typist. She was also an experienced horsewoman, sculptor and musician, and an expert shot with both a rifle and bow and arrow. Still an avid reader, she pursued a constant study of the Bible and of psychology. She was to use her knowledge of the latter in dealing with the Colonel.

Finding him in the throes of deep depression, she helped him escape the self-condemnation and sense of failure which had plagued him. She encouraged him to be thankful for every experience which had come his way, insisting that each could serve as a stepping stone to something higher.

Mrs. Harper agreed that the Peggy Ware School should be located at some place other than Buck's Pocket. So together they searched for another spot which would offer both scenic beauty and a source of water power. They found an ideal location just south of Mentone where they discovered a "little mountain" about three miles long and shaped like an hour glass atop Lookout Mountain. Toward the eastern end of the little mountain, which rose two hundred feet above the brow of Lookout, the clear waters of Little River tumbled over a picturesque waterfall. There were great boulders and fragile wild flowers in the midst of dense towering trees. There were giant rocky bluffs and panoramic views of Little and Big Wills Valleys.

There in the middle of the forest above the western brow of the mountain they visualized the school buildings which would soon be standing on those grounds and they dreamed great dreams together. The simple "Peggy Ware School" developed into an elaborate plan for a series of hundreds of schools throughout the Appalachians, with the central unit being established here, ten miles northeast of Fort Payne. The whole network would comprise "the Master Schools." Eventually the community center schools would not only provide free education for all the mountain children but would also sponsor chautauqua, lyceum and musical concerts, lectures by educators, statesmen, ministers, club members, physicians, and others as well as outstanding motion pictures. But the main purpose of the complex school system was to be the education and character building of boys and girls. They would also be taught the dignity and the joy of work and would develop into master craftsmen.

Planning as though they had a vast fortune to invest, they never paused to consider obstacles which might block their way. To replace the sobering, practical influence of Sally, there was now the blind, adoring encouragement of Vivian Harper, who lauded each new idea he expressed as "Wonderful!" or "Magnificent!" No one had ever shown such confidence in him, such unbounded faith. His imagination ran wild; his aspirations and hopes seemed limitless.

After the Master Schools were all established and staffed with master teachers, they would establish a university on this mountain. Together the two founders of schools and dream castles chose the site where the great institution would be built and named it "University Point." But in the meantime they would be developing the Master School the first year. They would erect a radio station atop Sentinel Rock and broadcast old time southern folk songs. During their second year they would also arrange for filming *Peggy Ware* and an immediate search would be started for a local girl to play the lead part. They dreamed on and on. And they genuinely believed their dreams would come true.

With less than $100, but with faith greater than the mustard seed, Colonel Howard proceeded to buy the top of Lookout Mountain. Many owners were happy to sell and agreed to extend credit for most of the sale price. Beginning with two large tracts containing an aggregate of 350 acres belonging to James A. Croley, he managed to buy most of the land he desired. For several years smaller tracts were added as they

150

became available, if the necessary funds could be obtained. With their aim set at acquiring 1,000 acres, they announced in the fall that 750 had been bought.

The Master Schools were incorporated on July 16, 1923, with the legal work being done by John B. Isbell, of Fort Payne, who also obliged his old friend by becoming one of the trustees. The other four trustees and their addresses were: Milford W. Howard, Los Angeles, California; Stella Vivian Harper, Brunswick, Georgia; Claude M. Howard, Camden, Alabama; and Mamie B. Hanson, Los Angeles.

An expert publicist, Colonel Howard had begun making speeches about the proposed school almost from the time he stepped off the train. He spoke at the Baptist Church the first Sunday night after his arrival and several days later addressed the Civitan Club. Soon afterward he spoke at the local theatre, at a picnic at Skirum, and made three public appearances at the showing of his movie in Montgomery. Then he addressed the Modern Woodmen of America in Fort Payne and Parent-Teachers Association of Collinsville and returned to the Baptist Church to speak to the Baraca Class.

Colonel Howard's latest project was the topic of much conversation by July 23, when the first underbrush was cleared for the little school building. He carefully measured the 24 by 25 foot dimensions and placed markers at the four corners where the rock building would stand. The hard working and generous mountain neighbors caught his enthusiasm and offered freely their time and labor. They not only believed in this man who promised to bring great things to their area; they loved him. Their staunch loyalty would make him even more determined to succeed.

Their attitude toward Stella Vivian Harper was a different matter. Colonel Howard talked and acted like a mountaineer, which he claimed, with some pride, to be. He was among his own. Mrs. Harper, however, fairly *radiated* culture, and gave the distinct impression that she was somewhat above these honest, warm-hearted mountain farmers upon whom she and Colonel Howard depended so heavily.

With supplies, tools, and carpenters ready to begin construction, it was announced ahead of time that the first term of their school would begin in September. Then they discovered what "dog days" were. It rained half of the first month. Then they planned a "working" and invited the people of the community to help with the shingling and flooring. A large crowd of both men and women turned out, but it rained for half the day. A date was set for the people to return to finish the job and it rained almost all day.

Colonel Howard worked in the hot, humid weather with almost superhuman strength, determined to get as much done as possible in every daylight hour that was free from rain. Even Mrs. Harper worked hard, picking up the rough building stones until her hands were blistered and sore. As soon as the exterior of the school house was completed, work was begun on two dormitories 18 by 25 feet, and a dining hall 16 by 26 feet. These buildings were all sided with pine slabs and it was planned to build stone walls around them later. They were covered with pine shingles furnished by Miles Bailey, who, with the help of his wife and seven children, operated a saw mill adjacent to the school property. Although they found it impossible to complete the dormitories or to finish the inside of the school house, they erected a fifty foot flagpole and prepared for Dedication Day, to be held on the first Sunday in September. The featured speaker for the big occasion was to be the governor of Alabama, William W. "Plain Bill" Brandon.

Dog days were not yet over. The early Sunday morning skies were overcast by dark, ominous clouds. By mid-morning it began to rain and intermittent showers continued throughout the day. But the people came anyway, from both Lookout and Sand Mountains, by horseback, in wagons and buggies, and—sloshing through newly made ruts—in their Model T's. By ten o'clock 1,000 people had gathered at the base of the huge Sentinel Rock. At the top of their giant natural stage, nearly 100 voices sounded the old four note, fa, sol, la, mi musical scale. Led by "Uncle Tom" Smith, the long-time editor of the Fort Payne *Journal*, the singers held their old Sacred Heart song books and lifted their joyous voices in "How Firm a Foundation," and "Amazing Grace, How Sweet the Sound." Echoes from the mountain peaks returned with notes from a distant invisible choir.

Governor Brandon arrived to join heartily in singing the second song and was ready to begin his address when a sudden downpour sent everyone scurrying for shelter. In a short while, however, the sun burst through the clouds and the rain stopped as quickly as it had begun. The crowd gathered again and invocation was pronounced by Joseph W. Harper, son of the dean of the Master School.

The governor then ascended to the top of Sentinel Rock, where he was introduced in glowing terms by Colonel Howard, who proclaimed him the best governor Alabama ever had. The governor, in turn, lauded Colonel Howard and his plans for the Master Schools to provide girls and boys with a free education. He also took this opportunity to refer to criticism he had received during his term of office for his free use of the pardon power. He believed, he said, in giving an unfortunate fellow a chance, and declared that fully 75 percent of all the criminals in the state prisons were there because of the lack of proper education and training.

Following the governor's address, a bountiful dinner was spread on flat stones but another brief shower delayed the meal. With the return of the sun, everyone ate and then Governor Brandon led the crowd in his favorite song, "I am Bound For the Promised Land," sounding the chord and beating time like a singing master. Then he made his farewells and headed back to catch the afternoon train.

Colonel Howard spoke to the crowd, declaring that he had had a dream, a vision of being able to help boys and girls who were unable to secure an education for themselves and that he had found the end of a rainbow right there on the "topmost peak" of Lookout Mountain. He promised the consecration of his life, the revenue from his last two books and the "moving picture," *The Bishop of the Ozarks*, to the service of the Lord and to the success of the Master Schools. Then he asked for a free will offering for the school about to be opened, after which Stella Vivian Harper spoke on the aims and purposes of the schools.

The last speech of the day was made by Congressman Miles C. Allgood, who highly commended the Master School idea and pledged his support in every way possible. At the conclusion of the speeches, the people filed past to shake hands with the two founders of the school and began wending their way down the rugged mountain slopes.

After the crowd left, Colonel Howard examined the money and pledges received through his free will offering request. This act of asking for money was, he thought, his greatest act of humility ever, but he was overjoyed to find about $100 in cash and pledges for over $700 more. Though he had on many occasions received more than this whole amount in fees, he had never been as thrilled to receive any amount of money. It was one of those times when emotion welled up within him and he bowed his head and wept.

Colonel Howard and Mrs. Harper used the cash donations to pay the workmen and rode to Fort Payne for a large supply of groceries for the school, relying on the pledges to pay their bill. Looking forward to the opening of school, they were as happy as any of the children, and about as inexperienced as they were in managing and financing a school.

Classes began that week inside the incomplete and unfurnished school building with over thirty students. The teachers included Mrs. Harper, Garfield McCurdy, Miss Lucile Price, and Mrs. Lillian Rush Smith, of Birmingham. For a brief period, Joseph Harper joined the faculty, as did his wife, who taught music. Miss Mae Prestwood, of Fort Payne, and Miss Catherine McMenamin, of Kansas City, taught briefly in 1924. Miss Price, daughter of Mr. and Mrs. Ben Price, of Valley Head, had taught at DeKalb High School the previous year and was persuaded to join the Master School faculty against her parents' advice. Young and attractive, she was chosen by Colonel Howard for the leading role in the movie he intended to make, based on *Peggy Ware*, and was coached for the part by Mrs. Harper.

Students who were enrolled at some time include the following: Dorothy Lloyd (Mrs. Harper's half sister), Ruth and Ruby Keith, John and Cecil Bloodworth, Emmet Shaw, Frank Akins, Emmet Lively, Alice McCurdy, Mae Goss, Bill Garrett, Bill Horton, Houston Craig, Augustus Bailey, Ted Miller, Homer Brock, Arnold Hicks, Ishmael Payton, Clifton Brock, Chester Green, Odell Yancy, B. C. Wester, Melvin Ray, Horace Lively, John and Seaton Boldworth, Tom Smith, William McDonald, Alfred and Edward Tree, Murphee Smith, and Melvin Edge. Vernon Cook was, appropriately, a cook for the school, and was reputed to have been especially good at making wholewheat biscuits. He was assisted by Bill Stout.

The food at the school consisted primarily of vegetables, supplemented by lots of oatmeal, milk, butter, eggs, and some fruit. Freshly ground flour was obtained for the wholewheat bread, intended as a substitute for meat. Coffee was banned, along with tobacco.

Dr. W. A. Richardson, a Fort Payne dentist who made a liberal contribution to the school, also agreed to take care of the pupils' dental work without charge. Dr. R. B. Chastain, a Valley Head physician, offered free medical treatment to the faculty and pupils. Many others made various donations of services and goods. Robert Wright, of Fort Payne, gave the school a Seth Thomas clock and someone donated a Corona typewriter for Mrs. Harper's use. Magazine subscriptions were donated and boxes of books were shipped to the Master School. The Birmingham Public Library sent some well-worn volumes and a large number of new textbooks were donated by the Johnson Publishing Company of Richmond, Virginia. Hens, sorghum, milk, potatoes, and other food products were donated by mountain residents. In response to a request for large quantities of milk, Mr. and Mrs. W. W. Prestwood, of Fort Payne, donated a big healthy cow named "Jersey." Fruit trees for the school orchard were furnished by the Southern Nursery of Winchester, Tennessee, the Longshore Brothers of Collinsville, and P. G. Pendergrass and Son of Fort Payne.

In order to further publicize the school and obtain funds until it could become a self-sustaining institution, Colonel Howard and Mrs. Harper published a small booklet, *The Master Builder*, each quarter from October, 1923, through the following year.

The boys and girls, all having less than a seventh grade education, appeared anxious to learn and were also willing workers around the school. Much of the land near the school was cleared for strawberry patches and an orchard. On one occasion, the boys volunteered to help a neighbor pick his cotton. But there was also schoolwork to be done each week day. On pretty days classes sometimes adjourned from the little building to a clearing in the woods or to the top of Sentinel Rock, where they had a panoramic view which included portions of three states and seven counties. There were spelling bees, debates, kangaroo courts and plays which included one based on *Peggy Ware*.

There was also time for fun and games at the school. A basketball court was constructed in the fall and the Master School team challenged teams from Fort Payne and Valley Head. A tennis court which was added in the spring proved to be popular with the students. On weekends the boys could fox hunt or shoot wild turkeys. Once a group of students looking for wild fowl found a wild hog instead and staged a "hog-killing" time on the mountain. During the extremely cold winter of 1923-24, there was enough snow for several snow battles at the school.

Each morning the flag was raised to the top of the flag pole, where it could be seen from many miles away before being lowered at sunset. Church services were held on Sundays and vesper services each day at dusk.

The period of coeducation at the Master School was brief. On November 15, Colonel Howard announced that, for "good and sufficient" reasons, the girls' boarding department would be discontinued. At some future time, he promised, a girls' school would be opened, but it would be separate and distinct from the boys' school. This explanation was made, he said, in answer "to false rumors started by malicious minded persons." But male students continued to come from both Lookout and Sand Mountain and from several counties adjoining DeKalb.

During this era of improving means of transportation there were many rural roads which were often impassable. Infrequently traveled mountain roads were usually among the poorest in the state. However, visitors came from near and far to see for themselves what kind of school Colonel Howard had established in the mountain wilderness. One group of Gadsden women, members of the Axis Club, planned a visit in December but sent word that they couldn't get there because of impassable roads. Some visitors came out on horseback, as did Misses Roberta Haston and Willie Dean from Valley Head in November. Among the most prominent people to inspect the school were Dr. Frank Willis Barnett, historian and Birmingham *News* feature writer and Mrs. James Longstreet, widow of the Confederate general. Some groups, including the Fort Payne Civitan Club, visited the school in a unit.

Among the local people who frequently called at the

Master School were Joe Biddle, Blev Crow, J. E. Cordell, Mr. and Mrs. Mac McCurdy, W. M. York, Misses Beatrice and Mary Lee Crow, Rev. and Mrs. Charles H. Moorman and their daughters, Eva and Clara, and Mr. and Mrs. Elijah York. Many of the pictures of the buildings of the school were made by "Lige" York, who was an excellent photographer.

Visiting frequently from the Fischer settlement were Hardy and Frank Fischer and their wives. Among those from Valley Head were C. T. Larmore, Ben White, Miss Louise McKown, Mr. and Mrs. N. S. Davenport, Mrs. J. W. Wright, T. W. Holleman, George Hixon and Ben Price. From Fort Payne came Mr. and Mrs. Joe Wheeler Cook, Mr. and Mrs. Press McCurdy, A. E. Hawkins, J. A. Johnson, and Dr. William Warren. Mr. and Mrs. Wilbur Graves, Monroe Bailey, and Odell Turner were among the Fyffe visitors. Professor A. B. Hall, of Geraldine, Mrs. D. M. Miller of Cherokee County, Mrs. Charles Lowry, of Clinton, Oklahoma, Euclid Rogers, of Collinsville, and many others traveled up Lookout Mountain, usually by way of either Tutwiler Gap at Valley Head or through Beeson Gap at Fort Payne, to visit Colonel Howard's Master School.

In order to provide a more direct route to the school, Colonel Howard started efforts to make a passable road up Wade Gap. Requesting both labor and cash contributions, he set Wednesday, November 21, as the day for a big community "working" on the road. Aiding him in overseeing various phases of the work were N. S. Davenport, M. A. McCurdy, Jess Long, Earl Cochran, W. V. Jacoway, Carl Thomas, L. M. Price, and Commissioner E. E. McCurdy. A large number of men turned out with plows, road shovels, road drags and teams, hoes, mattocks, and picks. By sundown a large section of the mountain side had been dug down and dragged ready for grading. From then on into December, Colonel Howard and some of the faithful volunteers returned every day that weather permitted to help open up Wade Gap.

Weary from six months of arduous activity and lonely for Sally, Colonel Howard left Fort Payne shortly before his sixty-first birthday for a prolonged stay in California. In addition to spending some time with his wife and their son's family, he also intended to conduct an extensive campaign to obtain funds for his struggling school.

After a happy reunion with Sally, Clyde, Perle, and the three grandchildren, Colonel Howard rested during the Christmas holidays and then set out to acquaint the people of southern California with the Master Schools, Inc. of Alabama. In January, he made arrangements for personal appearances in Hollywood and at Long Beach. In between showings of his movie, he made talks about his mountain people in north Alabama and his hopes for providing a free education for all their children. While at Long Beach, he also addressed the Knights of the Round Table and attempted to appeal to their philanthropic instincts without actually asking for money. He began his February efforts with a personal appearance at the Ambassador Hotel theatre in Los Angeles, where he addressed the audience. Next he appeared as the guest of honor and main speaker at a banquet held by the Adventure Club at the Virginia Beach Hotel. Then he addressed the 400 member Woman's Club of Hollywood and the Hollywood chapter of the D.A.R. As his last engagement, Colonel Howard accepted an invitation to speak at the Los Angeles Public Forum at the Ambassador Hotel theatre, on Sunday, February 24. At all his engagements, the audiences were courteously interested and he received many good wishes, but very little money. He would have to raise funds for his school some other way. He again bade farewell to his family and friends and left the land of sunshine and orange blossoms to answer the irresistible call of his mountain top in Alabama.

Meanwhile, the students and his mountain friends had been preparing a surprise for Colonel Howard. After the holidays the boys began cutting down trees, hewing logs, piling stones, and clearing the site for a rustic "study" for him high upon a stone cliff. They were aided by Joe Biddle, a native of England who was a skilled carpenter and mechanic, a good musician, an active patron of New Union School, and a staunch supporter of educational causes.

Biddle stayed at the school for several days while working on the little building which Colonel Howard would later call "The Cabin." Located just west of Sentinel Rock, it had six windows, a large open fireplace, and a door with a latch string on the outside. There was a crane where a kettle could be hung over the fireplace and a large turkey-wing fan was fastened beneath the stone mantel. Beside a small pail there was a long-handled gourd to drink from and over the door a primitive gun rack held an old-fashioned fowling piece and a hunting horn. From the rustic porch one could see the railroad tracks stretching northward at the base of Lookout Mountain. West of Little Wills Valley, a great forest-covered ridge extended down the valley. Beyond the ridge lay a series of valleys with lower ridges between them. There were Big Wills Valley, Dug Out Valley, Sand Valley, and then the great plateau of Sand Mountain.

A special homecoming program was planned for Sunday morning, March 9. Joe Biddle and Blev Crow were chosen to be in charge of the exercises, which were to consist mainly of singing and speeches. A basket lunch would be spread at noon.

Straight from the balmy weather of southern California, Colonel Howard stepped from the train at Fort Payne into a chilling winter gale. The wind continued its icy blasts as he made his journey up the slippery path which wound among the creaking bare trees of the mountain. But his greeting upon his arrival at the school made up for the bad weather when he was welcomed back by excited students and several good friends anxious to tell him of their grand surprise. He blinked back tears as they told him of the program to be held in his honor.

Sunday morning was cold and dark, with winds blowing in roaring gusts. The rain started early and came down harder and harder as Colonel Howard looked out a window of the little stone school house. Greatly disappointed, he sighed, "No one will come."

But they did come. By ten o'clock they began to arrive, splashing through the cold rain bearing carefully covered baskets of food. By eleven almost everyone in the community was there to greet "Colonel" as most of them called him. He was to realize—on that glorious gray winter day—that, even if he never accomplished anything else here in the land of his latter-day dreams, he had gained the love and trust of these warm, loyal, and wonderful people.

However, as self sufficient and generous as these friends were, they simply did not have the vast cash reserves needed to keep the Master School financed. Donations continued to come in but bills for food and supplies mounted even faster and land payments also came due. The school could not continue to exist, much less expand into the complex system envisioned when the plural title was chosen for the Master Schools, Incorporated, without lots of money.

Nonetheless, Colonel Howard was still determined to see his plans materialize for the electric power system, the broadcasting station, the school chapel, the filming of *Peggy Ware*, and the expansion of the schools. Thus he arrived at a plan to conduct a $100,000 campaign right away. He would attempt to find 100 men willing to make $1,000 investments in his schools.

The third and final issue of the *Master Builder* was prepared and the new drive launched. The little booklet also carried a long open letter to Henry Ford, pleading with him to set aside some of his reported $230,000,000 cash assets as an investment in about 2,000,000 southern boys and girls.

Then Colonel Howard began a series of speeches. First, he accepted an invitation to address the student body at the Alabama Polytechnic Institute at Auburn on Wednesday, March 13. Early Tuesday morning he left the cabin to walk to Allen's Switch, three miles away, to flag the train to Birmingham. Taking the afternoon train to Opelika, he arrived there about 9:30 p.m. Though Dr. Spright Dowell, president of the institute, planned to meet him and take him to Auburn, they somehow missed each other so Colonel Howard took a room at an Opelika hotel. The next morning an automobile was sent for him and he was taken to the president's office.

Upon learning that he had never seen the Tuskeegee Institute 25 miles away, Dr. Dowell offered to drive him there. Colonel Howard was amazed and greatly impressed by the size of the school. As he stood before the statue of Booker T. Washington, the great founder, he could not restrain his tears and silently prayed that he might build an equally great institution for his people.

They returned to Auburn just in time for lunch with the Lions Club. He addressed the student body in the afternoon and then returned to Opelika to catch a train back to Birmingham. He and Governor Brandon were to speak at the American Business Club's banquet at the Tutwiler Hotel the following night.

On that occasion it appeared that Colonel Howard might have reached a turning point in his struggle to fund his great educational project. Governor Brandon agreed to head the drive for $100,000 and pledged a $1,000 subscription to start it off.

160

The American Business Club of Birmingham, parent chapter of the 75 unit organization, made Colonel Howard the first honorary member of the club. A number of prominent business and civic leaders of the city expressed their interest in the Master School and encouraged him to continue his efforts.

But the bright glow of momentary flattery and encouragement was soon dimmed by the accumulation of debts for food and supplies and by the knowledge that the first notes on land purchases would soon be due. Very few large donations or pledges were coming in from the cities where he had hoped to raise such large sums. Still as determined as ever, Colonel Howard in 1925 added two new features to his dogged pursuit of financial backing for the Master School.

First, he launched a propaganda campaign, based upon a thesis he had first promulgated in his California speeches. He maintained that the Anglo-Saxon race was in the process of vanishing from the country and that the purest Anglo-Saxons remaining anywhere were those intelligent but under-educated people who had dwelled for decades in the Appalachian Mountains. The Master Schools would be the salvation of the inhabitants of this "world of forgotten men" and would help preserve both the race and its ideals.

From March 27 through May 8 the *DeKalb Republican* published a series of long newspaper articles entitled "The Crises," in which Colonel Howard presented statistics and arguments to prove that the old American stock of Anglo-Saxon ancestry was fast disappearing. He warned that if the disaster was not prevented, our government, as founded by our forefathers, was doomed; our splendid civilization would disappear; the descendants of our Anglo-Saxon ancestors would either disappear or diminish, as had the Indian race, or they would become hewers of wood and drawers of water for inferior stocks which were multiplying rapidly.

New York was no longer an American city, he declared, but one dominated and controlled by the foreign element, whose ideals were different from those of our Anglo-Saxon forefathers. In other cities, where the foreign element was not yet dominant, it held the balance of political power and was using that power to destroy our ancient ideals. According to Colonel Howard's articles, the "oppressed and downtrodden" had come to our country like a swarm of locusts, bringing anarchistic ideas, bombs, and dynamite to enjoy their new-found liberty by destroying our Sabbath and overthrowing the ideals of our forefathers.

He again revealed his mastery of words and his skill at argumentation no matter how far he strayed from sound reasoning, as with this assertion:

The idea that we can take a nondescript aggregation of foreigners and make them or their children good Americans is a biological fallacy.

Quoting voluminous statistics, Colonel Howard argued that the more highly educated people had fewer and fewer children while those on charity reproduced more rapidly than the educated and self-supporting. The Anglo-Saxons were committing race suicide. Like all other great civilizations which had fallen, we were producing children from our worst stock.

Bolshevism and atheism were being taught in many of our colleges and universities, Colonel Howard declared, as materialism continued to replace the spiritual concepts of our Anglo-Saxon forefathers. In order to counter these and other terrible influences of our "foreign-born mongrel population," the Master School concept should be supported. Here in the mountain regions of the south the present generation could become as "seed corn" for bringing forth another crop of true Americans filled with the ideals of America's Anglo-Saxon founders.

Thus it was that Milford Howard, turning in desperation to any method he could discover to gain financial support for the Master Schools, grasped at an issue which was dividing the country in 1924. The issue was race consciousness and prejudice, with its ramifications of anti-Catholicism, anti-Semitism and all the other negative feelings of one group of Americans for another. It was a time when the Ku Klux Klan was making a strong resurgence and effectively exerting its influence on local, state and national levels. Their support is credited with deciding the gubernatorial contest in Alabama later in the year. One Sunday morning the following April, 70 members of the secret organization turned out in full regalia to attend services at First

162

Methodist Church of Fort Payne. During the year 40,000 K.K.K. members staged a parade down Pennsylvania Avenue, past the national capitol. Until later excesses and frequent usurpation of legal authority, the group and its view of Americanism appealed to many leading citizens. Colonel Howard had seized upon a popular issue and the more he wrote, the more carried away he became with his own arguments.

In October a new publication, *The Saxon*, appeared as "A Magazine Devoted to the Purity and Perpetuity of the Great Race." In it, Colonel Howard warned that "BLACKS, BROWNS, AND YELLOWS" were threatening to mongrelize and destroy Saxon America. The population was less than one-half Anglo-Saxon, he argued, with the non-Saxons outbreeding the Saxons. Philanthropists were eagerly helping minorities destroy the "GREAT RACE." *His* was a voice in the wilderness of forgotten men, telling the world that here was a place where God had preserved a peculiar people who were destined to repopulate the country with a mighty race. His mission here on earth was to keep this little "Mountain World" from the outside mongrelized world, while bringing it all the helpful, useful things that modern civilization had to offer.

Colonel Howard ascribed his own ability to break the shackles of poverty and illiteracy to his racial heritage.

> I am a product of the Southern mountains, a rail-splitter, a black-smith, a wood-splitter, a tiller of the soil, a recruit from the ranks of the underprivileged, who by the grace of God has struggled until he has raised his head a little bit above the waves of illiteracy that have submerged his beloved people. It was my heredity that made it possible, for without this heredity, God's grace would have no foundation to build on.

To buttress his own arguments, Colonel Howard included a long article entitled, "Let My People Go," by Earnest Sevier Cox, author of *White America*. He discussed the "world-wide color problems," advocating recolonizing all Negroes in this country by implanting them in an African country.

Copies of *The Saxon* were mailed to newspapers through-

163

out Alabama. But instead of receiving the favorable reviews Colonel Howard had expected, they were ignored everywhere except at one paper where he had friends on the staff. The subscription price, "a free will offering," brought in very little toward the cost of publication and the Fort Payne printer had to wait two years before being paid.

Colonel Howard's other new idea revealed more positive thinking and brought more visible and longer lasting results. He proposed to develop the scenic area of the school property where the clear, cool waters of Little River[1] wound past sheer rock bluffs and banks covered with huge trees, wild rhododendron, mountain laurel, jasmine, and honeysuckle. Rustic summer homes could be built in this beautiful setting on a town site which he had laid out and named River Park. In order to sell a large number of these building lots to raise money for the school, a big auction would be held on July 4.

At a choice spot on a bluff overlooking the river, a $10,000 club house would be erected. Made of logs and native stone, it would have a large living room with a great open fireplace and a wide porch extending over the edge of a precipice above Little River 32 feet below. Just above the club house, where the water plunged over a fall, a dam would be built. Water power from the fall would be utilized to generate hydroelectric power and the lake would be stocked with fish. An Alpine Fishing Club would be organized with a limited membership of 100 at $250 each.

His plans grew daily as he walked the banks of Little River and envisioned the future. A hotel would be constructed some distance from the clubhouse; a picturesque golf course would be laid out; a bridle path would be opened for horseback riders and hikers; a chain of scenic highways would be started for the convenience and enjoyment of automobile owners. River Park, along with Valley Head, Mentone, and Cloudland, Georgia, would become part of the playground of the lower south, and would be properly publicized through the broadcasting station to be built atop Sentinel Rock. The movie version of *Peggy Ware* would be filmed soon. And, ultimately—out there in God's

---

[1] *Colonel Howard called it DeSoto River, but that name was not widely used.*

own quiet and beautiful mountains—a great "country university" would be built among the trees and giant rocks.

Colonel Howard increased his efforts to spread the word of the natural beauty of the area. He often spoke of the million dollars worth of scenery to be found there, referring to the following statement of Dr. Frank Willis Barnett in the Birmingham *News:*

The Master Schools have a million dollars worth of scenery on their Lookout Mountain property and this scenery is Fort Payne's greatest asset.

Meanwhile, some 20 boys were being cared for at the school. These students were also utilized as workers for a truck garden. The boys put out 1,000 strawberry plants, 150 raspberry plants, 10 bushels of Irish potatoes, a bushel of onion sets and patches of mustard, lettuce, spring turnips, cabbages, and other vegetables. Then a "working" was held and friends and neighbors from across the river and down the mountain helped set out almost 2,000 peach and apple trees for the orchard.

Classes were taught at night during crop-planting time and a class in expression was added, with Colonel Howard serving as instructor. A debating club was organized and two boys tested their forensic abilities in a public debate against Arthur Hixon and Britton White, two young schoolteachers from Allen's Switch. Colonel Howard presided over kangaroo courts and took his young charges to Fort Payne to observe the proceedings of a real court.

The dean of the school, Mrs. Stella Harper, left during May on a visit to relatives in Meridian, Mississippi. While there, she also engaged in some evangelistic work, making speeches on "Why Christian Education?" A semi-vacation was observed at the school during her absence, with the boys who remained to carry on the summer work being privately tutored by the other teachers. The faculty at this time consisted of Colonel Howard, Miss Price, and Miss McMenamin. The first Master School baby, a ten pound boy, was born to Rev. and Mrs. John Blasingame on May 4, 1924. The Baptist minister was helping with the carpentry and other work at the school while studying along with the boys.

The mountain people continued to accept Colonel Howard and his school with open hearts and willing hands. At his urging, further work was done on Wade's Gap, which Mrs. Harper renamed "Summit Pass." By means of volunteer labor and some aid from the county commission, the road from the gap to the school was also improved and made passable for automobiles.

A Master School Corn Club was organized at New Union School on April 19, with 30 members. Colonel Howard, E. T. York, Joe Biddle, and Erskine Crow were elected officers. Similar clubs were to be organized at Moon Lake and New Oregon, with competition between members for the largest yield from any single acre of corn. A large community fair was planned for the fall.

On Monday, April 29, 1924, the community spirit was evident when more than 50 people showed up with axes and picnic lunches to help clear the underbrush and cut down trees at the site chosen for the club house at River Park. After pausing for prayer and other dedicatory services, the men and boys began to wield their axes while the women and girls piled the brush. They stopped only at noon when the food was spread for the ravenous workers beneath tall shade trees at the river side. By late afternoon the area had been cleared, leaving an open view of the river and falls from the road. Pleased with their accomplishment, the workers made plans to return on Friday to clear sites for some of the building lots to be auctioned on July 4. Colonel Howard appeared very happy at the progress made by noon Saturday when he and Mrs. Harper ate lunch with Mr. and Mrs. Blev Crow at their lovely country place, White Oak Springs.

May and June were busy months at the Master School as more acreage was cleared of underbrush, and building lots marked off. Visitors arrived daily to see the little stone schoolhouse and the hustling activity around River Park. Many went on to the famous "Pot Hole" for an afternoon swim and others rode on toward Mentone to stop by Miss Clara Moorman's Studio Tea Room in her log cabin on the west brow of the mountain.

During the last week of June, Colonel Howard traveled to nearby towns in Alabama and Georgia publicizing the auction to be held on the Fourth of July. Newspapers advertised the

166

event weeks ahead. Blev Crow and his daughters erected a unique rustic store where food and candy would be sold, and a cold drink booth was prepared. A grandstand was constructed for Governor Brandon and other speakers. Commissioner David Jones sent tractors and graders to put finishing touches on the Summit Pass Road a few days before the auction. Henry Burnett, an expert at barbecuing, was placed in charge of preparing the sheep, goats, yearlings, and chickens for the free feast. Tables were built for the food. A brass band was hired and old time singers invited. More debts were incurred in anticipation of a huge crowd and the sale of several hundred lots.

Friday, July 4, dawned as a bright and glorious day without a cloud in sight. People began to arrive early and by 11 o'clock the largest crowd ever assembled on Lookout Mountain stood by anticipating the good food and excitement of the great day. As a number of lots were to be sold before lunch, Colonel Howard instructed his helpers to begin placing the food on the long tables while the auction began. Several men from the Southern Auction Company, of Albertville, began urging the crowd toward the first lot to be auctioned. But only a small number of people could be persuaded to leave the tables where long knives were carving through the savory barbecued meat.

Once the troop had gathered around the selected lot, where red flags waved from each corner, the preliminary sales pitch was given. Then the loud voice of the experienced auctioneer rattled off his fast, breathless spiel before halting abruptly for the first bid. When no one responded he looked over the faces in disbelief. His assistants worked among the onlookers, attempting to get an opening bid, but without success. Another lot was chosen and every effort made to get the sale started. But again there was only dismal silence instead of the expected eager bidding. After a hurried consultation with Colonel Howard, the embarrassed auctioneer announced that the sale would be postponed until after lunch.

There was even more disappointment in store for the group. For as soon as they had gotten out of sight to begin the sale, some of the eager bystanders, fearing there would not be enough food for so large a crowd, suddenly rushed to the tables and gave the word to start. When Colonel Howard returned there was not one scrap left. Overwhelmed by the chaos and disaster, he sat down and cried like a child.

After an hour had passed, it was evident that Governor Brandon, who had gone to New York to attend the Democratic convention, had been delayed and would not arrive.[1] It was also clear that the huge crowd had come merely to observe the auction and to enjoy the food. There would be no sale that day.

Wearily, Colonel Howard mounted the speaker's stand, located in a shady grove, and spoke to the faithful who still remained. Never mind this setback, he urged. Someday, on this spot he had named River Park, there would be built one of the most beautiful and unusual villages in the world. But now, at this disappointing and dark moment, he needed the help of those who could possibly contribute any amount to a free will offering toward defraying the expense of the barbecue.

Coins were dropped into a hat which was passed through the crowd and then quickly counted to determine the amount of the contributions. The offering would pay some of the debts incurred that day, but not all. Fortunately, trade had been extremely good at the stand where several people had been kept busy selling ice cream, sandwiches, and cold drinks. There should be several hundred dollars turned in from these sales. Colonel Howard returned to the dormitory, anxious to count the proceeds from the food stand to see if he could pay for all the supplies used that day. But most of the money was gone! One of the men who had run the stand had done his own collecting of a debt owed to him.

In California Sally waited in suspense for a telegram giving the results of the sale. She had feared the worst since having a premonition two days earlier that the sale would be a failure. When no word came, she took immediate action to help her husband in his time of adversity. Just two days later an envelope stamped in large letters AIR MAIL, and bearing 24 cents postage arrived at the Master School. It had traveled by rail from Montrose to San Francisco, and by plane to Chicago—to arrive as the first air mail letter ever received in the community. It created quite a sensation at the school and brought new hope

---

[1] Governor Brandon was casting Alabama's votes for Oscar Underwood at this long convention, which cast 103 ballots before nominating John W. Davis for president.

to Colonel Howard. Enclosed was a check for $200, enough to pay all the expenses for his holiday fiasco.

At this time, an elderly Civil War veteran who lived nearby sent word for Colonel Howard to come to see him. Marion "Old Doc" Keith had been among the mountaineers who fought for the Union army and was paid a government pension. A popular and well known resident of the community, the old soldier had a practice of nicknaming everyone. He had dubbed Mrs. Harper "Old Flax Head," which she was called—when she was not within hearing distance. Too feeble to attend the auction, the old man had been distressed to hear of its failure. He wanted to contribute $10, which he had saved, toward building the projected dam across the river.

So with this small sum in hand, Colonel Howard began construction of the dam at the falls near the proposed site of the club house. Joe Biddle, the former British sailor, was placed in charge of the dam. This versatile man, now approaching 70 years of age, was a master at concrete construction in addition to his other skills. First, holes were drilled in the river bottom for iron pipes; then large quantities of cement were secured from Valley Head. The Crows, Yorks, Culpeppers, Westers, and other men and boys of the neighborhood contributed free labor and "wheelbarrowed" cement for weeks.

They built a solid concrete and stone dam, reinforced throughout by a double row of steel rods, measuring 150 feet from one bank to the other. Colonel Howard was well pleased upon its completion, declaring that it would stand as long as there was a Lookout Mountain. In gratitude to its builder—and, as everything at River Park was given a name—he proclaimed it the Joe Biddle Dam.

With the dam completed and backwater forming a lake along the cleared banks, Biddle began building a log mill house on top of a huge boulder just below the dam. Then he erected an old fashioned overshot wheel, once common along southern mountain streams. A race was to be built later to carry water to the wheel to produce motive power for operating a mill and an electric plant.

Then it was decided to go ahead with the construction of the club house upon the picturesque bluff overlooking "Rainbow Falls," the dam, and the waterwheel. By selling club memberships, Colonel Howard could pay for the building, liquidate a portion of the indebtedness of The Master Schools, Incorporated, and help finance the school. The fall session was postponed until further development of River Park was completed—and until the school could obtain better equipment for classroom and field work.

During the summer of 1924, one year after planning the buildings for his Master School, Colonel Howard invited a young Birmingham architect, Gurley Burgin to spend a week at the school. While there he made blueprints from Mrs. Harper's designs for a clubhouse. After they were completed, Miss Price, the only teacher who had worked with the two founders of the school since its beginning, accompanied the three as they walked the mile from the school to the site for the clubhouse. After they reached the high stone cliff overlooking Little River, she helped Burgin and Mrs. Harper step off the ground and place stones to mark the corners for the large two-story structure.

Then they all stood back and envisioned the completed clubhouse and its rustic interior. The entrance would lead into a large reception room, or lobby, 40 feet long and 33 feet wide. Above would be a mezzanine leading to the guest rooms. On the west side a large porch, with the same dimensions as the lobby, would overhang the cliff and provide a clear view of the river.

Building the clubhouse was an ambitious undertaking during a period of recession by a man without a regular income, who already owed large sums of money for numerous tracts of land. But the lumber was ordered, the supplies bought, the carpenters hired, and that master craftsman, Joe Biddle, began his last job.[1] Expenses and debts began increasing at an alarming rate.

In November, Colonel Howard rented the new city auditorium in Birmingham for a Saturday night showing of his movie, charging $1.00 admission and delivering his address on the Saxon race between showings. While there he also made efforts to promote his Alpine Fishing Club among his influential friends in the business world.

---

[1]Injured in a fall while roofing Alpine Lodge, Biddle died on November 15, 1926, as a result of these injuries.

But the meager profits from a movie, occasional small donations and three or four memberships in his club could not even pay current bills. By December several notes on school property were overdue; Colonel Howard owed the workmen several hundred dollars; and merchants in Fort Payne and Valley Head were demanding money for supplies obtained from them. At first impatient, his debtors became angry and disgusted with the man who was building on such a grand scale and yet—apparently—could pay for nothing.

Colonel Howard planned a trip to make one more effort to sell club memberships and building lots. He knew some people at Rome, Georgia, and would begin there. With less than $5.00 in his pocket, he went to see a Fort Payne friend who had pledged $100 to the Master School over a year before but had paid only a portion of that amount. Attempting to conceal his agony of humiliation, he revealed his need for some cash to finance a fund-raising trip. Expecting at least a small amount of money, he was stunned when told that his friend's family was planning a family reunion for Christmas, that he had nothing to spare.

Crest-fallen, he staggered to the street in a daze and plodded slowly down the street he had traveled with such joyful steps over forty years before when he passed his bar exam. He paused before the courthouse where great crowds had gathered to hear him address the jury in prominent criminal cases, where throngs of people had gathered to listen to his political speeches. Lost in a fog of bewilderment, he stared at the first brick store ever built in Fort Payne—erected by a daring and adventurous young lawyer. He glared bitterly at the bank where he had once enjoyed unlimited credit, at the business houses, smaller in stock than his own had been, where he could now add nothing to his account.

A cold gust of wind swept his hair across his face and he winced with pain as a gravel cut his foot through a hole in the sole of an old, soiled shoe. Hobbling to a small store which sold only cheap shoes, he asked for and received credit from the proprietor, to whom he didn't already owe anything. Wearing the warm brogans from the store, he headed for the depot.

On December 21, 1924, Colonel Howard registered at a small hotel in Rome, requesting the cheapest room available. He

171

now had $3.00. He was lonely, despondent, and ill. At the end of a week he had made no sales and had neither the spirit nor the strength to make further efforts. A bill for only $7.00 was placed in his box; it might as well have been $700 as there were only coins in his pocket now. Admitting his plight to the manager, he was shown Christian charity that Christmas season and was allowed to stay on anyway. With his last dimes, he purchased loaves of bread, which he carried to his room and made his meals from until even the dimes were gone.

Shortly after his sixty-second birthday, he walked out the country road to the place where he had been born. As he stood there penniless, friendless, broken in spirit, a miserable failure, he pondered the meaning of the life which had begun there. Dejectedly, he gave a sigh of relief that his kind and loving mother was not alive to witness her son's agony and perdition.

Upon his return to the hotel he received a message to call Western Union. Some money had been wired from California, which he could obtain upon identification. He knew Sally had sent enough money for him to come home. "But if I go," he thought, "I shall never return to Alabama and will be leaving only failure behind me." Nor could he bring himself to obtain the money for some purpose other than that for which it was intended. Ignoring the message, he went back to his tiny bleak room. His trudging over many lonely miles had brought fatigue and going without food had left him trembling and weak.

Standing before his mirror, he shuddered at the strange sallow-skinned, disheveled man with bloodshot eyes whom he saw there. The gaunt creature looked more like some disturbed spirit than a human being. Colonel Howard locked his door and fell wearily across his bed, where he lay sobbing into the night.

It was the holiday season, a time for joy and sharing with one's family. Here he was alone, so alone! Yet—not really. There was a lifetime partner, always with him or lurking not far away. Wherever Milford Howard went, Failure stalked his path. He had met Failure in business, in politics, in writing, in his attempt to found a great school, and in his personal life as a father and as a husband. Had he not given his sons too much and too long, making them spoiled and pampered and lacking in self-discipline and self-reliance? As for his dear, loyal, devoted wife, who deserved so much, had he not failed to give her security for her golden years? Yes, Failure was with him now.

And those twin plagues which followed every lost dream, every defeat—Gloom and Despair—were with him now, tempting him to give up. All was lost; all was hopeless. They told him so.

The four of them were together again and they knew each other well. But, alas! There was a stranger there! The troubled man burrowed his head beneath his pillow, gasping the stale, dusty air. Still he could perceive those silent footsteps, made by plodding, invisible feet. He sensed that eerie, shadowy apparition and trembled in the presence of Death.

For hours he lay unconscious, ill in body, mind, and spirit. Finally he realized where he was and that he urgently needed help. That he had almost died, he felt certain, but he now had a new feeling of inner peace. At least he felt resigned to whatever fate held in store for him. If the work he had started on the mountain had to be completed by someone else, he was ready to accept anything Divine Will should decree.

As his life had been spared for some purpose, he felt he must leave that dismal room before it did become his death chamber. To Mrs. Harper, who had gone to Brunswick, Georgia, for the holidays, he dispatched an urgent plea for money. She wired back that she had none to send and urged him to trust the Lord to provide help. Assistance soon came from his usual patron saint, Sally, who had mailed him a check. He cashed it immediately and boarded a train for Tuskeegee to visit Claude and Jennie before making plans for the future.

At his son's home Colonel Howard regained some of his strength during the few days he spent resting and visiting with his grandson. Although Claude and Jennie expressed concern over his health when they saw how dissipated he looked he gave them no hint as to how near death he had been. Neither did he tell them about his financial troubles after he realized they had their own. He did get enough money from Claude to travel to Brunswick for consultation with Mrs. Harper about possibilities for reviving their school and paying off their indebtedness.

While in Georgia, Colonel Howard received another check from Sally which enabled him to pay some of the smaller debts. But if the club house were ever finished he would have to sell some more property. In discussing cities where buyers might be

173

found, he and Mrs. Harper decided that Miami, where the real estate business was booming, should be a likely place for prospective customers.

In January, 1925, Colonel Howard, Mrs. Harper, and her mother, Mrs. Lloyd, traveled to Miami in an old Ford, arriving in that thriving city with a total of $20.00 among them. Soon after their arrival, Colonel Howard was busy publicizing his project by talking to a reporter from the Miami *Herald*. Along with his descriptions of the mountain scenery and the picturesque building lots, he deftly dropped references to his terms in congress and to the books he had authored. He also carried with him a picture of himself as he appeared in his movie. A feature story about the ex-congressman and his ventures on Lookout Mountain in Alabama soon appeared in the Florida newspaper. In the following weeks several $1,000 lots and club memberships were sold, bringing in what seemed like a small fortune to the formerly destitute promoters.

Returning to Alabama early in March, Colonel Howard paid his labor and supply bills but found that if he finished paying all the land notes he would have nothing left to complete the club house. He reasoned that the notes were drawing interest while he increased the value of the property and that those holding the notes would not lose anything by not being paid right away. He chose to spend part of the money for work on the Alpine Anglers' Club House and other projects at River Park.

A little success at raising funds had once more aroused optimism. The planning and dreaming began anew. Colonel Howard announced that he would establish two summer camps. Camp Lookout would be organized for boys and Treasure Trove Camp for girls. A corps of trained assistants, life guards, swimming and athletic instructors were being secured to accommodate 400 children. Buildings would soon be constructed for Howard Institute, a school for boys who were high school graduates. Preparations would be made later in the year to bring in a prominent motion picture location company for the filming of *Peggy Ware* on Lookout Mountain. Finally, River Park, consisting of 220 acres on the river, would be further developed, with a strip of land on each bank designated as a parkway. It would become a selective summer colony for discriminating people, restricted to persons of the Anglo-Saxon race and Protestant religion.

W. N. Gramling, of Brunswick, Georgia, prepared the plat of River Park, with over 250 building lots. Several bungalows were started and many people, including Claude and Jennie, chose lots and began planning their summer homes.

Soon the money was all gone again, with the clubhouse still not quite complete and certainly not yet furnished. The fishing club, with less than a dozen members, had to be abandoned. The big rustic building was renamed Alpine Lodge. When opened for tourists it would begin to pay for its construction and would also help in the sale of lots at River Park. But that ever-present problem stood in the way. Where could Colonel Howard turn for more money?

Again, Sally was the answer to his prayers. Already planning to come spend the summer with him, she received his solemn message: she must mortgage their California home for money to complete the lodge. There was no other way. He had enclosed the necessary waiver to any rights he had to the property. Unhesitatingly, she borrowed every dollar she could get on the mortgage and made preparations for her trip. With young Milford driving her car, and with a camping outfit in the back, she soon was crossing the continent with a check to cover the completion of Alpine Lodge.

On a warm sunny day in May, Milford swung the Ford around a curve in a cloud of dust and sounded the horn as they approached the Master School. Sally bounded out of the car with the exuberance she had shown in her youth decades before. She still had, her husband thought, that same girlish figure, the same quick springy step she had the day they met at the courthouse. He rushed to meet her, this intensely loyal wife who had never lost her faith in him during any of his misfortunes.

As he peered down through misty eyes at her smiling face, he noticed instantly the marked change in her appearance. She looked so tired, so very pale. The wrinkles in her face were deeper, the circles beneath her eyes dark and wide. But there were no complaints, no indication of pain those first few days.

The summer of 1925 would always hold bitter-sweet memories for Colonel Howard. It was a time of reunion and togetherness, a period of heartbreak and dread. There was a hospital examination in Rome, Georgia, long hours of fearful waiting, a terrible diagnosis, a fateful prognosis. An advanced case of cancer. A short time to live. There was her amazingly bright outlook, her continuous optimism. The radium would help, she was certain. She would get well.

She did make a will however, leaving the California home to him—just in case. Afterwards, she would talk only of getting well and of plans for the future. She and their grandson helped build flower boxes in front of his cabin, using mortar and conglomerate stone. Promising to send him some rose cuttings from California, she carefully put a rock in place, telling him that was the "corner stone." He picked her up as though she were a child and kissed her, his heart breaking at the thought that she would never live to send the roses. She showed Milford where she wanted a coat of cement smeared on the box and with a sharp stick inscribed:

SACKIE—MILFORD
August 1st, 1925

Together they attended a Sunday gathering at Rock Bridge Church, where he delivered an address. Afterward she entered his cabin looking more radiant than she had in a long time. Calling him "Dad," as was her custom, she told him how wonderful she thought his religious talk had been and insisted, "I want you to preach." But he demurred, insisting he could never be an orthodox preacher. "Besides," he laughed, "I shouldn't be any kind until I can practice what I preach."

During her visit, Sally made two trips to Tuskegee to visit Claude and remained active, as well as cheerful, all summer. Though she rested often and tired easily, she still betrayed no signs of the pain she must have suffered. Rather, she claimed to be getting better and kept insisting she would get well.

But when the mountain became a colorful blend of gold and red with leaves rustled by the first cool breezes of autumn, Sally announced that she must go home. She could not be dissuaded and her husband knew she wished to be buried in California. That was the land of her childhood dreams and the place of her personal fulfillment in later life. Here in the sunset of her years she would not stay where bitter political battles had been fought, where terrible memories haunted her still. She must go home. In spite of her family's pleas, she would not take a train, preferring to travel in her car with Milford. First, they would go to Tuskegee and Jennie would accompany them home. Colonel Howard would tend to affairs at River Park and go to California later.

As he told Sally good-by, he held her in his arms and groped for words which would not go past the big lump in his throat. She smiled and said, "I'll see you soon." He watched sadly as the car wound down the mountain road. At the last turn she leaned out, threw a kiss, and waved a last good-by. Turning his back to the crowd which had gathered to see Sally off, Colonel Howard blinked back tears and walked toward his secluded cabin where he could release his torrent of emotions in solitude among the pines.

From Tuskegee and from cities between Alabama and California, came a steady flow of letters from Sally. Each was read over and over and then carefully added to a bundle stored in a small trunk in his cabin.

From Tuskegee:

I will write you a card everyday if I can so you will not be anxious or uneasy. You are fine and so dear to me. How I wish you could sell some land so you will be free from care. Dear, your interests shall always be mine, and what you do is more interesting to me than to anyone. We all love you and talk about you and wish you good luck. My heart goes with you wherever you go, and I wish you all the success in the world. Goodbye, and God bless you. With love always.

From Demopolis:

Stood the trip yesterday fine. Feel good this morning.

Mineral Wells, Texas:

This is a wonderful Sunday morning, and the hills are so beautiful . . . . I don't know how I would have managed without Jennie. She and Milford do everything for me, and I just rest when we stop. I spent a long time with you this morning, you have always and will be so dear to me. I pray all you do is for the best, and pray God you will soon have financial relief. This means you can be free, have some good clothes, and be independent, not feeling you have to "do or die." God bless you, I am with you. I will be so glad if everything turns out as you hope and you can spend this winter in California . . . .

Lordsburg:
   We will get home Wednesday or Thursday. I'll be glad for I can rest, and try to get well.

Montrose:
   My dear Dad, I won't write a long letter but just a few lines to let you know I am home and feeling "fair." The children are all "up in the air" so glad to see us. Virginia jumped up and down and said, "Granny! Granny!"

   For almost a week afterward she wrote daily. In the last letter, which he prized above all others she gave expression to her unwavering faith and made one statement which seemed so characteristic of her that it always stood out in his memory: "God has always been as good to me as I would let him be."
   Then he received the following message from California on October 16:

   Mama goes to the hospital in the morning. We are doing everything possible for her. Will keep you informed. She sends lots of love.

Soon afterward, on October 25, came this message:

   Operation noon today. Mama is conscious and asked me to wire you. The end is only a matter of hours.

   For weeks Colonel Howard had attempted in vain to raise enough money for train fare to California. Finally, after Sally entered the hospital a Fort Payne businessman agreed to purchase a lot. The deed was to be prepared and brought in the next day for the money. After making a sleeper reservation on

the night train, Colonel Howard returned the following afternoon with his packed bag. At the office, he was told to wait
while the man went home to get his wife's check, as she was
buying the property. After an agonizingly long wait, the man
returned, handed the deed back and said he might buy it some
other time. Trembling with anger, Colonel Howard tore the
deed in half and roared, "You will never buy a lot at River Park
as long as I live!"

It was almost time for his train. He had to get a ticket
somehow! Frantically he searched the streets for some friendly
or kind face to which he could relate his sad predicament.
Where was some good Samaritan who would give him a quick
loan as an act of mercy? At the last moment he got the money
and rushed to the depot. He held his emotions in rein until he
boarded the train and located his berth. Then his pent up grief
and frustration burst forth in a flood of tears as the whistling
train jerked forward.

As physically exhausted and emotionally drained as he
was, he could not sleep. With the clackity-clack of the train
wheels, events of the previous year flashed across his mind.
There had been such bright prospects with the land sales and
the renewed activity. The summer camps could have been such
a success with adequate backing and facilities. Swimming
instructors had been employed to help develop the camps and
to manage them. Robert Rodgers, holder of the world's high-
diving record and Robert Pearson, the Olympic long distance
underwater swimmer had arrived in May. There was such excitement on the mountain the last day of the month when Rodgers
dived into the gorge from the brink of DeSoto Falls! The Sunday crowd would long remember his bravery and diving skill.
But he would never give diving lessons at River Park. The
camps, like the fishing club, were laid to rest in a vast cemetery
of discarded dreams.

The final attempt to reopen the Master School had been a
calamity. In order to operate for a while two groups of boys
were accepted from Atlanta. The Rotarians were sponsoring
eight and paying their tuition and five were sent from the
Anson Dodge School for underprivileged boys. Garfield
McCurdy was employed to help teach the term.

When the Atlanta boys arrived at Valley Head, most made

their exit from the train through the windows and swaggered forth to see what kind of place they were invading. Fresh from reform schools and rejected by Atlanta high schools, they were ready for anyone who was ready for them. A brave effort was made to control the boys, to teach them fundamentals and to raise their moral values. Some were even furnished with shoes and clothing when winter came and their sponsors refused to clothe them. But finally the financial and mental strain became too much. The boys were herded aboard a train and sent back to Georgia. The Master School closed again.

And now he faced the greatest tragedy of his life. The sweetheart of his boyhood, the brave companion of his storm-tossed manhood was dying—or already dead. "We fought our hardest battles a continent apart," he sobbed. "Why did I long for the rugged mountain wilderness and fashion dreams I could not fulfill?"

Unable to sleep, Colonel Howard got out when the train stopped at El Paso and paced up and down the platform. When he saw a Western Union messenger approaching he suspected the telegram was for him.

"Are you Mr. Howard?" he was asked.

He nodded and answered affirmatively as he reached for the message. With his hands trembling, he read of Sally's death.[1] The funeral would be delayed until he reached California, the telegram said.

She was dressed in white, a plain little gold wedding ring on her hand. As Colonel Howard looked at her serene and peaceful face he thought of how much she still resembled a bride. Milford came to stand by his side, with bowed head and silent tears. The grieving husband and grandson were the last to see her before the coffin was gently closed.

Sally A. Howard was buried in a beautiful spot she had chosen in Forest Lawn Cemetery at Glendale, California. Nearby stood a little stone chapel, the Wee Kirk O' the Heather. As Colonel Howard stood by the graveside he made a silent vow. "A thousand dreams I've wasted but this one I'll make come true. Some day I will build a little chapel like this one you loved as a memorial to you and your name."

---

[1] *Sally died at Glendale Sanitarium on October 28, 1925.*

Afterwards the stark loneliness of the little rose-covered bungalow seemed unbearable. But his grandson came to sit with him to talk into the night about the one they had lost. Early the next morning he drove Milford to work and watched as "Bo" stood waving when he left him there. That was a scene he would often recall. He would never see his grandson again.

When he reached home, Perle asked him to come to their house next door to hear the lawyer read the will. "I don't want you to think we influenced her in any way," she said, "in the making of this *new* will." Stunned, he stalked across the lawn to find what disposal was to be made of these two houses and lots which had been put in Sally's name. He found that she had left him a life estate, with the property going eventually to their sons. He could not sell either house! He was supposed to meet monthly payments on the mortgage when he didn't even have train fare back to Alabama! Seething with resentment toward Clyde for this unexpected blow, he spun around and left his son's house without a departing word.

On the verge of collapse from the combined forces of grief, anxiety, shock, and disappointment, Colonel Howard was unable to realize at this time what would gradually occur to him later—that Sally thought she was doing what was best for him. She had attempted to make some provision for him in his old age in case his Alabama ventures continued to fail. She wanted him to keep the little cottage near their grandchildren. He could have a refuge here by the green Verdugo Hills, free from care and worry in his last years. Indeed, he was destined to need such a haven toward the end of his incredibly troubled life.

His thoughts at this time centered upon getting back to Lookout Mountain, to salvage what he could of his life and his investments there. Taking Sally's car to a dealer who offered him a fair price, he was about to close the deal when it was discovered that someone had removed the tag and the dealer refused to buy it. Thwarted again in his efforts to raise some money, he drove home as fast as possible, stormed into the little house, and grabbed his bag. Glancing back at his mahogany bookcases and desk, his Edison phonograph and records, he gave a resigned shrug, paused to gather some family photographs, and walked out into the darkness to catch a street car to Los Angeles.

Somehow he got back to Alabama and to his little log cabin on Lookout Mountain. Barely holding on to reality until he could reach his private sanctuary, Colonel Howard collapsed, semi-conscious and lay prostrate for hours, reliving the most wretched moments of his turbulent life. Alone in his purgatory, he suffered the torment of his mistakes and failures, the agony of self-condemnation, the anguish of having loved ones die.

He could remember little of the following weeks. There were anxious faces of friends. A doctor had examined and questioned him. There was tasteless food and nausea. But nothing had mattered. He had no strength to move, no will to live. Life was just a big hopeless void and he was a worthless trespasser.

While he was little more than withering vegetation and when he became violently, desperately ill, there was one who showed deep compassion, who ministered to him, who saved him, literally, from dying. Stella Vivian Harper fed him, talked to him, read to him, and gradually coaxed him back into the land of the living. He finally gained the strength and the will to walk once more in the sunshine, to look upon the magnificent panorama of the valleys, the ridges, and mountains, and—even to dream again.

The reason he had not had more success became clear; it was the inaccessibility of the place. What he needed to do was to get a road built on the brow of the mountain. It would be a great scenic highway stretching all the way from Gadsden to Chattanooga. It would be the longest summit highway in the world, traversed by thousands of automobiles, bordered with roses and dotted with vine-covered cottages set in beautiful orchards and vineyards.

Yes, he would build his highway.

The Scenic Highway

The first public announcement of his dream highway was made by Colonel Howard through the Gadsden *Star* in March, 1926. Later in the month, he appeared before the Gadsden Chamber of Commerce to seek its support for the great scenic highway which would traverse the backbone of Lookout Mountain from Gadsden to Chattanooga. This 100 mile long road on top of a mountain which had a river and waterfalls, and from which one could see miles of valleys and ridges, would become one of the greatest tourist attractions in the United States, he told the Gadsden businessmen. Millions of dollars would be spent each year by people choosing this vacation route into the heart of the southland. In addition, it would bring settlers and industries into the fertile region.

His speech was impressive and his logic convincing. The group immediately endorsed the project, making the Gadsden Chamber of Commerce the first civic organization to support the Scenic Highway. The members even agreed to launch a movement to build the highway by spending $800 for a big barbecue to be held at Noccalula Falls on April 9.

Colonel Howard awaited that event impatiently and with great expectations. He had been successful once more in influencing at least one group of people. Unfortunately, he could not affect his greatest enemy on so many occasions—the weather. The gray skies brought several morning showers and caused concern that the well-planned lunch and program would be a total failure. But people began to arrive even as the rains continued. They came from local communities, from Chattanooga and Birmingham; they came from small towns, the mountains, and the valleys. There was soon a happy and enthusiastic throng gathered around the speaker's stand to hear a description of the proposed highway and to learn of the immense changes it would bring. The people were inspired and well entertained and gave their approval to the famous ex-congressman's dream with shouts and applause. John A. Rogers, president of the Alabama Highway Commission, followed with a ringing endorsement of the project and volunteered as the first subscriber to a highway fund.

Delicious barbecue was then served by the ladies of the Axis Club, after which Dr. Frank Willis Barnett entertained the audience with one of his colorful speeches. At the conclusion of the program, the Lookout Mountain Scenic Highway Association was organized, with Milford W. Howard as president. An executive committee was chosen with representatives from Gadsden, Valley Head, Chattanooga, and Cloudland.

Newspapers in Birmingham, Gadsden, Collinsville, Fort Payne, and Chattanooga endorsed the highway project and published frequent articles concerning both the proposed roadway and its chief promoter, Colonel Howard. A Gadsden reporter quoted the former congressman as saying this was the only undertaking of his life where he expected no opposition, as everyone wanted the highway. That belief was short-lived.

At the first meeting of the executive committee, held on April 14, at the Hotel Patten in Chattanooga, tempers flared in a heated dispute between Colonel Howard and a well-known member of the committee. The latter proposed that the highway association raise $50,000 and spend the entire sum on efforts to induce the federal government to build a mammoth, paved highway, 100 feet wide. Colonel Howard, who wished for every cent raised to be spent on actual construction, expressed his unwavering opposition to raising money for a propaganda campaign. It was ridiculous anyway, he asserted, to believe they could induce either the state or the federal government to build a highway running through the woods along the crest of a mountain when there was another state-federal highway parallelling it at the foot of the mountain in Little Wills Valley. The clash of opinions and personalities ended with the resignation of the director, who declared he could never work with the association president. The rest of the committee remained intact and met again the following Saturday at Hal Howe's hotel at Mentone to discuss the location of the highway and other business matters. In between these two meetings, Colonel Howard addressed the Chattanooga Rotary Club, securing another endorsement of the highway and a promise of promotional and financial aid, along with a $100 membership in the association. By the time the officers met at Mentone, sufficient funds had been pledged to warrant their making a preliminary survey of the part of the highway which concerned Colonel Howard most, that section stretching southward from Mentone.

The Birmingham *Age-Herald* observed that the Scenic Highway idea "appealed to the imagination." But several experienced businessmen and F. E. Schmidt, a Mentone civil engineer, all accustomed to dealing on a more practical level, were convinced that a brow road all the way from Mentone to Collinsville would be almost impossible. They attempted to persuade Colonel Howard that it would be much more feasible to drop back to the middle of the mountain between these two places. But the association president was adamant: The Scenic Highway was going to be SCENIC and it was going to run along the west brow of the mountain.

Expertly wielding his ax at River Park, he seemed to accent his determination with repeated forceful blows as he fashioned a huge pile of stakes before organizing a surveying party to mark off the route of the southern end of the road. Through the cool morning breezes of May and into the scorching heat of mid-day Colonel Howard stalked slowly through the thick forest in his boots and work clothes. Fighting fatigue and minor illness, he kept up with the younger men every work day. Half finished by June, the group continued trudging through the thick snake-infested, waist-high underbrush, tearing clothes and ripping flesh on blackberry and saw briers and on scrub-brush plum thorns, while becoming encrusted with "beggar lice."

"Colonel," as most of the men called him, pushed his robust physique and giant's strength to the limit, demanding more than his share of the grueling labor of lifting heavy logs and huge stones. His friends looked on helplessly as he refused to slow the killing pace. His own concern was not for his physical well being, but for his peace of mind. The continuous, tiring activity helped keep his mind off himself, his great tragedy, his failure in life. Every pause seemed to bring a reminder that the fruits of a lifetime of effort were gone, that the faithful one who had loved him most and understood him best had been taken when he needed her desperately. He remembered, every time he thought of "Sackie," that even as she was dying she made the supreme sacrifice of mortgaging her home for him. Such thoughts could be pushed aside as he worked his way along the mountainside.

The nights were more difficult than the days. Alone in his cabin, he relived his most bitter battles and suffered miserably from remorse, doubt, and uncertainty. When he finally succeeded in banishing these ghostly skeletons and fell asleep, he became fitful and disturbed by hideous dreams, awaking suddenly to wipe the cold perspiration from his brow. In utter desolation, he often lay awake for hours, longing for the morning, the sunshine, and the constant strenuous labor of the day. For the first time in years he began to pray—in long and sincere sessions, during which the last shreds of skepticism died away, and he found a measure of surcease from his agony.

During this period he began sketching the beginning of an autobiography. Perhaps some other underprivileged boys would be inspired by it if he should succeed in doing something big and really worthwhile during his life's closing chapters. It would have to be some contribution to humanity, as it would certainly not be a great personal achievement. His was no success story. With all the mountain property deeded to the Master Schools, he owned nothing of value in the world. At the age of 64, he didn't have even a decent suit of clothes. Surely fate would crown his present effort with success and before he reached the age of threescore and ten he could point with pride to at least one outstanding achievement. If so, he would make this the climax of his story. He simply would not complete it until he had attained one great victory. His surveying and his efforts at publicizing the road continued. His trail of stakes finally reached the Gadsden terminus and he, personally, drove the last one in with a flourish.

He would show the doubters that an ideal location had

been found on the brow. The road's construction should be simple and it would be indescribably beautiful from a scenic standpoint. After seven weeks of pacing off the route one foot at a time, he was ready to present the details of his work to the directors of the highway association. Some of these men, however, were still not convinced that an easily constructed highway over his proposed route would be possible. Colonel Howard, on the other hand, was unwilling to make any compromise. An impasse resulted in several months of inaction during which continuous efforts were made to sell some River Park lots. Another auction failed to bring even a single bid on any of the property. He would have no market until some progress had been made on the highway.

Unable to pay off the land notes, he began to suspect a conspiracy against him. Certain enemies were not only blocking the construction of the Scenic Highway, but were also attempting to get the school property. After his unsuccessful auction, two of those whom he believed responsible for much of his trouble made him a rather substantial offer for all the holdings of the Master Schools. Although accepting this offer appeared to be the only solution to his financial plight, his stubborn pride dictated the resolute reply, "No, I'll starve first."

The hitherto patient and long suffering creditors began demanding their money. The unpaid notes comprised a total indebtedness of between $15,000 and $20,000 on property Colonel Howard believed to be worth several hundred thousand dollars. But without the Scenic Highway there was no market, and without a market it had no commercial value. He was discouraged but not yet defeated. A crisis was a time for action.

Thinking first of his personal life, he turned to his partner and companion who had already shared his ambitions, efforts, and failures. Stella Vivian Harper agreed to become his wife and they were married in Chattanooga, Tennessee, on November 9, 1926. Thereafter, he called her "Lady Vivian," a rather grandiose title for a woman choosing to share Colonel Howard's bleak future at this time. He was heavily in debt and beginning to show signs of misfortune and age. His Master Schools dream was apparently shattered and his efforts to start the Scenic Highway were at a standstill.

He could not overcome the obstinacy and opposition of

some of the association directors who refused to approve his plans. His only alternative, if he could not remove an obstacle, was to go around it. He decided to ignore the Lookout Mountain Scenic Highway Association altogether and to organize a corporation to take its place. Birmingham would be included in the cities sponsoring the new movement and help would be enlisted from civic groups there. A Birmingham businessman was induced to lend him $500 to launch this effort.

Following advance publicity and a number of personal contacts, Colonel Howard spoke in December to a group of approximately 100 Birmingham businessmen, representing various civic organizations at a luncheon hosted by the Knights of the Round Table. He boasted of the marvelously beautiful scenery along the proposed route of the highway, describing the waterfalls, the rugged cliffs, and the entrancing vistas over the foothills into the far blue mountains. It was, he told them, "the best craftsmanship of nature in the creation of the wholly lovely."

Aside from the fact that the highway would, for the first time, provide the people of Alabama with an opportunity to enjoy this long neglected asset, there was also a more practical reason for its construction. Several of the main highways converged at Chattanooga, with the biggest part of the southbound traffic traveling by way of Atlanta. There was no highway to attract them into Alabama. The Scenic Highway would not only draw tourists southward, but would appeal to travelers headed toward both the north and the west as the fame of the highway spread.

His eloquent arguments won the endorsement of the Birmingham group and two directors were elected to serve on the new board. From a similarly successful meeting at Gadsden the next day, he went on to Chattanooga and smaller towns in between to obtain support for the highway and to arrange for the selection of directors. On January 11, 1927, the Chattanooga-Gadsden-Birmingham-Lookout Mountain Scenic Highway Association was organized and incorporated in Birmingham.

At the first meeting of the directors, Colonel Howard was chosen president and J. B. Pound, of Chattanooga, made an enthusiastic speech predicting an immediate and spectacular success for the association. They would raise $250,000 for the

188

proposed highway, Pound declared. It would be open for travel by the first day of January, 1928, when 1,000 automobiles would form a grand cavalcade from Chattanooga to Birmingham. Colonel Howard and Lady Vivian rented an inexpensive room in Chattanooga with the last of his borrowed $500 and opened a highway association office near the Read House.

Securing the services of J. C. Wall, a well-known engineer and roadbuilder, Colonel Howard prepared for the preliminary work of locating the road from Mentone to Chattanooga. Just as it appeared there would be smooth sailing, trouble arose unexpectedly. Property owners on the east brow of the mountain began to clamor for consideration, claiming that the scenic attractions were just as great on that side of the mountain. For two cold and windy weeks in February, Colonel Howard tramped up one side of Lookout Mountain and down the other with the survey team, pointing out the natural advantages of the west brow and the disadvantages of the other side.

When the west brow route was officially adopted from Chattanooga to Gadsden, by way of Mentone, Colonel Howard felt he had won an important victory. Donations of both land and money were made to the association that month. Two of the largest contributors were Earl Cochran and Walter B. Raymond of Fort Payne, who donated $1,000 each as well as property for the right of way. Letters of support arrived daily at the association office, including one from Miss Mary Collins, secretary of the Collinsville Chamber of Commerce, which stated:

> We Collinsville people appreciate your efforts in the enterprise and we are solidly behind the highway association as it means so much to us individually and collectively.

After getting the highway started, Colonel Howard and Lady Vivian returned to River Park to spend the rest of the winter in a small log cabin across from Alpine Lodge. They were broke again, with only a meager supply of food and lonely— without even a radio for entertainment. Much of their time was spent in a dream world of imaginary journeys made together, as on long winter evenings Colonel Howard sat in the glow of burning logs and read aloud from some of his treasured books.

One Sunday in March, 1927, he read from a volume on travel which included a chapter entitled, "A Year On The Island of Capri." The description of the Mediterranean resort contrasted so sharply with their mountain home that cold day that Colonel Howard impulsively asked his wife if she would like to spend the next winter on the Isle of Capri.

"Oh, that will be glorious!" she exclaimed. "When shall we sail from New York?"

"Suppose we set the date for the first of October," he answered, half seriously. Together they examined the almanac and found that the moon would be full at that time. They dreamed together of a voyage across the Atlantic, with the moon making a shining pathway on the ocean at night.

But first, spring would come and the road would be built from Chattanooga to Gadsden, passing through River Park. Then the property would sell at a high price and his good fortune would be well deserved. He was responsible for the Scenic Highway Association and was the only man who had walked over every foot of the proposed route of the road. Schmidt had surveyed one end and Wall the other, but he was the only person who really knew the full route. It was truly *his* Scenic Highway.

The one issue upon which Colonel Howard was overruled was on the method of financing the road. He had favored the popular subscription plan for the whole project. But it was decided to get various sections stumped and provided with drainage by whatever means possible and then attempt to secure county aid for grading. As Colonel Howard feared, this was to result in a piecemeal completion, with the last section not being built until the 1930's, with paving proceeding through the 1950's, and with one seven-mile stretch still unpaved in 1976.

Work on the northern half of the highway started in the spring of 1927 and progressed at a fairly steady pace. A 22-mile section through Dade and Walker counties in Georgia was cleared and stumped with money raised in Chattanooga, plus $1,000 given by Adolph S. Ochs, of New York, publisher of the Chattanooga *Times*. The total cost of preparing this section was $5,500, or $250 per mile. The commissioners of Dade County agreed to grade and gravel the road in that county when they could. The county owned only one tractor, however, and prospects of its help any time soon were not good. B. W. Newsom, of Rising Fawn, promised to grade the road himself, all the way from Johnson's Crook to Jackson's Hill, a distance of 30 miles. From Mentone to Fort Payne, the work was slow in getting started. During the first year, only five miles were graded, with the right-of-way being cut for another five. Nothing was accomplished between Fort Payne and Gadsden until the 1930's when the final route was somewhat altered from that meticulously marked off by Colonel Howard.

To him, the five miles between Mentone and Wade's Gap were the most important. He labored there from early spring into the fall, in chilling winds, through stifling heat, and sometimes during rain. Twice he became ill from overexertion and exposure, but was soon back at work on his road. Edging slowly through the right-of-way during the spring and summer, he hacked at scrub pines and seedlings, sawed through tough virgin pines and tall oaks and hickorys, snaked off maples, poplars, elms, and locusts. Finally, the road was ready for grading.

F. E. Schmidt agreed to survey and plat some of the Master School property along the brow and to wait for his pay until some sales were made. However, he was busy with other work at the time and Colonel Howard was anxious to get the brow lots ready to sell. After hearing about a young civil engineer who was visiting his mother at Mentone, he contacted Frank Berry, who came over to survey and plat the property. The engineer told his uncle, Thomas Berry, of Rome, Georgia (brother of Martha Berry) about the brow property. His uncle was already interested in the property and contracted to buy all that had been laid out.

At the last meeting ever held of the Master School, Inc. trustees, the previous June, Colonel Howard had been empowered to sell school property and to make deeds, either in the name of the Master Schools or in his own name, and to dispose of the property and money from all sales as he saw fit. He could, therefore, legally use the proceeds of the transaction with Thomas Berry as he wished. As he retained some hope of resuming the school project as long as he lived, he left most of the property in the school's name, except for that of Alpine Lodge, Inc. In 1927, after four frustrating years of promoting

191

the Master School and the Scenic Highway, he felt entitled to a vacation furnished by funds from the sale.

Colonel Howard paid off all his debts and considered his work with the Scenic Highway as practically completed. The highway was far from finished but a significant amount of progress had been made. For a year and a half he had worked harder than any other man, serving as a sort of combination Moses and John the Baptist. He had given of his time, worked with his own hands, undergone untold hardships and privations, and had gone further into debt to get a little more than half of the Scenic Highway built. The association would elect a new president early in the new year and someone else could carry on where he had left off.[1]

As for him, he and Lady Vivian were going on their dream trip to Capri. They would visit Italy—and while in Rome, perhaps he would interview one of the most famous and powerful men in the world—Benito Mussolini.

---

[1]Colonel Howard never lost interest in the Scenic Highway and in his last after-dinner-type speech, urged the Lions Club, in March, 1937, to support a plan for reviving and completing the project.

Adventures In Europe

Lady Vivian had not waited until funds were available before making arrangements for their voyage. After corresponding with various steamship lines in order to find a comfortable but inexpensive ship, she had chosen the steamer *Minnesota*, a small German-made ship which had been captured during the war. An agent had suggested a choice stateroom which he promised to reserve upon receipt of a cash deposit. Without even a prospect of getting the money for such payment, Lady Vivian somehow managed to persuade the agent to hold the stateroom without a deposit.

After the sale of the property, the excited couple discussed ways of traveling as cheaply as possible in order to stretch their limited funds to cover expenses for a four month European tour. With a small amount of luggage and high hopes of adventure, they sailed at midnight, October 1, 1927, from New York for Bolougne, France, on the *S.S. Minnesota*, with a bright, full moon lighting their way.

After all their hardships and broken dreams, Colonel Howard and Lady Vivian were actually sharing the thrill of crossing the ocean for the first time and enjoying the excited anticipation of a carefree tour of Europe. Using material from interviews with other passengers, Colonel Howard wrote the first of a series of feature stories about the pleasures and experiences of vagabonding for the Birmingham *News*. This too, was a new adventure, as he had long desired to write articles for some prominent newspaper. They could also use the income his writing brought.

Landing at night, they got their first view of France by the light of a midnight moon which added enchantment to the unfamiliar scene and sounds as they stepped ashore. They were soon in Paris, where they visited the usual historical sights. But Lady Vivian could not restrain her eagerness to see the latest Parisian fashions. Soon, she was having the time of her life window shopping—not daring to enter the huge department stores, or "galleries." She kept reminding herself that dress-up clothes and extra luggage were taboo for vagabonds.

Traveling overland through southern France, the two nature lovers admired the pastoral beauty of the peasant country, with its quaint little houses and their small garden plots, well-trimmed hedges and profusion of flowers. Next came a brief visit to picturesque Switzerland where they gazed at the beauty of the famed Alps. Their eagerness to reach the isle of their air-castle dreams grew as they reached Naples and boarded their steamer for the short voyage to Capri.

It was late at night when they arrived, and the steep mountainside rising out of the Bay of Naples glistened with thousands of lights from the water's edge to the highest peak, inviting them to a fairyland of adventure. Because of a rough sea, the ship anchored some distance from shore and dozens of small boats were soon swarming around the larger vessel. Chattering Italian boatmen made elaborate gestures to attract attention to their individual "water taxis."

The boat Colonel Howard selected already had several tourists aboard and when the big Alabamian stepped aboard some of them gasped with fear they might capsize. The small vessel appeared to go down several inches as the 250 pound, six foot, four inch giant stood silhouetted against the sky. However, the boatman quickly assured them they were all perfectly safe and they landed without mishap a few minutes later. As they left the boat they were met by a guide named Antonio, who escorted them to a carriage. Then they proceeded up the mountain to the public square. Here, from the edge of a high wall, with an open view of the sea and the Riviera shore, they beheld the magnificent view and realized that their dream, made during a lonely winter at Alpine, had actually materialized.

Early the next morning Antonio took Lady Vivian villa

hunting and she soon found one named Floridiana which she immediately proclaimed as being "darling." The house was surrounded by a garden where terraces were lined with rows of gnarled olive trees and vine-covered walls, brightened by colorful splashes of roses and other flowers. Seven terraces back from the street stood the white stucco-columned Italian piazza overlooking the beautiful blue Mediterranean. Lady Vivian rented the villa and secured a maid's services for one month at a total cost of $60. Such extravagance for old "Yaller Jacket," now metamorphosed into "The Vagabond," bothered his conscience somewhat, he admitted. But after all, this was a once in a lifetime event, and perhaps their mountain neighbors back in Alabama would never learn of their luxurious living.

Always impressed and awed by artists and intellectuals, Colonel Howard and Lady Vivian quickly made friends with all their neighbors on the island resort. These fellow vagabonds included the following: a Bavarian artist and musician; an English nature painter; a German university professor of Greek, who with his wife had survived a shipwreck while on a voyage to Syracuse, Greece; a Nordic-German musician and composer who had been born in Germany, reared in France, and educated in Constantinople, who had formerly served as director of music at the Academy of Music in Paris and had lost a fortune through confiscation during the World War and had wandered as a self-exile ever since; an American writer from the south who was the son of a well-known journalist; and a Russian artist-sculptor-violinist, who lived in a basement room on the terrace below the Howard's piazza, a refugee from Communist Russia who had barely escaped with his life after losing his home, his studio, and a fortune in priceless possessions.

Colonel Howard and Lady Vivian enjoyed visiting with their new friends and their little villa abounded with southern hospitality. Long discussions touched on many topics, especially art, philosophy, and politics. During these few weeks this predominantly anti-communist group, composed of individuals who had found security and sympathy in a fascist land, greatly influenced the ever-vacillating political philosophy of Milford W. Howard. Especially influential was the quaint Russian refugee who soon became a familiar figure in his sandals, blue trousers, and artist's smock. After he insisted upon painting Colonel

Howard's portrait, the sittings were all arranged to enable the artist to share the Howard's noon meal, as it was evident that the victim of communism was nearly always hungry.

Colonel Howard and Lady Vivian left their villa often for sightseeing ventures. On one outing Antonio took them in a small row boat from Marano Grande to the famous "Blue Grotto." Once inside the grotto, the fisherman-guide laid aside his oars and startled his clients by bursting into a rapture of Italian melody—singing one of Caruso's songs. He explained to his pleased listeners that he had carried Caruso in the same little boat to the Blue Grotto, where the renowned operatic tenor had sung the same song just a few days before he contracted his fatal illness.

The most momentous event for Lady Vivian was the visit to the Isle of Capri by King Alfonso of Spain, accompanied by Crown Prince Humbert of Italy. With the parallel stripes of green, white and red of the Italian flags and the horizontal red and yellow bars of the Spanish flags waving from all public buildings, and the stores and shops elaborately decorated with bunting, the fiesta atmosphere added to her excitement. The tall American and his beaming, exuberant wife found themselves caught up in a jostling, shouting crowd moving slowly along a narrow street at the entrance to the Quissanne, where a formal reception was being held for the royal visitors. Deliberately pushing and inching her way through the mass of excited, screaming Italians, Lady Vivian persistently urged Colonel Howard on toward the waiting government limousine. When the royal party left the hotel, Lady Vivian was ecstatic! She was actually within six feet of a real king and prince, getting a good close-up view of both. Surely none of the emotional Italians in that surging throng was half so thrilled and happy as the red-haired American tourist.

Colonel Howard walked daily over the island, climbing its lofty peaks and exploring ancient ruins. He walked through the quaint narrow streets, most of them not more than six feet wide, and visited the strange little shops. Here he gesticulated and attempted to communicate with the shopkeepers, occasionally finding a bilingual person with whom he could talk. In such instances he always sought opinions about fascism and Mussolini. All agreed that Mussolini had restored law and order where there had been chaos and terror. But about Mussolini as a man, opinions differed, with most agreeing, however, that *Il Duce* was an enigma, a man of mystery.

When it was time to board the steamer once more, the Italian maid and several other newly formed acquaintances followed the Howards to the ship to bid them farewell. From the deck, the Colonel and Lady Vivian watched with moist eyes as the little island which had been their home for a month faded from view, both realizing that they would never see it again.

The *Minnesota* headed toward the Italian Riviera, where the American tourists visited Sorrento, Amalfi, and Ravello before going to Naples. In anticipation of visiting Rome's "city of the dead" which had remained buried beneath lava and ashes for more than 1,500 years, Colonel Howard had reread Bulwer's *Last Days of Pompeii* at Capri. While waiting at the Naples train station he hired a guide, Signor Michele Proverble, to accompany them to Pompeii and to pay their railway fare, all entrance fees and tips, for 100 lira—a little less than $6.00. The guide proved to be a scholarly and charming gentleman who had previously served a number of prominent Americans, including the William Randolph Hearsts. As he led them over the narrow stone-paved streets, Colonel Howard contemplated this ancient tomb of past civilization and visualized the skill, grace, and form of the Roman gladiators in the giant arenas.

Next came a two week stay in Rome—where the Colonel was to have his moment of glory. Before leaving on his voyage Colonel Howard had obtained from the managing editor of the Birmingham *News* a letter of introduction which contained a request for an interview with Mussolini. After arriving in Rome, he requested and received a similar written request from the American Embassy. Then, following the advice of an Englishman he had met on the train, he registered at a hotel where a friend of the dictator lived. At the first opportunity the Howards sat near the prominent Italian and his wife in the dining room. Colonel Howard introduced himself, explained his mission, and asked for help in obtaining the coveted audience with Mussolini. He was told that what he was asking would require time and patience—if he succeeded at all.

The Howards began their sightseeing and spent one afternoon attending a session of the Chamber of Deputies, where a new treaty with Albania was under discussion. They entered between long lines of smartly dressed young Italian soldiers and watched as the impressive looking chamber began to fill with deputies who talked animatedly as they greeted one another and made many gestures with their hands.

Promptly at 2:30 p.m. the president of the chamber took his seat and disposed of some routine business in a quick manner. There followed a brief period of conversation and moving about as the arrival of Mussolini was awaited. Then *Il Duce* strode briskly into the chamber, looking neither to the right nor to the left, and took his seat on a platform directly in front of, but slightly lower than that of the presiding officer. Folding his arms across his breast, he stared straight ahead as a hushed silence fell upon the room. The treaty with Albania was read and discussed, with no man speaking more than ten minutes. Within an hour all discussion was finished and the treaty was ratified by secret ballot. During the whole episode Mussolini sat as immobile as a statue, except when approached by a deputy who whispered some message or question to the dictator, after which he answered with a word or a nod.

The efficiency of this speedy parliamentary procedure was readily evident to the former congressman, who had participated in the slow-moving process of democracy. "A perfect administrative working system!" he exclaimed to his wife as they left the chamber.

At last, word came that the premier would see Colonel Howard at seventeen-thirty o'clock, or 5:30 p.m., and it was made clear that he should be prompt. Thirty minutes before time for the interview he was waiting in a large reception room watching officials with portfolios enter and exit, averaging one every five minutes. Suddenly, he began to feel the same kind of stage fright which always plagued him before a speech. His mouth became dry and his big hands trembled as he realized that in a matter of minutes he would be facing one of the world's most powerful men, the formidable Mussolini, whose pictures appeared daily throughout the world.

The marble, the gold, the glistening crystal chandeliers, representing the power and splendor surrounding him, made the former farm boy of the red clay fields of Georgia feel humble and ill at ease. The hands of a big clock kept moving toward the appointed time. A stiffly correct official in a gold-trimmed uniform finally opened the door and called, "Mr. Howard!"

They passed through several doors before reaching another large room, where the short, stocky man with an intense and penetrating gaze was the sole occupant of the spacious office. Mussolini stood rigidly silent behind a large, ornate desk as his tall, awkward visitor entered and stood speechless in the center of the room. Then the premier strode briskly toward Colonel Howard, grasped his hand, and said in excellent English, "You are Mr. Howard, an American citizen, representing the Birmingham *News*. I am delighted to greet you on your mission to Italy."

As Colonel Howard began to stammer a reply, Mussolini asked him to speak slowly, explaining that he had been studying English for only a short time. His guest saw an opening here to broach a subject designed to catch the premier's attention. "My education has been very much neglected," he said. "At the time I should have been in school, I was helping my father in his blacksmith shop."

"Oh, you are a blacksmith. Well, so am I," replied Mussolini, whose father had followed that profession.

The dynamic personality of the man who had risen from obscurity to a position as a major world power was to dominate that brief meeting—and he who was to have been interviewed posed the questions for the American.

"What do you think about fascism?" he snapped.

The evolution of Milford Howard's political philosophy completed its transformation into its final stage at that time and place. As the pompous and confident dictator focused his wide staring eyes on Colonel Howard, the new fascist convert eagerly responded, "Fascism is a new renaissance, destined to remold Italy, then spread over Europe, and perhaps become a working model for the world."

The answer evoked a wide, spontaneous smile from Mussolini, who then asked, "Are you going to write that for your paper? Will you say that to your American people?"

The Colonel had been thinking of the resemblance of the muscular, vigorous man to Napoleon. But as the magnetism of Mussolini's personality emerged while he changed from one subject to another with lightning-like rapidity, he was reminded of

Theodore Roosevelt. During a pause in the conversation, he commented that the Italian resembled the former American president.

Pleased at the comparison, Mussolini then spoke momentarily about the renaissance in literature and art that had arisen in Italy and spread throughout Europe. He was certain, he said, that Colonel Howard was correct in judging fascism to be a new renaissance. Then Mussolini bade his guest farewell and the brief interview was ended.

Colonel Howard left the huge Italian building lost in his hazy dream world where reality and facts could never enter. He would forever remain convinced that Mussolini's fascism was an ideal form of government for the future; and Milford W. Howard was to be its self-appointed prophet. Those few moments alone with Mussolini would not only fail to benefit Colonel Howard in the long run, but would serve as an unsettling influence on his increasingly fluctuating mental and physical stability.

Convinced that he had achieved a major journalistic coup by obtaining the audience with *Il Duce*, Colonel Howard did not know, nor would he ever realize, that he was being duped and skillfully used for propaganda purposes—at a time when Mussolini desired world approval and admiration.

In retrospect Colonel Howard is judged harshly for his gullibility and for his espousal of the detested principles of fascism. It might be noted, however, that the impressionable Colonel saw mostly the better part of the dictator's personality and reign of power. Mussolini, at the age of 44, in 1927, had exhibited no more cruelty or despotism than many of the most admired kings and queens of history. He had restored order where there had been utter chaos, had reduced unemployment, had improved relations with the Roman Catholic Church, and had adopted a program designed to win the support of responsible property-owning Italians. His nationalistic appeal to the Italian people to rebuild the glories of ancient Rome struck a responsive chord in the hearts of most of his countrymen. Though he mercilessly suppressed all opposition, he received much sincere support and millions acclaimed him with deafening shouts of *"Duce! Duce!"*

Not long before his death, Colonel Howard would learn of

Mussolini's ruthlessness in killing and conquering peaceful Ethiopians. Even then he could not bring himself to realize or admit his greatest error in judgement. One can only speculate as to his reaction, had he lived to see Mussolini's treachery in turning on an already collapsing France, his brutal conquest of Greece, or the final ignominious death of *Il Duce* and his mistress—after which they were hung by their heels in the streets of Milan.

But in 1927, when the story of fascism was unfolding, Milford Howard gratefully accepted an official photograph of Mussolini, standing in a dramatic pose making the raised stiff arm salute, and rushed back to his hotel room to complete his feature story for the Birmingham *News*. The article, over three-fourths of a page in length, appeared in the *News Age-Herald* on Sunday, January 8, 1928, under the banner heading of "ALA-BAMA VAGABOND INTERVIEWS IL DUCE." Even before this article was completed he had planned the outline of a book to be entitled, *Fascism: A Challenge to Democracy*.

The European tour was not yet complete, however. There was still a tour of London, and the Colonel was anxious to visit "Merrie England," from whence his early ancestors had come. Though her grandfather Lloyd was a Welshman, part of Lady Vivian's family was also of English lineage. They were both enthusiastic over the last part of their journey. It was still winter and their finances were so low by now that they were unable to see much of rural England. They went out, instead, to discover the London of Dickens and to visit such famous places as the Tower and Westminster Abbey.

Their stay in England proved to be anti-climactic and disappointing. London was bitterly cold, with a penetrating wind. The sun was hidden from view by heavy fog. The poverty and squalor they saw in the big city surprised and distressed them. They were ready to leave when they packed their bags early on December 24, to catch a train which carried them once more to their ship. The steamer drifted slowly down the Thames through the thick, heavy mists, heading for the open Atlantic and Colonel Howard's first Christmas at sea. The day was observed with a tree and gifts for the children and a royal turkey dinner and English plum pudding for everyone.

Aboard ship Colonel Howard almost completed his book

on fascism and contemplated vagabonding in his own country. Perhaps he and Lady Vivian could purchase an automobile and visit famous places in the United States, while he made a living writing feature articles for the Birmingham *News*.

Part II

Fascism: A Challenge to Democracy

Colonel Howard's book on fascism was poorly conceived and poorly written. He devoted only three pages to the interview with Mussolini, the single event most responsible for his writing the book. Two-thirds of the book consists of direct quotations from fascist sources, including Italian Historical Society publications, books written by Mussolini's minister of public instruction and speeches by Mussolini.

The author reveals his complete captivation by the powerful Italian dictator and his political and economic theories. He shows fervent admiration for Mussolini and his policies and predicts utopian success for fascism in Italy.

Mussolini's staunch opposition to socialism and communism, which appealed to wealthy Italians, is stressed. Free enterprise was best, according to the premier, because it was most successful for the state. Liberals considered economic freedom as a principle; fascists considered it a method. Colonel Howard was favorably impressed by the fact that Mussolini's government required religious education in elementary schools and decreed that the crucifix be returned to public school rooms. The author, who had been strongly opposed to birth control in his own country, also lauds Mussolini's opposition to any attempt to limit the Italian birth rate.

In brief, this book is an extremely flattering account of Mussolini as Colonel Howard perceived him, and an unequivocal endorsement of fascism. Milford Howard truly believed that fascism posed a real threat to democracy—and to all other forms of government.

The Vagabond

After their four months in Europe, Colonel Howard and Lady Vivian returned to River Park rich in experiences but low in finances. When they added up their assets and their liabilities, they found they had $20 to their credit. Alpine Lodge was still not finished, furniture was not yet purchased, and the watermill was not completed. In addition, an unexpected complication arose when Claude appeared without Jennie and Morris— and with a drinking problem.

Perhaps most couples their age would have been crushed by similar circumstances. But these two inveterate dreamers dwelled within a realm where the rainbow never faded; they were still as anxious to pursue the elusive treasures as they had been when they laid the first stone of their little schoolhouse. Ever since their brief tour of Switzerland, Lady Vivian had longed to build a colony of Swiss chalets along the bluffs of Little River near Alpine Lodge. Even though there was no money in the bank, she designed the first one and enlisted Claude's help in securing workers and supplies. The chalet was soon underway and it became evident that the local builders were very skilled artisans in stone and wood construction. Colonel Howard spent much of his time in some quiet spot writing. In between his Vagabond articles for the Birmingham *News*, he completed his book on the black shirt movement of Italian fascism, filling it with praise for Mussolini, "the most dynamic, spectacular figure in world politics today." He mailed the manuscript to the manager of the Italian Historical Society in New

York, ostensibly to get his opinion about it. As he had hoped, the highly pleased Italian answered in a very complimentary and flattering letter in which he promised to assist in securing a good publisher. Colonel Howard was advised to come to New York as soon as possible.

Early one morning in July, 1928, Lady Vivian drove Colonel Howard to the Valley Head depot to make the trip. He had come down the day before to make a reservation on the sleeper and his ticket was ready, with a telegraph blank pinned to it to denote the number of his berth. When the train arrived he bade his wife farewell and boarded the sleeper which was to carry him to New York in quest of a publisher. Handing the ticket to the conductor, he remarked that his sleeper reservation was attached to it. After unpinning the paper, the conductor glanced up at the Colonel several times and back to the telegraph blank, then burst out laughing.

"Have a seat, Colonel Howard," he said. "Have two seats if you wish!"

Delighted at the Colonel's puzzled expression, he explained by relating an often repeated joke about a Tennessee congressman with whom Colonel Howard had served. Shortly after Bob Taylor was elected governor of that state, the story went, John Wesley Gaines, a distinguished lawyer who prided himself on his ancestry, called on the governor for the first time.

"I am John Wesley Gaines," he announced, and then gave his father's name.

"Have a seat," Governor Taylor invited, adding that he was glad to see him.

Without pausing to be seated, the Honorable John Gaines proceeded to identify his grandfather and great-grandfather.

Finally the genial governor, who was somewhat of a practical joker, exclaimed:

"Well, have two seats, Mr. Gaines! You should have two!"

The conductor then handed Colonel Howard the paper, which read as follows:

Lower 2, car N. G., Valley Head, Ala. to New York City, reserved for Col. M. W. Howard, former member of Congress, author, globetrotter, the man who conceived the idea of a scenic highway atop Lookout Mountain, vagabonded six months in Italy, interviewed Mussolini. Please give him good service. Mayor Ellis, of Valley Head, Ala. sends greetings to Mayor Jimmy Walker of New York.

Colonel Howard joined in laughing at the joke conceived by Mayor John W. Ellis, who was also the Southern Railway agent and the telegraph operator. He also enjoyed the special attention accorded him the entire trip.

Upon his arrival in New York on Thursday, he realized he had considerable time at his disposal before his 10 o'clock appointment on Friday morning. Buying an armful of daily newspapers, he seated himself in the hotel lobby and read the latest word on presidential politics. The 1928 election was becoming the most unusual and controversial since Lincoln's first race.

The next morning he met with representatives of the Italian Historical Society. He had first learned of this organization while in Rome and Lady Vivian had contacted the manager of the society upon their return from Europe. At that time they accepted an invitation to have lunch with two members of the group and thereby established a liaison with these influential Italian-Americans. Now they were ready to aid him in getting his book published and were authorized to make him a lucrative offer for a six-week lecture tour during the winter.

After leaving his manuscript with a publisher, Colonel Howard had lunch with a group which included Count Ignazio Thaori Di Revel. (He could hardly wait to tell Lady Vivian about dining with a real Italian count!) They discussed fascism, Mussolini, Al Smith, Herbert Hoover, and the Italian vote in the forthcoming election. The count, who was a Wall Street broker and president of the Fascist League of North America, explained that the league was strictly non-partisan in American politics. His group, he said, discouraged any organized political activity on the part of its members but noted that there were 1,000,000 voters in this country of Italian descent.

Within a few days, Colonel Howard was leaving for Alabama, bursting with pride and eager to tell Lady Vivian about the lecture tour and to give her the good news that his book would be published before the year ended.

An excited and vivacious Lady Vivian chauffeured the

Colonel from the depot to their log cabin across from Alpine Lodge. She had drawn the plans for this little building, which was wholly constructed by 15 year old Frank Kirk. Working with the skill and maturity of a man, the youth had resented Lady Vivian's strict supervision as she directed his every move, showing him just where to place each rock in the chimney. He complained to others that she drove him "absolutely insane" while he worked and insisted on calling him "Boysey," although she knew he detested the nickname.

During the year of 1928 Colonel Howard often sat in a chair behind the cabin with a handful of sharpened pencils at his side, a pad of yellow lined paper on his lap. Here he delved into the immense repository of his memory and employed his vivid imagination to dash off a Vagabond story for the *News* each week.

Written in a natural flowing, folksy style, these Sunday features were often reminiscent of the humor and wit of Samuel Clemens. Occasionally the strain of melancholy which continued to haunt Colonel Howard was evident in these articles, though he made an effort to keep most stories in a gay and carefree vein. He wrote voluminously from the standpoint of a vagabond, a philosopher, and a "student of life," on subjects he knew well and on new experiences gained from his travels about the countryside. He wrote of mountain scenes and rural homes, of the various species of trees and the different rock formations, of the birds and their songs. He toured the gulf coast, describing Mobile's beautiful azaleas, its docks and sea wall, predicting the development of a fabulous American Riviera, the playground of the south. He wrote of famous people such as Clarence Darrow, whom he hated, and Winifred Black, whom he admired. But more often he wrote of simple people, and through several of his best stories he immortalized a colorful old Indian known on Lookout Mountain as "Granny" Dollar.

This independent and testy old woman, who had passed the century mark, inhabited a little cabin on Master School property, with her 17 year old hen (which she claimed laid an egg every day), and her mongrel dog, "Buster." An amazingly strong woman, the large six-foot Indian tended a garden and worked in her flowers regularly. She frequently entertained visitors with fascinating tales about her childhood as the oldest of

26 children (her father had two wives at the same time), of her escape from making the "trail of tears" march, of living in Atlanta when it was a village called Marthasville, of losing her fiance in the Civil War, and of finally marrying—at the age of 79. Granny Dollar was a favorite with the Vagabond and his readers.

In preparing his articles Colonel Howard wasted little time as his big hand raced along to keep up with his thoughts. After choosing a topic, he often branched off into several unrelated subjects which he happened to think of, and frankly admitted that he never knew where his pencil was going when it got started. Looking up an exact date or quotation was far too much trouble. His memory was fairly reliable and he saw no need to worry about small errors or inaccuracies. His readers would perhaps find a grain of wheat somewhere in a peck of chaff—and it was the grain he was concerned about.

As soon as he ended an article, the Colonel prepared it for mailing. The omitted words of hastily scribbled sentences were never added and those misspelled or unfinished words were never corrected. Someone at the Birmingham *News* office had a difficult job each week.

The Vagabond articles revealed Milford Howard at his best as a writer. His mastery of the English language, his ability to express ideas, and his excellent descriptions were most evident in this type of non-fiction. Even though he often skipped from one topic to another and sometimes bogged down in philosophical ramblings, nearly all were well-written human interest stories.

They pleased the managing editor of the Birmingham *News*, who wrote:

> Without seeking to flatter you, Colonel, you have given our paper a note of splendid wholesomeness, . . . If you ask me, I'll say, as I have said before, that you are writing quite the most human material that is being written for our paper today and you have a big following.

Most of the Vagabond articles carried banner headlines and ranged from one-half to three-fourths of a page in length. A fairly typical article was the one written in 1928 entitled "The

Vagabond Discovers a Boys' Paradise Near His Own Retreat,"
about the first Mentone camp, the Lookout Mountain Camp for
Boys. In it he injected a little personal philosophy and ended up
on the subject of King Akhenaton. Near the beginning he
departed from his topic to discuss his experiences with tooth-
pulling and dentists. (The founder of the camp was a dentist,
Dr. J. A. Gorman.) The following exerpt is an example of the
wit of this unschooled vagabond author:

In fancy I go back to my boyhood days when my
mother would tie a string around one of my teeth almost
loose enough to drop out of my head, while I squalled lust-
ily, and then too tender hearted to pull it herself would tie
the other end to the bed post, make a gesture in my direction as though she were going to slap me, causing me to
dodge the threatened blow, and, when I discovered the
trick there hung the tooth to the end of the string.

As I grew older my father, who was a splendid blacksmith, applied a pair of "pullers" he had fashioned in the
shop, strong enough to pull an elephant's tooth, and I can
feel them now clamp down on the tooth of a frosty morning, as I closed my eyes and resigned myself to my fate.

In later years when dentists came into vogue and I
went to have a tooth pulled, the up-to-date one to whom I
journeyed with my aching molar, suggested it would be
criminal to pull the tooth, explaining how he could pull
the nerve, leaving the tooth to be filled.

I allowed him to undertake the job. First, he had to
drill the tooth so he could get to the nerve and I suffered
such agony as I had never known before. Finally he completed this barbarism and took a gimlet looking instrument
and proceeded to bore down into the tooth and twist the
nerve out, just like we used to twist a rabbit out of a hollow log when we were boys, with a hickory stick forked or
split at the end. The first attempt, he got only a part of the
nerve, like we used to get a big handful of fur off the rabbit. So he had to go back the second time, and when he
got through with me I was more dead than alive. I don't
know how I ever walked home, but I did, and the next day
I had to take the train to Washington City. By the time I

reached my destination I was beside myself with loss of sleep and agony. I hastened to a dentist's office, and he extracted the tooth just in time to save my life.

During this period Colonel Howard also worked briefly on the autobiography he had begun two years earlier, and to which he would make additions spasmodically for about five more years. This work was to provide valuable and enlightening information about his childhood years. The first few chapters were as well written as anything he ever wrote, but as time passed, his interest apparently waned and so did the value of his intermittent biographical sketches. Dwelling more and more on abstract philosophy, he gave little space to many important people and events in his life. Omissions were obvious and errors were frequently made in dates—although they were more often left out entirely. His state of mind at a certain period could be discerned more readily than the exact sequence of major events in his life. Details were to this author just so much trivia; a person's view of life—and death—were much more important.

Colonel Howard had two motives for writing his autobiography. First, he thought he would one day realize a profit from its publication. Secondly, he had a lifelong desire to be remembered after his death and he hoped to end his manuscript with the story of some final achievement or outstanding accomplishment. It often occurred to him, however, that he might never really succeed at anything worthwhile. As he sat writing in the spring of 1929, the thought came to him that he might not even finish his autobiography. "Perhaps the unfinished tale may be left for other hands," he wrote, "when you are gone far away where they do not write autobiographies as we mortals understand them."

He did not add much to his manuscript beyond this time. His life seemed more and more difficult to write about. Both his mind and body were showing the effects of the terrible strain to which they had been subjected. In bringing his autobiography to an end, he found himself groping for an appropriate parting message as he felt himself "slipping, walking away into the night." Turning to the words of Victor Hugo, he declared, "They are wiser than mine; they are more eloquent than mine."

You say the soul is nothing but the resultant of the bodily powers. Why, then, is my soul more luminous when my bodily powers begin to fail? Winter is on my head, but eternal spring is in my heart. I breathe at this hour the fragrance of the lilacs, the violets and the roses, as of twenty years. The nearer I approach the end, the plainer I hear around me the immortal symphonies of the world, which invite me. It is marvelous yet simple. It is a fairy tale, and it is history.

As he continued writing his Vagabond articles, Colonel Howard received great satisfaction from the publicity and the monetary compensation he received, and especially from the many friendly, admiring letters he received from his readers. Yet he did not at this or any other time consider himself a successful writer. In 1928 he wrote about his lack of guidance in his literary efforts.

I have often thought what a great boon it would have been for me if I could have had the guidance of a competent, sympathetic, honest teacher in my poor efforts to express myself on paper. I had no guide-posts to mark the way, and to tell me when I was on the right road or on a lost trail; no one upon whom I could rely for helpful criticism; no one capable and honest to tell me I did nor did not possess the ability to become a writer.

What a great service some teacher could have rendered me. Perhaps I might have been taught the technique of writing, so that now instead of being a mere scribbler, violating every known rule of construction, I might have been (who knows!) a real writer.

God knows I had the longing, the urge to write, as thousands have, and it is worth a king's ransom to any one of them to have a great teacher who can guide them if they have talent, or tell them frankly, it is hopeless. If I had been told that by someone who knew, it might have saved reams and reams of good white paper, and my own soul the tortures of pursuing an unattainable future.

I am perfectly aware of the fact now, however, that I shall never be a writer, that I shall never have the approval of the critics because I am lacking that technique I might have acquired in the days long ago, so I must go through the remainder of my days just a vagabond scribbler, with the single hope that I may occasionally write something out of the storehouse of my experience that may be interesting or helpful to others.

On another occasion, he wrote concerning his efforts at writing feature stories:

I see so many human interest stories all about me that I want to write every one of them. But after I write one that moves me tremendously I feel how poorly I have done, and I wonder why I ever thought of trying to be a scribbler at all.

While Colonel Howard pursued his writing career and gardened, Lady Vivian tended her "Italian" flower garden, planted with seeds brought back from their trip, and helped Claude oversee the construction of the chalet. After this first summer home was completed it was sold to Lady Vivian's mother's sister, "Aunt Martha" Miller, of Rome. Encouraged by this initial success, Colonel Howard signed a contract with Claude in June, granting his son a 50 percent interest in any Master School land he might develop and sell. Claude soon afterward opened an office in Alpine Lodge for his new real estate business, which he named Little River Development Company.

Alpine Lodge was completed at this time and inexpensive rustic furniture was obtained or built in. A large dining room table was made of a willow base and a natural black walnut top. The hickory sideboard contained a dumbwaiter designed by Lady Vivian to bring food up from the kitchen. Beds and dressing tables were built of bark-covered hickory poles and slabs.

Other chalets were soon built at "Little Switzerland" by several Birmingham residents. Mr. and Mrs. Charles A. Fell were among the first to build. The J. G. B. Fletchers built a two-story rock home with balconies and Mrs. Dora C. Fell constructed a pioneer log cabin with a mud and stick chimney. At last River Park was beginning to grow, with Alpine Lodge at its center. Colonel Howard began calling his mountain retreat Vagabondia.

Lady Vivian referred to it as Vagabondia Rhododendron Garden.

Efforts were made to promote Alpine Lodge as a summer resort. Advertisements boasted of the lodge's 3,500 square feet of balconies and porches. It could accommodate about 50 guests, and cabins were also available. Modern facilities included electric lights, telephones, running water, and a sewerage system. The food offered included mountain-grown vegetables and berries, Armour's best meats, and bread made from freshly ground flour and meal. Chalybeate water was available at a local spring for those who desired it. Although recreational facilities were available nearby, the quiet and peaceful atmosphere was stressed. Form letters were mailed to physicians in various cities, asking that they recommend Alpine Lodge to patients in need of a restful vacation. Rates were very reasonable: a room and three daily meals cost $18 a week for adults and children over six years old; those between two and six paid $6.00 and there was no charge for children under two.

Among those who visited Vagabondia during the summer of 1928 were Dorothy Lloyd, Lady Vivian's sister, and another teenager, Maxine Stephens, daughter of Colonel Howard's sister, Octie. The two girls shared a room at Alpine Lodge and became good friends. As they sat eating at the big dining table on the day of her arrival, Maxine was astonished when "Big Unk," as she called the Colonel, suddenly burst into tears. Her emotional uncle explained, after a few moments, that she resembled her deceased mother so much that he had almost felt she was there. During her month's stay at the lodge Colonel Howard often called her Octie.

Journalists and writers were always extended a special welcome at Vagabondia and their articles on the beauty of the mountain scenery and the hospitality found at Alpine Lodge provided much good publicity. Dr. Frank Willis Barnett and Dolly Dalrymple, both feature writers for the Birmingham *News*, were among the first to write about Vagabondia. The Colonel was pleasantly surprised when the noted writer, Winifred Black, came by one day, planning to stop for just a thirty minute break while on a tour across the nation gathering material for a series of articles on the theme, "My Country, 'Tis of Thee." She ended up though, staying from Friday until Sunday, visiting over the Lookout Mountain area and attending church on Sand Mountain. As a result of her visit, she wrote two articles, one on Granny Dollar and one on the Pea Ridge Singers, for the San Francisco *Examiner*.[1]

Late in the summer, Mrs. Katherine H. Chapman, an Alabama author,[2] journeyed to River Park from Selma. Arriving on a bright Sunday morning, she found a concert in progress at Alpine Lodge. A Miss Davis, of Birmingham, who was serving as hostess of the Mentone Hotel, had planned the event as a surprise for Colonel Howard. Joseph Moreno was playing the organ, accompanied by Miss Pearl Steward, one of Birmingham's leading violinists. At the conclusion of their program, Mrs. Chapman requested "Tell me, Love, Oh! Am I Dreaming?" after which Colonel Howard expressed his appreciation for the lovely concert. As he spoke, the writer had her first opportunity to observe the Vagabond. She noted that he was tall, spare, and bronzed, with little gray in his thick dark hair. She observed his long sharp teeth and flexible lips, the mouth, she thought, of a born orator. His beak of a nose and his lids drooping over keen eyes reminded her of an eagle which was, it occurred to her, suitably environed in the spacious wilds.

Mrs. Chapman was taken to her upstairs room before she joined a group of guests at the large table which bore a generous supply of chicken, vegetables, fruits, buttermilk, and peach pie. In the afternoon she visited the cabin where the Howards slept and had breakfast and where the Colonel did his writing. He had shed his collar and cutaway coat, worn during the morning's musicale, and sat working on his next Vagabond article in a white shirt and gray striped trousers.

When a bell rang at the lodge he grabbed his collar and coat and they all returned for the evening meal. The table talk that night ranged from Boston to Los Angeles, from Mussolini to Winifred Black, from Valentine Smith to Ben Ames Williams, and touched a number of times upon the prospects for establishing an artists' colony at River Park.

---

[1] *Robert Ripley, in the tenth year of his cartoon feature,* Believe It or Not, *read her articles and made Granny the subject of one of his cartoons.*

[2] *Mrs. Chapman wrote a number of novels and plays. One book,* The Fusing Force, *was made into a movie.*

On Monday morning, while the Howards were gone to their garden, Mrs. Chapman explored Vagabondia, venturing first over the swinging bridge which crossed the river, then investigated the mill and overshot wheel. She picked galax leaves and wild flowers and caught a glimpse of the rainbow which often formed in the spray above the falls, prompting Lady Vivian's name for Rainbow Falls.

Returning to the lodge, she found the Colonel looking very much like a vagabond. In faded and frayed khaki, he stood at a table under a tree near the well, cutting great piles of cabbage to make kraut. Explaining that this was a very wholesome, life-prolonging food, he declared his intention of salting down gallons of it and then eating it twice a day.

In the afternoon Lady Vivian drove her guest over the area she called "Little Mountain" making a stop at Granny Dollar's little cabin. Barefoot and wearing a blue denim mother hubbard, Granny was gathering vegetables in her garden. Welcoming her visitors, she laid her basket aside and showed them her storeroom, which held an ample supply of potatoes and onions and where rafters were strung with peppers and herbs. Instead of her usual pipe, Granny was sporting what appeared to Mrs. Chapman to be a long magnetized snuff stick. It rolled about in the gaps between her teeth and even though she appeared to make no effort to retain it, the stick stayed put whenever she bent over or talked.

Colonel Howard showed Mrs. Chapman the Master School buildings and his log cabin and she walked around the site where he and Lady Vivian hoped some day to construct a "temple of art." From "Inspiration Point," she looked over the valleys and ridges at the view of seven counties and three states.

On the morning of her last day at Vagabondia the writer was invited to ride to Fort Payne with Lady Vivian, who was going for some supplies. Having already been assured that her hostess was an experienced driver, who had twice driven across the continent, Mrs. Chapman had no fear as they sailed along in a cloud of dust, reached the old covered bridge, and turned off onto an abandoned road—to save a little time. But the seasoned chauffeur suddenly drove over a stump, causing the two startled ladies to bounce into the air as the old car jerked to a sudden stop. An unperturbed Lady Vivian strolled around inspecting the damage and climbed back in, announcing calmly that she had "only bent a bumper." As they sped along the Scenic Highway Lady Vivian gave a running discourse on psychology, interspersed with the names of people who lived along the way. "That's Mrs. Snedocar's house . . . there's the Tutwiler camp . . . the Berrys come over from Rome to stay there every summer." They raced past Mentone down the mountain to Valley Head and along the highway into Fort Payne, in time—it appeared—to return to Alpine Lodge for lunch.

Stopping first at a garage, Lady Vivian requested the attendant to "Please straighten the bumper and see what else I need."

Squatting down to look underneath the car, the man grunted and exclaimed, "Lady, you need aplenty! What'd you run into?"

After she explained she had hit a stump near River Park, the mechanic stared incredulously.

"Well then, Lady, you've been saved for a purpose!" he said. "The whole engine's just barely dangling to your automobile. With luck, I might get it fixed in about five hours."

As they would be there for quite a while, Lady Vivian showed her guest several points of interest, including Fort Payne's main industry, the big W. B. Davis Hosiery Mill and the employee clubhouse. While Lady Vivian shopped, Mrs. Chapman sat at a table in Haralson's Drug Store making notes for a newspaper article. She was beginning to suffer from the oppressive August heat and to long for the coolness of the mountain when Lady Vivian rushed in announcing that they were going to go listen to an opera singer.

"Who is the singer and why is she in Fort Payne?" asked Mrs. Chapman.

"She is Margaret McCartney and she's here for a while to stay with her mother, who fell recently and broke her hip. Margaret graduated in voice at Brenau Conservatory and sang with the Atlanta Civic Opera Company," Lady Vivian explained. "The Schuberts heard her sing in Atlanta and offered her a fine contract and she will soon be leaving for New York. Colonel lived next door to the McCartneys once and has been fond of Margaret since she was a baby."

Mrs. Chapman was introduced to a tall, friendly girl with

215

large blue eyes and brown hair which was parted in the middle and drawn primly into a small knot. She sat enchanted as Miss McCartney sang beautifully with a splendid, full, well-trained voice, even with the disadvantage of playing her own accompaniment and sitting facing a wall. Mrs. Chapman complimented the singer enthusiastically and invited her to appear on the next program for the Alabama Writers' Conclave, explaining that musicians and composers of the state were recognized as well as writers.

On her last evening at Alpine Lodge Mrs. Chapman and other guests were seated with the Howards on the wide veranda overhanging the gorge when an electric storm began and provided them with flashes of views of the mountain and river. Between bursts of thunder the steady roar of the falls could be heard above the sound of heavy rain. Lulls between these boisterous frolics of nature were filled with animated conversation. But the "good nights" were said early as Mrs. Chapman rose to comment, "Early to bed and early to rise makes a woman hope she may make the 6:30 train at Valley Head in the morning."

Before she went to sleep the storm had passed and the moon was shining on the river. She awoke at dawn to hear an oriole singing by her window and rushed downstairs where the other guests had gathered to see her off. Colonel Howard, who disliked farewells, and evaded them when possible, was not around, but Lady Vivian was ready to drive her to the station. They drove once more through the creaky covered bridge and the departing guest caught one last view of the big lodge as they rounded a bend in the road.

About two weeks later Claude drove Vagabondia's old Model T through a heavy downpour of rain, taking Colonel Howard and Margaret McCartney to the Writers' Conclave at Montevallo. They left Fort Payne at 6 a.m. in order to arrive in time for the Colonel to speak at the Montevallo Exchange Club luncheon. The president of the club, J. L. Appleton, had sent the invitation by special delivery letter.

Colonel Howard and Claude were accompanied to the meeting by Dr. O. C. Carmichael, president of Alabama College and Dr. Barnett of the Birmingham *News*. The Colonel found Dr. Carmichael to be a big, outgoing and fascinating man and was impressed by the educator's observation that of the eight

216

state-supported colleges for women in the United States, seven—including the one at Montevallo—were located in the south.

Upon reaching the Methodist Church, they went to the basement where the luncheon was being held and were greeted by a young man with, "How are 'you all' today?"

"Your name is Appleton," Colonel Howard announced, "and you are a hillbilly from DeKalb County."

"How do you know that?" he asked in surprise.

"I can tell by the way you say 'you all' and your features show your relationship to Dr. Thomas H. Appleton, of Collinsville."

Well into his "Italian Period," Colonel Howard spoke on fascism and Mussolini. Afterwards he felt satisfied that all the Exchangites had been interested in his subject.

The banquet that night was the climax of the sixth Writers' Conclave, an annual event started by Katherine Chapman. The theme was Old England, with heralds and minstrels, as well as a boar's head and other choice viands. Ale and stout also represented the days of Dickens and Scott.

Dr. Carmichael was toastmaster and many witty toasts and responses were made while the Colonel's usual case of stage-fright developed. Though he had spoken in the halls of congress, on the lyceum platform, in schools, colleges and universities, before men's clubs, women's clubs, open forums, and churches, he had never felt more honored than at this time, when he, a "mountain scribbler," was about to address a group of writers and authors.

In his speech he declared that he had but two purposes in his life at that time: One was his own spiritual development and one was the rendering of service to others. He could relax again when he sat down and listened to Margaret McCartney sing "like a mockingbird" to the hushed audience. He felt immensely proud, as though he were momentarily taking the place of her own father, who had died a few months before.

The Colonel had an opportunity to chat with Miss Minna McLeod Beck, head of the art department of Alabama College, who became interested in his idea of establishing an artists' colony at River Park. She accepted his invitation to spend a week at Alpine Lodge during the fall and to consider teaching a five-week summer art school there the following year.

Another event of that summer was the 4-H Club camp held at River Park. The young county agent, R. C. Christopher was in charge of the group of 120 boys who spent a weekend at Alpine.

In the fall Colonel Howard decided to experience some real vagabonding. He sold the Model T and bought a handsome new sedan on the installment plan. He also purchased a complete camping outfit, costing a little over $100 and consisting of a large and a small tent, folding cots, table, chairs, and gasoline stove. Leaving Alpine Lodge on Monday morning, September 10, he and Lady Vivian headed for Berea, Kentucky, to take Dorothy for her fourth year at the academy there. A tinge of autumn was in the air as they said their good-byes to Aunt Martha, who was left in charge of the lodge, to Claude, and to guests and friends.

When they reached Chattanooga Lady Vivian and Dorothy wanted to do some last minute shopping. The Colonel reasoned that every woman starting on a trip and every girl going off to college just had to shop. They all enjoyed a good 25 cent lunch before taking to the road again.

All the driving was done by Lady Vivian, who took the wrong road several times going through Sweetwater Valley and it was dark before the travelers reached Knoxville. The driver was familar with that city, however, and had no trouble finding a tourist camp sponsored by the Lions Club. The Daniel Boone Automobile Camp was located in a large grove of giant oak trees about 14 miles from Knoxville along the trail the famous pioneer followed from North Carolina into Kentucky.

Dorothy helped her sister prepare scrambled eggs and other simple fare on a stove in the community kitchen, after which the two females retired to bed in a cabin which they rented for $1.25. But Colonel Howard preferred to sleep on a cot under the stars on his first night vagabonding. He slept soundly there, even when a heavy dew moistened his face and dampened his hair. Curled over his ankle was a little abandoned white kitten with which he had secretly shared his supper.

The next morning his companions realized they had forgotten something in Chattanooga and had to run into Knoxville for "just a minute." Colonel Howard knew about women's minutes and remained at camp with a book—which he read halfway through by the time they continued on their journey. When they rode through Middlesboro, the Colonel pointed out a bank which occupied the corner lot he had bought some 40 years previously, during the boom there. He had paid the fabulous price of $100 per front foot and then sold it shortly afterwards for $300 per foot, reaping a good profit on one of the very few profitable investments of his lifetime.

When they reached Berea they pitched their large tent on a shady knoll and the Vagabond began writing about the trip while Lady Vivian summoned a photographer to make a picture to accompany his article. In this sketch he explained why he was a vagabond.

I have become a vagabond because my life has been one of struggle, since I was a 10 year old boy, and I have nothing to show for all the toil, the strivings, the disappointments, in a material way, except a large tract of land on Lookout Mountain that I have given away to the Master Schools. All that I can really call my own are the intangible, invisible things, and as I face life at 66, I am convinced that the things I have struggled for all my life, money, property, honor, are not worth a tithe of the effort I have put forth, even if these things had not slipped through my fingers, and I were still grasping them in my hands like a miser, and could do so until death relaxes my fingers.

I am thoroughly convinced, with Thoreau, "that to maintain one's self on this earth is not a hardship, but a pastime, if we will live simply and wisely," and in pursuit of this ideal, I have deliberately chosen the life of a vagabond, and am writing this sketch sitting by a tent, surrounded by most of our earthly belongings, as Lady Vivian prepares our elaborate breakfast of oatmeal and toast made of rye bread, to which we shall add some fruit.

. . . Nor am I going to apologize to anyone for my lack of ambition, for I have quit apologizing. I am assuming that a vagabond of any age has earned the right to live his life as he sees fit, and to throw both ambition and physic to the dogs if he desires to do so.

For the first time, Colonel Howard visited the campus of Berea College, established in 1853 and attended mainly by students from the southern Appalachians. He was thrilled as he watched 2,600 boys and girls march into the chapel singing:

> All hail the power of Jesus' name
> Let angels prostrate fall.
> Bring forth the royal diadem
> And crown Him Lord of all.

The next morning they "broke camp" and got ready to leave for the rugged mountains of Harlan and Leslie Counties, Kentucky. The Colonel took a last look at the little college town, listened once more to the ringing of the school chimes, and became lost in his thoughts of what *might have been* at the Master School on Lookout Mountain.

After a few days of camping in Kentucky, the two vagabonds returned to River Park and began preparations for the lecture tour. Colonel Howard received a copy of a letter which the Italian Historical Society sent to all its members.

The most important immediate task of the society is the national lecture tour of our honored member, former Congressman Milford W. Howard, of Alabama. Colonel Howard, whose new book, "Fascism: A Challenge to Democracy," will be published by Fleming H. Revell & Co., in November, has kindly consented to give a series of lectures on Fascist Italy under the auspices of the society on an itinerary which will stretch from Alabama north to Chicago and thence east as far as Boston and return. The tour will cover a period of six weeks, starting November 11.

An effort is being made to bring him before the largest possible number of American organizations in the cities on his itinerary. This tour has the endorsement of his excellency, Ambassador D' Martino, and the consular officers of all the cities of the route are giving us helpful cooperation.

An example of the kind of personal assistance which our individual members can offer was given by J. J. Costellini, of Cincinnati, who as a member of the Chamber of Commerce of that city, personally recommended Colonel Howard to the forum committee of the chamber, with the result that he was booked for an engagement.

Many of our members who hold membership in American organizations in their cities can similarly assure an engagement for Colonel Howard before their own organizations.

The result of a Howard lecture with its inevitable publicity will be to create a much more friendly atmosphere and understanding for the Italian people in your community.

In October Colonel Howard installed a "radio receiving set" at Alpine Lodge, built a big fire out of hickory logs, and sat back to enjoy the marvelous miracle of the transmission of sound waves. Delighted to find a grand opera broadcast from Chicago, he listened intently to the second act of Carmen with closed eyes, feeling as though he were actually sitting before the stage. Staring dreamily into the big glowing coals of fire, he thought of all the thousands of people in different parts of the country who were listening to the same music. In vain, he tried to comprehend this amazing phenomenon.

"What causes sound waves to travel so fast?" he pondered. "How far does it travel before it falls? Is it ever lost?"

The radio provided them with entertainment as the Colonel and Lady Vivian awaited the beginning of their tour, which was to start with an address to the Rotary Club of Knoxville on Tuesday, November 13. Just before time to leave, however, a telegram was received cancelling the Knoxville engagement. Instead of leaving on Monday, they entertained Dr. Barnett while the Birmingham *News Age-Herald* photographer, Walter Rosser, took pictures around River Park for Sunday's rotogravure section.

Departing early Tuesday, they reached Somerset, Kentucky, the first night, Berea the second, and Cynthiana on Thursday. They checked into a small hotel here in the heart of the bluegrass country and Colonel Howard wondered what he could find to write about in this little town. Lady Vivian went out to explore and returned in half an hour with the breathless announcement that the old log courthouse where Henry Clay tried many lawsuits was still standing.

The Vagabond rushed out to find it, certain of a good story. He found that the old courthouse, built in 1790 while George Washington was president, had been converted into a home. He was permitted by the owners to go through the building where Clay was admitted to the bar in 1801, and where his voice had been raised on behalf of many defendants.

That night he addressed Cynthiana's Rotary Club, where he had been invited by E. D. Van Hook, chairman of a committee for the promotion of international good will and understanding. The Colonel attempted to do his part by assuring the Kentuckians that all Mussolini asked of the world was a spirit of friendship as Italy worked out her destiny and solved her problems.

At Lexington, in the Gold Room of the big La Fayette Hotel, he addressed approximately 500 members of the Woman's Club of Central Kentucky. Before his speech he caught a glimpse of Lady Vivian busily cornering reporters from the two daily papers, the *Herald* and the *Leader*, and the president of the club. He suspected that she might be showing them the old "to whom it may concern" letter from the Birmingham *News* which she carried at all times.

When he arose to speak to the huge sea of ladies' faces and hats, the old subconscious fear and stage fright seized him as Colonel Howard stammered, "Madam president and ladies," but after a few moments the overpowering fear subsided. He was soon enjoying his chore of enlightening this group of cultured women about fascist Italy, which he felt he had accomplished at the end of one hour.

The flattering articles in both Sunday papers, one of which referred to him as "one of the south's most distinguished orators and newspapermen," showed Lady Vivian's influence quite as clearly as had the program chairman's introduction the night before. His wife was becoming more and more skilled as a self-appointed press agent.

They arrived at Marietta, Ohio, late Sunday afternoon and immediately selected a hotel. Assigned to a comfortable room, the vagabond scribbler found it entirely satisfactory. But his acting secretary-press agent appeared disappointed and hinted at thoughts of changing rooms the next day. After breakfast Monday morning the Colonel began writing an article on Kentucky, insisting that Lady Vivian go out to see the town or seek entertainment in some way until he finished. As she left he called out, "Please don't interrupt me until 12 o'clock!" But just as he had gotten well underway with his story there was a loud knock on his door. Startled, he sprang to open it to see what was wrong. There stood Lady Vivian with a bellboy at her heels, announcing victoriously, "We are moving to an elegant suite of rooms, at the same price—the same price, mind you!"

After following his wife, the bellboy and the luggage to the suite, he sat down and tried to organize his thoughts again, while wondering just what Lady Vivian had said to the proprietor. He decided after a moment, however, that he didn't really want to know.

The next day Colonel Howard spoke to the Marietta Kiwanis Club and looked about the city for Vagabond material. Shunning the statistics of industry and population which were given to him, he chose for his topic the largest elm tree in America. He found the circumference of its base to be 62 feet and he had a picture made which showed five huge branches, each as large as most big trees. It was estimated that the tree was already a large one when Columbus discovered America. Other research revealed that Marietta was the oldest city in Ohio, having been settled in 1788 by a group of 48 pioneers who named it in honor of Marie Antoinette, who was then queen of France.

Lady Vivian's research, meanwhile, turned up an American scholar and writer who had received her doctorate at the University of Rome, majoring in Italian, and who had interviewed Mussolini several times. Dr. Fredericka Blankner, whose poems had appeared in the *Forum*, had recently been awarded a Harvard literary prize for an essay on Lorenzo de' Medici and made a big impression on the Howards because of her attainments and by her sympathy with fascism.

The Colonel and Lady Vivian next stayed at the Roycroft Inn at East Aurora, where he worked on his newspaper column in the lovely Rembrandt Room. The next day they drove across the nation's border and Lady Vivian exulted over setting foot on Canadian soil, then emitted a steady flow of adjectives and superlatives when she first viewed Niagara Falls. Still, she concluded, with all its grandeur, Niagara was not as beautiful as Rainbow Falls and River Park.

After a night in Buffalo, Lady Vivian was out early the next morning visiting various stores and shops where she might find someone of Italian descent. Before long she had discovered Bessie Bellanca, proprietress of a flower shop, who was helping organize a chapter of the Italian Historical Society. The Italian-American presented the Anglo-Saxon visitor with a bouquet of violets which she happily pinned to her coat.

While in Buffalo the Howards attended a meeting of the New York State League of Women Voters. Here they observed a spirited debate on birth control, after which a resolution was approved which called on the legislature to legalize methods of birth control and the distribution of information relative to it. The Colonel was saddened by such stupidity. They also attended a debate between Clarence Darrow and Will Durant, author of *The Story of Philosophy*. Darrow, who took the affirmative side of the question, "Is a Man a Machine?" did not appeal to Colonel Howard any more than he had the last time he saw him. Even when he himself had been a radical he couldn't sympathize with what he viewed as the ultra-radical philosophy of Clarence Darrow.

From Buffalo they moved on to Rochester, with Lady Vivian admiring the lovely snow scenes as she drove along attempting to read every sign they passed. She constantly called the Colonel's attention to something—scenery, sheep, a "precious" child, or "cute doggie." He could never figure out just how she managed to see more than he did when *she* was driving. But he smiled as he thought what a wonderful traveling companion she was. If it snowed it was marvelous; if it rained it was so mystic; if it sleeted, the sun would soon shine; if they had a puncture it was an adventure.

In Rochester, Colonel Howard watched the snow flurries from their hotel room while Lady Vivian strolled along the sidewalk in galoshes and raincoat on her way to see the Italian vice-consul, carrying their letter of introduction. He was glad that she relieved him of such burdens, and knew she wouldn't miss it for the world. The manager of the Italian Historical Society had suggested that the vice-consul might arrange for them to meet the son of Gabriele D'Annunzio, the famous Italian novelist, poet, and politician, who had such a way with women. Perhaps that was one reason for her hurry, he mused.

She was soon back again, bubbling over with enthusiasm. D'Annunzio was in New York! She was sure they would be entertained by the Italians, perhaps at a big dinner, and he would be there, of course. Colonel must buy a hat. And he needed a tuxedo. But first they were going to lunch. She had made an engagement with the Italian consular agent of Rochester. He was coming by the hotel to take them to his club in a few minutes.

The next night Colonel Howard spoke to the Jewish Young Men's Association. Tobias Roth, the executive secretary who had been responsible for their coming to Rochester, had entertained them the previous evening.

With a snowstorm raging the next morning, Lady Vivian had chains put on their tires and insisted that if other people could drive to New York they could too. It was 400 miles and she wanted to be there for Thanksgiving. It would be "precious," she thought, to have Gladys Baker, the newspaper-woman from Alabama, eat Thanksgiving turkey with them.

So off they drove, into the blinding snow. It became frustrating to Lady Vivian when she couldn't read all the signs. She occasionally brought the car to a stop while she attempted to finish reading one. When she tried to read one without stopping, the car headed straight for a snow bank and the Colonel grabbed the wheel just in time to prevent an accident.

Driving through sleet and snow, they reached the big metropolis the day before Thanksgiving and went immediately to the office of the Italian Historical Society. There they found a telegram from Claude, saying all was well at River Park, and a boxful of copies of the new book on fascism. It was again a thrill to see a beautiful, freshly bound book bearing his name and he smiled through his tears as Lady Vivian clutched one to her heart rapturously.

Colonel Howard was soon on a train headed back to Buffalo to speak at a big banquet at the Statler given by the Italian Historical Society in honor of Commendatore Emanudo Grazzi, royal consul general of Italy, who was aboard the same train. More than 100 prominent leaders of the city were at the depot to meet their royal visitor and to escort him to the city hall, where Mayor Frank Schwab presented him and Colonel Howard with keys to the city of Buffalo. Distinguished government officials, judges, and consuls of foreign countries joined Colonel Howard at the speaker's table that night. Through the courtesy of the society, he presented each of them with an autographed copy of *Fascism: A Threat to Democracy* and made an unusually brief speech in order to catch the midnight train back to New York. He had to be in Philadelphia the next day.

At the West Philadelphia station he was met by an Italian gentleman who drove him to an elegant hotel where he met and had lunch with Dr. and Mrs. Mario Orbini. Then he was taken to a school building in the Italian quarter of the city, where he made a speech in the large auditorium. On a tour of other sections of the newly constructed school, the Colonel was shown a special desk in the eighth grade room. It was explained that this was the seat of honor for the best student and had been presented to the school by *Il Duce* himself. It bore a bronze plate inscribed "*Dono Di* S. E. Benito Mussolini."

After he returned to his New York hotel, Colonel Howard spent Monday morning reading sermons by leading clergymen of the city, including Dr. Henry Sloan Coffin and the Reverend Harry Fosdick. That evening, by Lady Vivian's arrangement, he met Miss Lillian Gibson, of England, who had been teaching Mussolini English for two years. The tutor expressed great admiration for the dictator, but confided that she didn't understand him.

The Colonel was soon headed for Massachusetts for an appearance before the Boston College Club. Next, he made an address at noon to the Springfield Exchange Club. That night he spoke at Central High School under the auspices of the Italian Women's Club and caught a train back to New York. At his next engagement there, he lectured at Columbia University while Mussolini's teacher sat with Lady Vivian in the audience. Excited and nervous, the Vagabond's wife was overwhelmed by the fact that he was actually a guest speaker at this noted institution.

At Newark, New Jersey, Colonel Howard appeared before a large Italian audience one night and at the Elks Hall the next. From there he took a train to Sharon, Pennsylvania, to speak to the local chapter of the American Institute of Electrical Engineers. Then he caught a late train to Binghamton, New York, for a speech the next day.

During all this time, Lady Vivian was having some adventures in New York. First, she boarded the wrong subway and got lost. A young man who helped her find her way hinted at thoughts of suicide and gained her sympathy and an appointment to meet the Colonel. After the derelict had trudged through falling snow, appearing on time but smelling of whiskey, Colonel Howard gave him money for a clean bed and bath, a new shirt and a haircut and shave. The youth was told to return two days later to show his desire to improve. They never saw him again.

Lady Vivian also got her first permanent wave, something the Colonel had heard about but didn't think much of. It pleased him that the hairdresser had telephoned to ask for an autographed book, however.

But Lady Vivian's most thrilling experience of the whole trip was in meeting Dr. Henry Knight Miller, editor of *Psychology Magazine*. She had long looked upon that publication as *the* authority on her favorite subject and eagerly read every word of each monthly issue. After succeeding in getting an appointment with Dr. Miller she appeared at his office with pictures of Alpine Lodge, Dr. Barnett's articles from the Birmingham *News*, and copies of Colonel Howard's books, ready to present a novel idea to the famed psychologist.

By the time the Colonel returned from Binghamton, she had made arrangements for a summer school of psychology to be held at Alpine Lodge, sponsored by *Psychology Magazine*, with a faculty headed by Dr. Miller. The official announcement would be made in the May issue of the magazine and details would be given in June. Lady Vivian's happiness was boundless as she talked of the plans for the school she had dreamed of ever since they had built the lodge. With Dr. Miller's help, she was certain that River Park would become the outstanding psychology center of America.

To honor Colonel Howard for his distinguished services the Italian Historical Society gave an elegant dinner at the Hotel Biltmore on Thursday, December 13, under the patronage of the royal Italian consul general. Engraved invitations were sent to about 60 guests, including bank presidents, Columbia professors, and a supreme court judge. Each guest was presented with an autographed copy of *Fascism: A Challenge to Democracy* through courtesy of the publisher.

To avoid the heavy New York traffic, the Howards left their hotel on Seventy-Sixth Street early in the morning. Driving down Broadway to Canal and through the Hudson Tunnel, they reached Newark, New Jersey, in less than an hour. Three days later they arrived at Cincinnati, where the Colonel was to address the chamber of commerce the following day on "The Real Mussolini."

While resting in the hotel lobby, Colonel Howard looked over the morning paper which carried his picture and an announcement of the meeting. Lady Vivian took a walk in the rain, looking at the bright and colorful store windows so gaily decorated for Christmas. She became suddenly aware that she was homesick for Alpine Lodge and River Park.

Leaving Cincinnati immediately after the luncheon, they drove 100 miles before stopping for the night. They arose early and drove all the way to Chattanooga on a bright and clear December day. After buying a few gifts, they started on the last lap homeward, with Lady Vivian passing almost everything on the road in her rush to get there. By mid-afternoon they were approaching River Park and Lady Vivian tooted the horn all the way to Alpine Lodge. Claude, Aunt Martha, and a group of friends gathered around the car to welcome them home.

They had traveled 2,653 miles, had seen interesting sights and shared many adventures. Their only mishap had been the loss of $35 expense money, which Colonel Howard, unaccustomed to carrying cash, had carelessly stuffed into his shirt pocket. However, he could still play Santa Claus on the mountain, thanks to the Birmingham *News*.

Before leaving on his trip, Colonel Howard had written to the newspaper's welfare department requesting aid for one needy mountain family and the *News* had carried a special appeal to its readers to provide clothing and toys for the Vagabond to distribute at Christmas. Gifts and contributions could be sent to the newspaper office.

When Lady Vivian drove to the express office to get the box from the Birmingham *News* she found it was much too large to put in the car. She located a truck to haul it for her and it took four men to lift the huge box. In addition there were six packages which had been shipped directly to Colonel Howard. The *News* had also mailed a $50 check to help provide a bountiful Christmas for the community.

People of all ages gathered at the little rock school house on Christmas eve. Albert Howell and Frank Hixon built a roaring log fire and brought in a stock of extra wood. Lady Vivian and Letta York decorated the tree and sorted the gifts. Claude helped them distribute the packages while Colonel, dressed in his red suit and white beard, played the jovial role of old St. Nick.

There was something for everyone, warm clothing for young and old, and toys for the children. A special big doll went to a ten year old afflicted girl, who was often depressed and in great pain, and a four year old caressed the first doll she had ever owned as a tear slid down Santa's cheek. Colonel Howard's favorite gift was a pencil he didn't have to sharpen—his first mechanical lead pencil.

Afterward the three Howards talked into the night, with the Colonel reminiscing about various events in Sally's life. Every holiday season there was an even greater ache in his heart for the faithful partner of his early manhood and his troubled middle years. He told his wife and son of an idea which had come to him and the three of them decided that night to build a Sally A. Howard Memorial Chapel on Sentinel Rock. They would have a huge electrically lighted cross placed over it with the words, "In the Cross of Christ I Glory."

In January Colonel Howard began planning another vagabond trip, to gather material for his articles. But he wanted no more of the big cities and the snow of the north. This time his thoughts turned to the warm breezes of the Alabama coast and he decided to go to Fairhope, Alabama. This time he and Lady Vivian were taking Aunt Martha, her daughter, Mrs. Isabel Knotts, of New York, and Claude. They left Lookout Mountain on a cold morning when there were giant icicles hanging along the bluff walls overlooking Little River. After a night at Brewton, they drove through Pensacola and on to Fairhope, arriving just as a heavy rainfall began.

When they looked out the next morning over the blue

water of Mobile Bay, it appeared that spring had already arrived. The grass was green and bright after the night's rain; the japonicas were in bloom; and the mockingbirds were having a merry concert while the bluejays protested in raucous, discordant cries.

To Colonel Howard it looked like a good day to explore on his own with the freedom to wander at will or to sit alone in meditation when he felt like it. Leaving the others to seek their own entertainment, he went down to the docks where he boarded a small steamer, the *Eastern Shore*, for Mobile. As he sat in the cabin of the boat, his thoughts went back to a time many years before. His granddaughter, whose birthday was the same as his, December 18, was seven years old at the time and had come into his room with a puzzled expression.

"Grandfather, do you do as you please?" she enquired.
"Yes, Virginia," he answered absentmindedly.
"About everything?" she asked very earnestly.
"Well, I suppose I do," he said a little doubtfully.
"About *everything* in the world?" she questioned.
"No, Virginia. I don't do as I please about *everything*."

She turned away with a look of disappointment, leaving him to wonder what was on her mind.

Now, with the others remaining in Fairhope, he was happy that he was free for a day to do as he pleased, carrying his pad and pencil for writing and a copy off *The Heart of Burrough's Journals* for reading.

During the hour and a half cruise across the bay the Colonel sat enjoying the glorious day, watching the sunshine dance across the white caps, and feeling the strange thrill the tang of salt air brought. It was good to visit the ocean occasionally, but he tired of it after a while and his heart turned to his mountains for constant companionship. He never tired of them. The mountains were never the same. Unlike the coast and the sea, they were an ever changing panorama. The mountains would always be home.

Part of the reason for this trip was an experiment which didn't work. Claude also did as he pleased; his vacation in the company of others did not have the desired effect. Saddened and disappointed, Colonel Howard was soon back at his beloved retreat seeking solace and strength through meditation and communion with nature. Suffering the anguish of mental depression, brought on by the behavior of his wayward son, Colonel Howard found it increasingly difficult to write light-hearted and gay vagabond articles. The baby son whom he and Sally had so adored was still—at times—a source of pride. His charming personality complemented his handsome face and lean, agile body. His intelligence and leadership had advanced him to captain in the army. His kindness, consideration, and ingratiating manner worked wonders with the Colonel, Aunt Martha, and many others—when he wanted something. But his unpaid debts, alcoholism, and love trysts at first perplexed his father and then almost devastated him.

In February, as Colonel Howard began a sketch on Elbert Hubbard, the famous lecturer, publisher, editor, and essayist whose son he had visited in East Aurora, Colonel hinted at his personal grief. He had been hoping, he said, to have the proper conditions under which he might relax and record his memorable interview with Elbert Hubbard, Jr. He continued:

> I would have chosen a time of peace and calm of spirit if left to me, rather than one of those Gethsemanes of mine when my heart is bleeding and crying out, "If it be possible, let this cup pass; nevertheless, not my will but thine be done."
>
> Today is such a time with the Vagabond when he is suffering vicariously . . . .

He did not reveal the source of his most recent tribulations. Nor did he publicize the fact that, in order to make Claude more steady and responsible, he had signed over to him six River Park lots and 20 acres on the brow belonging to the Master Schools, Inc. And certainly he did not know that this would be another well-intentioned effort which would fail.

For a while the Vagabond articles required more effort, yet ended up more rambling, colorless, lacking their usual sparkle and wit. But they provided a steady and much needed income and the Colonel managed to complete his feature article each week.

In March the Vagabond sketches began to have a companion article, a travel and human interest series authored by "The Vagabond's Hobo." There was an odd but interesting story behind them. The previous October Colonel Howard had received a letter from a man claiming to be a hobo without a friend in the world. The self-described derelict had been happily married once to a wonderful young girl, who had died soon afterward. He married again, seeking happiness a second time, but discovered his wife was a schemer who managed to get possession of all he owned. Disillusioned, he left home and took up the life of a hobo. Feeling that no one in the world cared whether he lived or died, he found the Vagabond articles warm and appealing and desired to communicate with the author. The Colonel answered immediately, telling his hobo that he now had a friend, and pinning his last dollar bill to the letter.

In March the two new friends met when the hobo left his train at Valley Head and trekked up the mountain and along the Scenic Highway to River Park. He was no common hobo, but another self-educated person of considerable intelligence. The two nonconformists liked each other immediately and spent two days conversing on a wide range of subjects. Each sent an account of their meeting to the Birmingham *News*, where they were printed on the same page. Thus began the writing career of the Vagabond's Hobo, whose real identity was never revealed to his readers.

Some people believed that Colonel Howard wrote both articles and he received a number of letters written to his hobo. These messages were forwarded to specified postoffices to the other writer. The Hobo's style was different from the Colonel's, as were his interests and knowledge. The Hobo was well versed in Indian lore and languages and knew about other matters with which the Vagabond was unfamiliar.

Born in Virginia in 1854, the Hobo had attended Lincoln's first inaugural and remembered a tall, angular man with black beard, vaguely resembling a scarecrow, waving long arms to the crowd. Buchanan, the outgoing president, had sat during Lincoln's address with his head down, as though staring at the ground, "his face looking as long as a horse's head," the Hobo remembered.

In April, 1929, Colonel Howard wrote his most tender and

232

memorable article. It was a story about his first—and favorite—grandchild, Milford. Beginning with when he was "a tiny, feeble bit of humanity," the boy had shown great affection for his grandfather. It was to him that he called out, when he began to lisp his first words, with the name "Bampooshie," later shortened to "Pooshie," and sometimes, when he wanted to be really chummy, just "Poosh." As other grandchildren came along, he taught them to say Pooshie. The Colonel recounted some memories of his grandson's birth and early childhood.

Perhaps it may be almost an obsession with me, but I want the seed of my body to live as long as man inhabits this planet.

So when the first grandchild came, and a boy, we named him Milford Robert, the Milford for me, the Robert for his other grandfather, and in him I saw myself reproduced.

He was a frail fellow, came near losing his eyesight, and was a great sufferer, which left him nervous and delicate. It seemed that he would never survive the period of adolescence, but he did, gradually growing more robust as the years went by.

When my two sons married they brought their brides to my home. There the grandchildren were born, and it was one big family and I was the patriarch.

In infancy and early childhood, Milford felt a peculiar something for me that I have never quite understood. It was I as much as his mother who was greatly devoted to him, who could soothe him in his sufferings and get him to sleep when all others failed.

A thousand times, yes, thousands of times, he used to say when he was a little fellow, "I love Pooshie best." . . .

We lived on a big farm three miles from Fort Payne, and I bought him a beautiful mare, bridle, saddle, and outfitted him with raincoat, rain hat and all other prerequisites . . . .

Colonel Howard expressed his and Sally's fondness for Milford as he grew older. One of his most cherished possessions, he revealed, was a gold watch Milford had paid for himself and sent as a surprise gift. His last memory of Milford was of his smile as he waved and shouted, "Good-by, Pooshie. I'll see you again before long."

The reason for the story was the tragic death of his namesake. A telegram had arrived from California with the heartbreaking message: Milford had died on March 3, 1928, from head injuries caused by a falling rock. He had surgery after the accident and had lived two days without ever having regained consciousness. A letter brought more details: Milford had volunteered to help fight a raging forest fire and a big boulder became loosened in Pickens Canyon, striking him on the head.

The Vagabond's own words failed him. He could neither subdue nor express his feelings after this sudden disaster. Turning to Eugene Field, he quoted "Little Boy Blue" to help convey his mood of the moment. Many of his readers, including former political opponents, were touched and saddened by the announcement of young Milford's death and they flooded Colonel Howard with letters of sympathy.

Just as he seemed to face every major crisis in solitude, he had been alone and troubled when this shocking message came. Lady Vivian, fired now with a crusading zeal for the advancement of her pet subject, was engaged in a two month series of psychology courses she was teaching in Jasper and other small towns. Claude had moved out of the lodge. Although he was only a few miles away in a cottage on the brow—with a woman he had been seeing for several months—he might as well have been a thousand miles away. His separation from Jennie had been bad enough but now he was trying to get a divorce. He was giving up a wonderful, loyal wife, and was disowning his only child—and Colonel Howard's only living grandson.

Even his Italian involvement, with its promise of influence and excitement, was beginning to sour. The letters delivered to him at River Park began to bear an increasing amount of criticism directed at his expressed admiration of Mussolini and fascism. One person, a former close friend whose words stung deeply, suggested that Colonel Howard had praised the Italian dictator and his totalitarian form of government because it had been profitable for him to do so.

Actually, he had made no profit from either his speaking tour or his book. Though he and Lady Vivian valued the rich experiences of their six weeks trip, his strenuous efforts and hurried pace had gained him no profit after expenses. As for his book, *Fascism: A Challenge to Democracy*, more copies had been given away than had been sold. The book had been on sale in Birmingham for three months and not one single copy had been sold.

He had reaped no financial windfall from his meeting with Mussolini or from any of the ensuing results of his trip to Italy. His money problems were still with him; but he was quite accustomed to living frugally. It was a new type of concern with which he must cope now. His good friend, Dr. C. D. Killian, had just advised him that he was not a well man, would probably never be any better, and might need very serious surgery.

Why did fate continuously deal him these heavy blows? With physical problems added to his mental agony, Colonel Howard felt, as David had, that life for him was "a dry and thirsty land where no water is." He had told his wife years before that he had drunk life's cup of sorrow to the bitter dregs and there could be no more poignant suffering for him. Little had he known what grief was yet to follow. Each time he thought the storms were subsiding and expected to enter a calm and peaceful sea for the remainder of his voyage through life, a new storm appeared over the horizon.

More and more his thoughts centered upon his advancing age and upon the subject of death. The realization that he would soon reach his "threescore and ten" preyed upon his mind. Someone had fixed that number of years as life's allotted span, a fact which gave him an appalling feeling that the end might be just over the next hill. It was in this frame of mind that he brought to an end the now rambling fragmentary autobiography he had worked on occasionally for several years.

After contemplating the age of 70 "deadline" for some time, the old Howard fighting spirit resurfaced and he solved his dilemma of how to escape the constant threat of nature's decree. He did not intend to recognize it! In the evening of his life he confronted the prospect of dying with his own conclusions "that I shall not die, . . . that there is no death, and that death is an impossibility and an utter absurdity." Until his death eight years later, he was to dwell more and more on the subject of immortality. He believed very strongly in life after death, as evidenced by the following statement:

> I have a consciousness, an awareness, that I am
> immortal, even as God is immortal, and that I am everlast-
> ing unto everlasting.

He also determined that his Vagabond articles would not
reflect the dark forebodings of his own future. He would try to
make them brighter, more optimistic, full of a rich philosophy
for living. One of the reasons for the success and popularity of
his feature stories was this positive and optimistic quality.
Another bit of charm the Vagabond displayed was his injection
of humor at unlikely places. Once, in the midst of a very deep
philosophical discussion which delved into both reincarnation
and immortality he paused for the following observation about
his body:

> I have no desire to dwell in this body forever. Not
> that I am dissatisfied with my body. I am proud of it. I
> thank my maker for the body He gave me. It is a strong
> body, capable of enduring great hardships, full of vital
> energy, great driving power, tremendous strength. And it is
> not so bad to look upon, if one admires the rugged moun-
> taineer, for I am that in body as well as in my heart. So I
> am perfectly satisfied with my body. I would not exchange
> it for any other body I ever saw. It just suits me, although
> it has been quite unruly at times, but I doubt not I have
> managed it better than I could have managed any other
> body.

One of Colonel Howard's visitors during Lady Vivian's
psychology lectures was William Patrick Lay, of Gadsden, who
accepted an invitation to spend several days at Alpine Lodge
with his friend. This outstanding businessman was naturally
interviewed as the subject of a forthcoming Vagabond sketch.
In seven full columns, the story was told of how Captain Lay
was responsible for the following accomplishments: securing the
Gulf State Steel Company for Gadsden; building the Printup
Hotel; building the first electric plant in the city; and incorporating the Alabama Power Company in 1906 with a capital

stock of $5,000.

Most days during Lady Vivian's absence began with the same routine. He prepared his breakfast of fruit and oatmeal, took a walk to commune with nature and prepare himself mentally and spiritually for the day, then wrote on his sketches or answered letters until the mail was delivered. The warm letters from his readers helped provide Colonel Howard with momentary escape from some of his burdens. The kindness and sincerity of so many people also boosted the self-esteem of this troubled man who deemed himself a failure.

I have sometimes, in these sketches, hinted at the complex, almost obsession as the psychologist would say, that has haunted me for years: the feeling that I had not used the talents God had given me properly, and the fear that I should go hence "empty handed," as some hymn writer has put it. So, it is no wonder that I am so deeply moved when some one tells me or writes me that I have brought to them a gleam of inspiration.

As Colonel Howard sat alone or strolled along a winding trail in meditation he searched for other ways to make his life more meaningful to others. Thinking first of the beautiful rhododendron and mountain laurel blossoms of Alpine, he announced a rhododendron festival for the months of May and June. Everyone was invited to come to Vagabondia to enjoy these wild mountain flowers. He also made vague plans for establishing a "sanctuary for birds and weary souls" on 500 acres of the Master School property. Those seeking refuge from mental and financial strain would be given a plot of land for a home and garden. He was beginning to receive a few inquiries when Lady Vivian returned to prepare for the summer school of psychology.

Just before her triumphant arrival with $100 she had made from her lectures, the bank where they had deposited the money to cover the last car payments failed. Instead of buying new clothes for herself and the Colonel as she had planned, Lady Vivian had to spend most of her earnings to pay off the note on the car. But even this disappointment could not keep her spirits down now as she was about to realize her great dream of having outstanding psychologists from leading colleges and universities come to River Park.

Money had been borrowed in order to get Alpine Lodge ready for the school. After they received wide publicity during the activities of July, they would probably sell enough property to pay their debts and take a vacation, the Colonel reasoned. He too, had been swept up in Lady Vivian's excitement and gay anticipation by June 30, when most of the faculty was due to arrive.

Lady Vivian drove down to meet the Sunday evening train. The Colonel preferred to miss the commotion of the first night and went to his cabin retreat near the Master School. Soon after the train had passed by he heard the roar of cars and taxis speeding along the highway toward River Park. When Lady Vivian passed by she blew her horn long and victoriously.

The Summer School of Psychology, which opened on July 1, 1929, at Alpine Lodge proved to be a big success from the standpoint of attendance. River Park was swamped with people, as some 80 students arrived from 26 states and six foreign countries. Tents and other additional equipment were hurriedly purchased and more help was hired at the lodge.

The faculty included the following: William MacDougal of Duke University; Dr. Durant Drake of Vassar College; Donald Laird of Colgate; Lawrence W. Rogers of New York University; Mehran Thompson of Michigan; Dr. Alfred J. Fox; Dr. Henry Knight Miller and Arthur H. Howland of New York; and Judge Daniel Simmons of Jacksonville, Florida.

On infrequent breaks in class routine, the River Park visitors went swimming in Little River or basked in the sun on the huge boulders along the bank. Their biggest entertainment was saved for the last Sunday of the month when several hundred Sacred Harp singers gathered at the lodge. With many psychology students hearing this type of music for the first time, the crowd sang "Amazing Grace, How Sweet The Sound," "How Firm a Foundation," and many other old gospel songs. Then such tempting foods as fried chicken and egg custards were spread on long tables in the grove across the road and the visitors were treated to another southern institution.

During most of July there was intense scholastic activity at the school as the students coped with their strenuous courses of study. Lady Vivian was divinely happy and seemed to be beaming every moment, while Colonel Howard followed the proceedings rather dubiously. It appeared to him that the learned professors were attempting to present a four year course in tabloid form in one month. He concluded, at the end of July, that most of those who had come seeking knowledge had become lost in a hopeless daze—while a few had learned *what not to do*.

After the closing exercises of the School of Psychology the visitors all made their departures, the tents were folded and the cots were stored away. An exhausted Lady Vivian went on a visit to North Carolina to recuperate and Colonel Howard was left alone with his new debts. Not a house nor a lot had been sold, nor any prospects found.

For almost four months he was to wage a lonely battle against illness, loneliness, and depression. Spending much of his time in his little cabin, the Colonel began an experiment through which he sought to improve his physical and mental health by achieving a higher spiritual level. He rarely saw his son, who started building two small houses on his lots near the lodge, getting most of his supplies on credit at Valley Head.

Borrowing money from Aunt Martha, Claude also bought some horses and made elaborate plans for developing a golf course. The Merimeechi Golf and Riding Club got little further than providing Claude and his friend with riding horses, however. When her son's summer camp was over, Claude's paramour left her rented house on the brow and returned to Birmingham. He then prevailed upon Aunt Martha to rent him a room but instead of paying her he continued to borrow money.

In October Colonel Howard left his isolated home on "Sanctuary Mountain" and made his first trip in six months to speak in Birmingham to Post Number One of the American Legion. While there he conceived the idea of a legion camp on his property and offered to donate the land for such a project. The commander and approximately 40 other legionnaires were invited to come to Alpine Lodge to look over the area before making a decision. The group accepted and spent a day and night at the lodge. It was decided to form a committee to investigate the possibility of establishing the Howard-Legion Lookout Mountain Camp. However, the stock market crash later that month and the ensuing depression halted all efforts toward making the camp a reality.

On another trip made in October, Colonel Howard visited Dr. C. W. Daugette, president of Jacksonville Teachers College and featured his host and the college in a Vagabond article. He wrote of the Daugette's brick mansion, built with the aid of slave labor, where the distinguished guests had included William Jennings Bryan, Elbert Hubbard, Champ Clark, and Bishop Richmond Pearson Hobson. The Colonel added the personal note that the first congressman he had ever seen had been Brigadier General Henry Forney, brother of Mrs. Daugette's father, Major General John H. Forney. He also traced the history of the college, which had been established by act of the legislature in 1883, with an appropriation of $2,500 annually.

Shortly afterward, Colonel Howard made a speaking tour which carried him to Arkansas and Ohio. While at Fort Smith, Arkansas, he visited his nephew, Herbert Howard, eldest son of Wallace. Afflicted as his father and mother had been, Herbert, too, was dying of tuberculosis.

In November, the Colonel wrote another article praising Mussolini and the accomplishments he had achieved in his seven years of power. Shortly before leaving to spend two weeks with Lady Vivian and her mother in Florida for the Christmas holidays, Colonel Howard wrote his last Vagabond article. In a sketch less than half the length of most, he reminisced about the family of eight in which he had grown up, noting that he and Edgar[1] (a professional photographer) were the only survivors.

The Vagabond ended the article and the series with one of his favorite subjects—Granny Dollar. The busy centenarian had just sent him word, he said, to get her some new fruit trees to set out in the spring. Her old trees were failing, she had explained, and she wanted to be sure of having enough fruit in the future. In discussing Granny's secret of longevity, Colonel Howard explained it as being her vital interest in life and her vigorous physical activity. "When Granny dies it will be in the winter," he predicted, "when she is shut in by the bad weather and has little to do."

The days of the Vagabond were over. The traveling about

---

[1] Edgar died in Oneonta in 1952 at the age of 79.

the country, the lectures, and the after-dinner speeches were almost at an end. His writing, though of a more subjective type, would continue as Milford Howard entered into the final and saddest chapter of his turbulent life.

The End Of The Rainbow

The 1930's should have been the golden years for the tired, aging man. All his life—as the sad barefoot boy, the shy "Yaller Jacket," the cocky young lawyer, the colorful, controversial congressman, the superb orator and speaker, and as the folksy Vagabond—he had dreamed his dreams and had worked relentlessly. Always, he had envisioned a time of fulfillment, when he would be acclaimed for some great achievement or contribution to his fellow man, after which he would find rest and peace, with time for leisurely reading and reflection. But it was not to be.

During the last seven years of his life, Colonel Howard experienced severe illness, major surgery, and a near-fatal conflagration, became estranged from both his son and his wife, and suffered from hunger and want during the depression. This time of mental torment and physical discomfort was also a period of prolonged and intense meditation as Colonel Howard attempted to prepare himself spiritually for death. Bombarding an already confused mind with the most complex and controversial religious and philosophical questions of the ages, he was, at the end, a broken man, a mere shadow of the physical and intellectual giant he once had been. He was also still seeking what he had never found—peace.

As the years bear me swiftly forward now, where they used to drag when I was younger, I realize the heart weariness of David, the passionate craving for peace when

242

he cried out, "My soul thirsteth for Thee!"

I know that a longing for peace is a longing for God.

As his productive years slipped by, the Colonel saw that he was never to reach a glorious pinnacle of success, never to experience a thrilling moment which would compensate for so many failures. In looking back over his life, he found little which made him proud.

I see much begun, but nothing finished, for one thing. Great expectations and empty realizations. Beautiful castles in the air, to be blown away by the hot winds or obscured by the mists. Glorious rainbows of promise, but no "pot of gold at the end." Ever and always a bigger man than I has mocked me, urged me to scale the heights and be what he told me I was capable of being, and then my hands would tremble, I would lose my hold and fall back a failure. And then when I was down he would torment me, and sometimes when he would see me utterly discouraged and heart broken he would speak words of cheer and hope and try to comfort me. And, oh, at such times I have dared dream great dreams of the man I was going to be.

In January, 1930, Colonel Howard returned from a holiday trip alone, leaving Lady Vivian with her mother in Lakeland, Florida, where she would be spared the frigid mountain winds of winter, and where she would have the nourishing food he could not provide. Alone again, he read, meditated, and prayed. Pursuing some hazy theory based upon a combination of religion and metaphysics, he attempted to affect all the cells of his body with positive thinking and happy emotions—to recharge these cells, like batteries, with cosmic energy channeled through prayer. He sought desperately and ineffectively to avoid a dreaded operation.

With Dr. Killian advising him to enter a hospital for surgery, he stubbornly continued his lone vigil at River Park and conducted his "great experiment." Ill and lonely, he sometimes broke the monotony of dreary winter days by writing letters to old friends, as he yearned for the days when mail deliveries brought messages of cheer. None of these letters was answered.

Only Lady Vivian wrote to him.

The Colonel's housekeeping chores required little time. He cooked what meager food he had, washed the few dishes used, laundered his clothes, and then began his reading, meditation, and prayers.

He soon became haggard and thin, even though he assured friends he was feeling better. Generous neighbors, also suffering the effects of the big depression, shared their own food supplies, sending a sack of potatoes, a jar of milk, or some other food to Colonel, believing lack of food to be his main problem. But even when he ate more he continued to become thinner and more gaunt.

As the depression tightened its grip on the country, the Colonel's only asset, his property, became a liability when taxes became due. He attempted various methods of selling lots and devised an elaborate plan for establishing a summer recreation colony at River Park, with the formation of a syndicate to take charge of the properties of both Alpine Lodge, Inc. and Master Schools, Inc. His attempts were fruitless. He could not find buyers or investors in 1930.

Through Aunt Martha and others, the Colonel also learned of Claude's financial difficulties. His son had been unable to sell two rock houses he had built on his lots and still owed for the supplies used in building them, as well as his debts to Aunt Martha. After she had to pay his note, which she had signed with him, to her sister in Rome, Mrs. M. E. Floyd, for $2,500, Aunt Martha finally asked for a mortgage on Claude's property, which he promised to give her.

On June 30, 1930, a series of legal actions took place which was to precipitate a nine year court battle. On the same day that his creditors filed suit against him, Claude picked up his final divorce papers and deeded all his property to Myrtle Hickey McCormack, receiving as payment a $2,500 check and a Stutz automobile. The couple headed for Florida, where they were married on July 5, and spent a three month vacation in Panama City.

After Lady Vivian's return in the spring, she persuaded the Colonel to consult Dr. A. W. Ralls, a prominent Gadsden surgeon. He was admitted to Forrest General Hospital, where he was treated for a week and advised to have an operation which would be dangerous, but was necessary if he were to live long. At the end of a week, the Colonel left the hospital, still unable to bring himself to undergo the surgeon's knife. By September, he had lost 60 pounds and was more willing to have the operation. However, his finances had not improved at all and he could not pay for the surgery if he couldn't sell any property.

When Dr. Ralls examined Colonel Howard again he stressed the urgency for immediate surgery, insisting that he be admitted to the hospital that day and be scheduled for surgery the next morning, even though that would be on Sunday.

"I'm as poor as Lazarus," Colonel Howard admitted. "I can't pay you a cent right now, and I may never be able to."

The great surgeon, who had known of his patient for many years, was not going to deny him the medical attention he needed.

"You don't need any money at my hospital, Colonel Howard," he assured him. "You are welcome here without it."

The kindness of two men, at this time of his greatest need, helped the Colonel overcome his bitterness against those who denied him even their friendship. The other, who helped him financially, was Sumter Cogswell, the mayor of Pell City.[1]

Concentrating on Dr. Ralls' kind, intelligent face and his strong, skillful hands, Colonel Howard awaited his surgery in surprisingly good spirits. He had even persuaded himself that the operation was going to remove some difficulty which had held him back from being the man he wanted to be. By the time he was placed on the operating table at 9 a.m. Sunday morning, he was eager for the new adventure.

Afterward, he was placed in the best private room in the hospital, where for several days he was conscious of little except the presence of white uniforms and colorful fall flowers. As his strength slowly returned, he gained an awareness of feeling rested and realized that this was the first physical rest he had ever known. It was a strange experience for the Colonel, having no immediate worries or concerns while being fed and waited upon by others. After four weeks of hospital care, he was pronounced sufficiently recovered to travel to River Park and Lady

---

[1] *The main street in Pell City, once named Howard Avenue, is now Cogswell Avenue.*

245

Vivian was notified to come for him. Colonel Howard struggled to hold back his tears as he expressed his appreciation to Dr. Ralls and inquired about his hospital bill. The physician turned abruptly away and refused to discuss the cost of his extended treatment. No bill would ever be sent to Colonel Howard for the surgery and hospital care.

After recuperating at River Park for two weeks, the Colonel was driven to Birmingham by Lady Vivian and underwent minor surgery there. During the fall he slowly regained his strength and took long walks admiring autumn's bright red and yellow splashes on the mountainside, listening to the crunch of his footsteps against the stillness of the forest trails, checking familiar hickory and chestnut trees for his animal friends' winter food supply. Yes, he was happiest on his mountain, and found the largest measure of tranquility he was ever to know among its rocks and trees.

But there was no escape, even there, from the pressing financial problems of the times. There was often no food on the Howard table, no money with which to by any, and no income from any source to look forward to. At such times, the Colonel and Lady Vivian often visited the John B. Isbells of Fort Payne, the Blev Crows of Mentone, or other friends and ate ravenously when lunch was served.

During the winter, while Lady Vivian was gone again, Colonel Howard cared for his own needs, with occasional assistance from kind mountain friends. Always deeply touched by death, he was distressed by the loss of Granny Dollar, who died at the approximate age of 106, on Sunday night, January 25, 1931. As he had predicted, it was in the middle of winter and she had been unable to be outside.

An oak casket was made by several men of the community and the Colonel persuaded county officials to pay for the use of Emmett's hearse. In spite of a cold rain, most of the community attended her services at Little River Baptist Church, where the Colonel eulogized this unique woman. She was buried in the adjoining cemetery by the side of her husband, Nelson Dollar, who had died in 1923.

After the funeral there was a discussion as to what should be done about Granny's faithful guardian, the old mongrel dog, Buster. He was despised by all the men and women and feared by all the children, some of whom had scars to prove his viciousness. Not only did no one want him, but no one would have him. He soon showed that he didn't want them either. When some of the neighbors tried to enter the cabin to see about him, they found the almost-toothless dog attempting to gnaw the door, growling angrily and showing the gums which once held dangerous teeth. He could neither be coaxed nor driven from this position.

The Colonel and others held council and decided to chloroform Buster and then bury him at the foot of a large boulder in Vagabondia. There Colonel Howard conducted services over the mortal remains of Granny's bodyguard. After reading "Tribute To A Dog," he talked to the assembled mountain people about their dreams of eternity and of a heaven where all would be harmony, joy, and beauty.

"What sort of a place would this heaven be," he asked, "if it were inhabited only by such folks as you and me? What would heaven be without flowers, birds, and dogs?"

He closed the service with a prayer that all those assembled might be as faithful as Buster had been.

He and Lady Vivian struggled through another depression year, with both spending the winter months with Mrs. Lloyd in Florida. Upon returning to Lookout Mountain early in the year, the Colonel learned that his son was having little success either in business or with his legal battle and was suffering physically from increasingly frequent alcoholic binges. Beginning in 1932, he was admitted to a government hospital a number of times for long periods of treatment.

In the summer of 1932 the Colonel became interested in the Boy Scout organization, through the efforts of a son-in-law of his old friend, John B. Isbell. W. M. Beck,[1] a young lawyer in his fourth year as scoutmaster of Fort Payne Troop 24, interested the Colonel in furnishing his scouts with a permanent campsite. In August he deeded the local Boy Scout council three and one-half acres of land on the west side of Little River.

---

[1] *W. M. Beck, Sr., was also largely responsible for the establishment of Camp Comer Scout Reservation in 1963, on 1058 acres of land near the original scout cabin. In 1976, he was in his forty-sixth year of active scouting leadership.*

The Colonel followed the activities closely as Scoutmaster Beck and his 22 industrious young men[1] spent three weeks camping in the woods and building a large cabin. With the scoutmaster supervising the construction and his congenial wife in charge of the cooking, a remarkable job was accomplished. Dedication exercises were held on Sunday afternoon, September 25, 1932, with C. A. Wolfes acting as master of ceremonies. A large crowd of interested citizens from Fort Payne, Gadsden, and other nearby towns heard several scout leaders speak. Colonel Howard delivered the main address, during which he announced that he was giving 15 acres to the Northeastern District Council for a district camp site. The boys of Troop 24 later voted to name their lodge Camp Howatan in honor of the donor of the land, a tribute for which he expressed deep appreciation.

Colonel Howard was to show further interest in scouting by deeding 120 acres of the Master Schools, Inc. land to the Boy Scouts of America in November, 1933. In the deed, the grantor expressed his desire that the property be used by the organization to further leadership training and character education. He also requested that the area be maintained as a bird sanctuary and that other harmless wild life be conserved. This area had 850 feet fronting on Little River and should have made an ideal camp site. However, the Boy Scouts were also affected by the depression and the national executives concluded three years later that they were paying taxes on land they could not afford to develop. The land was deeded back to the Master Schools, Inc. in October, 1936. Exactly three decades after Colonel Howard's contribution of this land, it was bought back as part of the 1,058 acre tract for which the Choccolocco Council paid $87,450.

During 1932 the Colonel made several other speeches, including one to the Chattanooga Business Women's Club, where he spoke on Soviet Russia and Mussolini's Italy. But his speaking engagements were much more rare than in previous

---

[1] The boys were: Wolford Clayton, Deward Crow, J. Paul Crow, Wayne Mann, Fred Raymond, Walter B. Raymond, Bill Shugart, G. I. Weatherly, Jr., Glenn Owen, Leon Riddle, Alfred Hawkins, Richard Hawkins, Cecil White, Hobert Thomas, Jr., John Pendergrass, Allen Ory, W. B. Lowry, Charles Kershaw, Bryan Driskill, Billy M. Davidson, Lewis Cross, and Perry Bryant.

years. Due to failing health and increasing mental confusion, his great oratorical ability was decreasing. In addition to the minor illnesses to which he succumbed more easily in these later years, he also became more accident prone. In November he suffered a fracture in his left arm from a fall at River Park.

Perhaps to prove that he was able, or to escape Claude's mounting troubles, Colonel Howard made one more attempt at vagabonding and lecturing late in 1933, spending two months in Vermont and Rhode Island. Part of the time he and Lady Vivian camped in the state parks, cooking their own food. During this time he continued writing a manuscript started two years earlier on "Vagabonding at Seventy," a religious work which reflected his spiritual searching during this period.

While in Rhode Island he was asked to make a written deposition to questions submitted to him relative to the civil suit against Claude. In his statement he revealed that his son's wife had been aware of his financial difficulties before she married him, as he, Colonel Howard, had discussed them with her in an effort to discourage the marriage. In December Lady Vivian and the Colonel returned to River Park before going to Lakeland, Florida, for the Yuletide holidays.

In January he returned to River Park to make arrangements to sell most of the lots he still owned in the subdivision to a Florida buyer. All other efforts to sell any of his property—even choice lots at the most minimal prices—had failed. Now, faced with losing much of his property because he couldn't pay taxes on it, he was forced to sell the most desirable part of it. The Alpine Lodge Inc. property, including the cabin in which the Colonel had lived and four or five others, was purchased by Miss Alice MacVicker, of Miami, for $4,615.83. The new owner changed the name to Alpine Lodge For Girls and established a girls' summer camp.

As he always did whenever he could get some money, the Colonel first paid all his debts. These, combined with overdue taxes, left him very little cash and no good home. Later in the year he moved his few possessions to the lonely one-room cabin near the Master School. Here he spent the following winter alone, hurt and bitter toward Lady Vivian because she would no longer attempt to share his frugal life on the mountain. Though she had remained loyal through years of adversity, she herself was no longer young and had health problems of her own. She now refused to live in his tiny isolated cabin where there would be very little food to eat. The Colonel was doomed to a period of agonizing loneliness, bitterness, and disappointment. Many former friends, unable to understand him as he became further detached from reality, tended to avoid him. Puzzled and dejected, he thought he was being shunned because of his failures.

The one bright ray to penetrate his dismal spirits at this time was the development of DeSoto Park, established the previous year in response to a movement in which he and Thomas Berry had been active. The park started off with 950 acres of land, including 380 donated by Berry and 50 given by Mrs. Fred Huron, with the rest being purchased from various landowners.

The Colonel watched the boys of Civilian Conservation Corps Camp 472, of Fort Payne, as they cleared brush and built roads in December. With 175 boys and 10 foremen, including Frank Berry, the work progressed rapidly. Colonel Howard delighted in watching something being accomplished, even if he weren't the one doing it. The boys ate a hearty warm meal and he was made to feel welcome when he joined them, which he often did for his only substantial food of the day.

The Colonel observed during 1935 as the roads were cherted and cabins built of heavy hewn timbers. Telephone lines were put up, a well drilled and the park surrounded with "hog-tight" and "horse-high" fence. Almost every day that weather permitted work to be done, the Colonel walked over to watch the activity, wishing he were young and strong enough to participate—and eating as though he were.

Colonel Howard's efforts to get a poorly typed copy of his manuscript on prayer published were unsuccessful. Neither could he find a publisher for his handwritten, "Vagabonding At Seventy." Using a part of his autobiography and adding several new chapters, he wrote the manuscript for "Reminiscences of Fort Payne," and took it to J. A. Downer, who had recently purchased the *DeKalb Times,* to type for him. Busy with his new business, the editor had little time to decipher the difficult-to-read writing of the Colonel's and was slowly plowing through the manuscript when Colonel Howard became impatient and picked it up. He had the *Times* run an announcement of his intention to print a limited number of books. Those who wished to subscribe for copies at $1.00 each were asked to contact the Colonel. He apparently failed to get enough subscriptions to print his book.[1] Another announcement in the paper stated that the Colonel had some copies of his book on fascism which could be bought at half the publisher's price, which had been $2.00.

The Colonel made a few lectures in 1935, but could not find a market for any of his writing. Finally, he started a column in the *Times* in September, entitled "One Man's Opinion." With his mind more closed to reason than ever, he plunged into this new journalistic endeavor just after Mussolini had invaded Ethiopia, still a supporter of the fascist dictator. He was frustrated and alarmed because the general public could not perceive Mussolini's role as the world's only hope for escaping domination by the communists. In predicting that, if England dared go to war with Italy over Ethiopia, Italy would humble "proud, imperial England," he declared, "I am shooting wild, but this is one man's opinion." He still wasn't finished.

Here goes another shot. Democracy is doomed. It has been my opinion for a long time, and I might as well say it. All the world will be either Fascist or Communist.

Deluged with angry complaints, the kind, quiet-spoken editor wondered how to go about "firing" his former idol, who had inspired him to attend and graduate from law school himself. But the Colonel, who had also felt the ire of enraged readers, solved the problem by appearing at the newspaper office and suggesting that he discontinue his column. "One Man's Opinion" had lasted six weeks.

After he had started the column, but before his "wild shot," Colonel Howard delivered his last rousing speech to a large crowd and heard once more that wonderful, stimulating sound of loud, ringing applause. On September 26, 1935, he addressed a Republican rally at the DeKalb County Courthouse, speaking for an hour on "The Threat to the Constitution and

---

[1] *Unfortunately for local historians, this manuscript must have been destroyed, as it was not discovered with his other manuscripts.*

the Rising Tide of Communism." The master orator of half a century was respectfully received and applauded frequently during this—his last—major address.

There were few such satisfying experiences or happy days left for the Colonel. His attempts to persuade Claude to admit being guilty of fraud—to let his creditors collect from the proceeds which could be obtained from the disputed property—had almost succeeded once, but had finally failed. Claude and Myrtle separated in June and she received a divorce, on grounds of cruelty, in December, 1935.

In the fall term of circuit court, 1937, the creditors finally won their case against Claude and Myrtle, but she continued the legal battle, appealing to the state supreme court. Two years later that court affirmed the lower court's decision and Claude's deed to Myrtle was declared null and void. The five creditors, including Aunt Martha, were declared entitled to the relief prayed for in their original bill. When the register offered the 12 lots and two houses for sale on November 22, 1939, the high bid was $1,500, paid by Aunt Martha Miller.

Unable to provide for Lady Vivian, Colonel Howard's bitterness increased, nevertheless, over her absence and in April, 1936, he obtained a divorce on grounds of voluntary abandonment. In desperation for companionship, he dared dream that an unmarried daughter of a friend might become his wife and look after him if he promised to leave her all the land he owned. He summoned the courage to approach Beatrice Crow by addressing her younger sister, Dorothy. As he sat with his eyes closed, as if reading the future through a trance, he related to the child that she might have a brother-in-law who would leave them some property which would become very valuable some day. But the young lady to whom he directed this unique proposal was not interested in marrying the 74 year old Colonel for his mountain property.

No matter how great his need, there was no relative to whom he could turn for help—no one except his former daughter-in-law, Jennie. It was she who came to see about him and offered him help when he felt most deserted and despondent.

The Colonel had always loved Jennie and admired her resilient spirit. After her marriage had been dissolved, she enrolled at the University of Alabama and earned her A. B. and M. A. degrees and engaged for a short time in youth work with the Episcopalian Diocese of east Carolina. In 1934 she had become assistant dean of women at the university.[1] In July, 1936, Colonel Howard made a new will leaving all his earthly possessions to Jennie and explaining why.

... I hereby will and bequeath and demise to Jennie M. Howard all my earthly belongings, my real estate, my personal property, books, manuscripts, copyrights, chose in action, money, certificates of ownership in Boulder Park Subdivision, etc. All of my property is to belong to her absolutely and unconditionally to be administered, used, sold or disposed of in any way that she chooses.

I am naming her as the sole beneficiary under my will for two principal reasons. The first is that she is the only human being that came to my rescue after I was deserted, neglected, left alone, despised and even hated by those who have shared my generosity and bounty for years. Some of them simply forgot me; others have so crucified me that I felt I could not go on longer, and then Jennie came. God sent her in answer to my prayers. She is one of the only two people I have ever known whose loyalty I would count to the death. The other was my dear brown-eyed Sackie. They were kindred spirits in loyalty.

The second reason is that I still believe, as I have always believed that I am God's trustee of a great property, with tremendous possibilities and a great future. I shall not live to see it fully developed but I do not want to see it all come to naught upon my demise. Therefore I am giving it all to Jennie knowing that she will be just as faithful as I have been to carry on, and use it according to her wisdom, in carrying out some of the ideas she and I will talk over and elaborate as we work together if it be God's will that I be spared. However, I set no restrictions upon her in any manner. If in her wisdom she wants to dispose

---

[1]*Jennie Howard was still assistant dean of women at the University of Alabama when she died on April 6, 1950, at Druid City Hospital of congestive heart failure.*

of everything, and not be burdened by its development, and repaid by ingratitude and criticism as I have been, I shall want her to do so.

The death for which he was making preparations almost came that winter when the little log cabin caught fire on a cold night and the Colonel was overcome by smoke. A neighbor arrived just in time to rescue him from a fiery death. Little was saved for him to carry to the only home left to him, the 75 year old cabin where Granny Dollar had died six years before. His mountain friends had already been concerned about his health and mental condition. Now they prevailed upon him to mortgage some of his property, to go to California or some other warm climate until his health improved. He arranged for a loan and soon had the money in hand for the trip.

But money was for dreams—not for running away. And he had such an important dream yet to fulfill. If he didn't build the Sally A. Howard Memorial Chapel now, he would never build it and he would never have honored the name of the best and dearest woman in his life. He had found just the right spot, on a little hill.

The chapel would be patterned after the Wee Kirk O' the Heather (a reproduction of the Annie Laurie Church in Scotland) which stood on a grass covered hill near the graves of Sally and Milford. With a clear mental image of the completed chapel firmly fixed in his mind, his old stubborn determination returned. Unmindful of the weather, he trudged through wind and chilling rain to secure labor and material to begin building his chapel in January.

His friends were astonished and Dr. Killian was horrified. Such an undertaking by an ill and impoverished man in the middle of winter was sheer madness! He should at least use the material he had bought to build himself a warm, substantial house to live in.

But he was more adamant than ever. If he died during this endeavor, at least he would be pursuing his dream. For six weeks he acted as foreman, standing on wet, sometimes frozen ground to direct the work of carpenters who needed wages badly enough to brave the weather. After the sixth week his funds were gone and he went to Fort Payne to borrow $25

254

from the bank to pay his men. Although he had always, eventually, paid his debts for 50 years, he was told he would have to get someone to endorse his note. Already chagrined at the necessity of an endorsement, he suffered the additional humiliation of being refused by the first four he asked before finding someone who would sign his note.

Somehow the Colonel soon had his little church completed, except for several special features. He found some beautiful stained glass windows which cost only $11 apiece at the factory and wrote letters to 12 relatives and friends of Sally's asking each to contribute a window for the chapel. A wonderful Hammond organ was priced at $1,490, but he felt certain he could arrange to buy it on the installment plan. He hoped that money would be forthcoming from some source to erect the large cross above the church, which would be lighted with electricity to serve as a beacon for miles around.

Again, he had to compromise. The completed chapel had clear glass windows, an inexpensive organ, and a simple wooden cross above. However, its construction was a meaningful accomplishment for a broken and ill man who had realized few of his dreams during his lifetime. The huge boulder which formed the rear wall made a unique structure. Yet the view of the front was very much like the one Sally had admired at Forest Lawn Memorial Park at Los Angeles. The pulpit was made of stones from Little River and words from Sally's last letter were printed upon a huge beam above it. "God Has Always Been As Good To Me As I Would Let Him Be" would be Sally's message of reassurance to countless worshipers and visitors. His own contribution consisted of one word printed above the others, "Immortality."

The simple stone chapel was dedicated on Sunday afternoon, June 27, 1937. Colonel Howard delivered the memorial address on "Immortality," and talked on the same subject each Sunday during July and August. Sally had asked him to preach and he was doing so now in the Sally A. Howard Memorial Chapel. He knew she would have been proud.

The Colonel was pleased when Jennie and Morris came to see the church in August. His only living grandson was now a handsome lieutenant in the army and was accompanied by his wife. With them was one of Jennie's brothers, the Reverend Kenneth Morris, an Episcopal missionary to Japan.

Colonel Howard planned a big auction in August, to sell property to pay the debts incurred in completing the chapel. Again his efforts failed and not one lot was sold. He was broke, in debt, and practically homeless.

No one believed the frail old man could survive another winter in Granny's cabin. Again he was urged to go to California. But he had a dread of leaving his mountain, a fear that he would never return.

Finally the Colonel relented and accepted a loan which would enable him to travel to California to visit Clyde, whom he had not seen for 12 years, during his birthday and the Christmas holidays. He was certainly not going to leave the impression that he didn't plan to come back, though. In telling the mountain people about his plans for the trip, he added that he would try to make arrangements with a film company to return to Lookout Mountain with him and finally make a movie there of *Peggy Ware*. After all, he had meant to do so for 14 years.

On a cold December day he put a few possessions in a little bag and peered through a small window, watching for a neighbor to stop by to drive him to the depot. The wind whistling through the cracks between the aging logs made his eyes water, for surely those were not tears of sadness on the eve of a new adventure.

Among the stark trees, moaning and creaking as gusts of wind swept over the mountain, a series of scenes from the past gradually began to form:

He could see Governor Brandon addressing the huge crowd at the Master School dedication; a class of boys and girls were reciting lessons to Lady Vivian in the shade of a great oak tree; Sally and Milford stood making the stone planter in front of The Cabin; he stood in the school building wearing his red Santa Claus suit handing a doll to a little girl; Joe Biddle was directing carpenters in the construction of Alpine Lodge. Then a faint apparition drifted to his side and spoke in Granny's slow, cracking voice, "Lord, Lord, Chile!"

The car drove into sight and the Colonel walked the short distance to the road, where he stood with his back to his friend for a few moments. Raising his right hand to the trees and the wind, he said softly, "Good-by, Lookout Mountain."

The train ride was like a jumbled dream of vague sounds and sensations, with the Colonel hardly aware of his surroundings. He had left his mountain and he had no spirit now, no will to fight any more battles. There were not even any dreams left—just memories. And so many of them sad. Someone had once written an appropriate description of what life was really like. The words raced through his mind:

Life is made up of tragedies, sorrows, disappointments, sin, grief, disillusionment, toil, sickness, and finally, what we call death. Scattered along the pathway are moments of pleasure, sometimes even happiness and joy.

Then he remembered: *He* had written that—many years ago. Everything was so long ago. The pretty brown eyed girl with the bouncy step . . . Sally . . . Sally . . . The train had become so hot . . . His head was spinning so.

He was helped off the train and could see the faces over him. There was Clyde . . . and Perle . . . "Were these pretty young ladies his granddaughters, Virginia and Mary Ann?"

Colonel Howard was taken to Clyde's home and put to bed on December 15, with a temperature of 103 degrees. A doctor diagnosed his illness as bronchial pneumonia and Clyde realized it would be difficult for his father to recover. Lady Vivian was notified and came to be with him. Stubborn to the end, the Colonel refused for ten days to go to the hospital. After developing lobar pneumonia he consented, finally, to be taken to Los Angeles County General Hospital. There, at 1:15 on the morning of December 28, Colonel Howard lost his last battle—but was at peace at last.

According to his last request, his body was cremated so that his ashes could be placed inside the giant rock at his memorial chapel on Lookout Mountain. The cremation took place at Hollywood Crematory, on December 29, 1937.

It was planned to return to Lookout Mountain with his remains early in the year, but by July no one had made the trip. It was Lady Vivian who finally made the lonely journey to bring back the ashes of her former husband in order that his last wish might be carried out. Showing unusual loyalty to his memory, she did this knowing that he had divorced her and left her out of his will.

On July 25, with only a few others present, the Reverend Brady Justice, pastor of the Fort Payne Baptist Church, officiated at memorial services. The words spoken on that occasion were not recorded. However, as the minister was a personal friend and confidant of Milford Howard's, he may, perhaps, have expressed some thoughts this complex man had hoped would be said. For Colonel Howard had recorded, many years earlier, what he hoped might be said of him.

Here lies a man who felt that every man was his brother. He never turned away from the fallen, the desolate, the forsaken ones. He was a poor financier because he could not hold a grip on his purse strings. He tried very hard, sometimes, to live right. He always wanted to try, but somehow he often fell down. But although he was battered and bruised he got up every time he could and tried again. He never planted a thorn in any man's path, but as often as he could, he dropped a rose. He believed in all men, and foolish as it may seem to us, he felt that all men were Divine, and that this God in man would sometime, somewhere, bring them all safely back home.

An attractive bronze plaque was placed over his final resting place with the following inscription:

MILFORD W. HOWARD
Dec. 18, 1862
Dec. 28, 1937

"I shall dwell in the house of the Lord Forever."

With his mortal remains at rest for eternity on Master School property on his beloved Lookout Mountain, Colonel Howard had gone on that last journey which he had contemplated so philosophically a decade earlier.

I never yet was fully ready to start on a journey. It will be so when I receive my summons for the last journey.

I will leave a lot of things unfinished. But it won't matter then. At such a time nothing matters. And nothing seems really worthwhile. After we are gone things adjust themselves so easily. And the thing we were doing, that seemed so important, is taken up by someone else, or left undone, and it makes little difference which. Our little tiny speck that we proudly call "a world" continues to rotate in its little infinitesimal orbit, unnoticed by the rest of the universe.

Bibliography

Published Works

Hicks, John D. *The American Nation*. Atlanta: Houghton Mifflin Company, 1943.

Howard, Milford W. *Alpine Lodge*. Advertising pamphlet distributed in early 1930's. Copy in Howard papers, DeKalb County Library, Fort Payne, Alabama.

Howard, Milford W. *If Christ Came To Congress*. Washington: The Howard Publishing Company, 1894.

Howard, Milford W. *Fascism: A Challenge To Democracy*. Chicago: Fleming H. Revell Company, 1928.

Howard, Milford W. *Peggy Ware*. Los Angeles: J. F. Rowny Press, 1921.

Howard, Milford W. *The American Plutocracy*. New York: The Holland Publishing Company, 1895.

Howard, Milford W. *The Bishop of the Ozarks*. Los Angeles: Times-Mirror Press, 1923.

Howard, Milford W. *The Master Builder*. Fort Payne: The Master Schools, Vols. I, II, and III, October, 1923; January, 1924; and April, 1924.

Howard, Milford W. *The Saxon*. Fort Payne: The Saxon Publishing Company, 1925.

Howard, Milford W. *The Vanishing Anglo-Saxon*. Printed address delivered at Municipal Auditorium in Birmingham, November 8, 1924.

Journal of the House of Representatives, 54th Congress, First Session, 1895.

Journal of the House of Representatives, 54th Congress, Second Session, 1896.

North Alabama Conference College. *The Bulletin*. Vol. I, No. 3. Birmingham: North Alabama Conference, May, 1905.

261

Atlanta *Constitution*: November 17, 1894.

Boston *Ideas*: November 12, 1921.

Birmingham *Age-Herald*: January 31, 1910.

Birmingham *News*: February 25, 1895; October 26, 1924; December 18, 1927; January 6 and 8, February 5, April 15, May 3 and 6, June 3, 17, and 24, July 1, 8, 15, 22, and 29, August 5, 12, and 26, September 2, 9, 16, 23, and 30, October 7, 14, 21, and 28, November 4, 11, 18, and 25, and December 2, 9, 23, and 30, 1928; January 6, 13, 20, and 27, February 3, 10, 17, and 24, March 3, 17, 24, and 31, April 7, 14, 21, and 28, May 12, 19, and 26, June 2, 9, 16, 23, and 30, July 7, 14, 21, and 28, August 4, 7, and 18, October 20 and 27, November 17 and 24, and December 1 and 15, 1929; January 22, 1931; January 5, 1933; May 31, 1936; January 3, 1938; and April 9, 1950.

Collinsville *Courier*: March 11, April 15, November 11, December 2, and November 11, 1926; January 6, February 10, and April 14, 1927.

DeKalb County *Herald*: October 30, 1925; February 5, March 12, April 9, 16, and 30, September 10, and November 19, 1926.

DeKalb *Republican*: June 28, July 5, 12, and 19, August 23, September 6, 20, and 27, October 11 and 25, November 8, 15, 22, and 29, and December 6, 13, 20, and 27, 1923; January 3, 10, 17, 24, and 31, February 7, 14, and 21, March 6, 20, and 27, April 3, 10, 17, 24, May 1, 8, 15, 22, and 29, June 26, and 28, July 10, 17, 31, August 14, and October 9, 1924; March 5 and 19, May 21, June 4, and Sept. 17, 1925.

DeKalb *Times*: August 29, September 12, 19, and 26, and October 3, 10, and 17, 1935; January 6, March 25, and August 5, 12, and 26, 1937.

Fort Payne *Democrat*: November 2, 1927.

Fort Payne *Journal*: April 4, 11 and 18, May 16, June 13, July 18 and 25, August 22, September 5, and October 24 and 31, 1890; January 16, February 13, March 6, 13 and 27, April 3, June 19, August 14, September 18 and 25, October 2, and December 23 and 30, 1891; June 8, 15, 22, and 29, July 6 and 20, August 3, 7, and 10, November 16 and 23, and December 7, 1892; July 19 and 26, August 2, September 6, October 4, and November 29, 1893; January 10 and 17, March 21 and 28, April 4 and 18, May 9 and 16, June 6 and 27, July 18, August 2, 8, and 15, September 12, 19, and 26, October 3, 10, and 17, November 7 and 28, and December 26, 1894; January 30, February 13 and 27, July 17 and 31, September 4 and 11, October 9 and, November 13, 1895; January 8, February 5, May 20 and 27, April 1, May 20 and 27, June 24, July 8 and 22, August 5 and 26, September 2, 9, and 30, October 14, 21, and 28, November 18, and December 2 and 16, 1896; January 20, March 10, April 7 and 21, and August 18, 1897; February 9, April 13, May 11, July 13, August 10, 24, and 31, September 7, 21, and 28, October 26, November 9 and 23, and December 7, 1898; February 22, April 12 and 26, May 24, June 14, July 5, October 4, November 22, and December 20, 1899; February 28, May 17, July 20, September 26, October 10, and December 19, 1900; January 2, February 20, March 13 and 27, June 12, July 24 and 31, August 28, September 4, and November 20, 1901; May 21 and July 23, 1902; July 1 and December 9, 1903; June 8, July 6 and 13, and October 5, 1904; April 5, 12, 19, 26, and May 31, 1905; April 25, May 9, June 6, and September 19, 1906; March

6, April 17, June 12 and 19, July 17 and 31, and August 14, 1907; January 22, February 5 and 19, April 15, June 24, July 1, 8, 15, 22, and 29, August 5, 12, and 26, September 9, 23, and 30, October 7, and November 25, 1908; January 27, March 10, 17, and 31, April 21, May 26, September 1, October 6, 10, and 27, and November 17, 1909; February 2 and 16, March 9, May 18, July 20 and 27, August 17, 24, and 31, September 7 and 14, and October 5 and 19, 1910; February 22, March 15, June 28, July 5, August 2, 9, and 30, September 13 and 27, October 4 and 18, and November 1, 15, 22, and 29, 1911; January 10, February 21, April 24, July 17, August 28, September 25, and October 23, 1912; August 13 and 27, October 29, and December 31, 1913; May 20, June 24, August 5 and 19, September 9, 16, and 30, and December 2 and 30, 1914; January 20, February 10, March 17, May 19, June 30, July 7, September 22, and October 20, 1915; April 2 and 16, May 21, July 23 and 30, August 27, September 10 and 24, October 15, November 5 and 26, and December 3 and 17, 1919; December 1, 1926; November 30, 1927; March 28, May 16, June 6, and August 22, 1928; June 11, September 24, and October 16, 1930; January 28, April 22, and June 24, 1931; March 9, June 8, September 28; and November 30, 1932; August 16, October 11, November 1, and December 20 and 27, 1933; January 24, March 7 and 14, July 4 and 25, and September 26, 1934; February 27, April 3, 10, and 17, May 1, 8, and 15, June 26, July 10, 17, 24, and 31, September 18, and October 16 and 30, 1935; March 24, May 10, June 23, August 11, and September 8, 1937; January 5, July 20, August 3 and 17, and November 23, 1938; and September 18, 1940.

Fort Payne *Tribune*: January 31, April 25, and December 12, 1929.

Gadsden *Times-News*: September 11, 14, and 28, October 2, 5, 9, 16, and 23, and November 16, 21, and 27, 1894; June 30, August 28, September 1 and 8, and October 2, 1896; July 12, 15, 19, 22, and 26, August 12, and September 7, 1898.

Minneapolis *Tribune*: September 2, 1921.

Mobile *Press*: April 7, 1950.

Sand Mountain *Signal*: March 29, August 2, September 13, and October 25, 1895.

Legal and Public Documents

Administration Book 3, page 348. Petition for letters of administration in the estate of Jennie M. Howard. DeKalb County Probate Office, Fort Payne, Alabama.

Certificate of death for Jennie Howard. Department of Public Health, Montgomery, Alabama.

Certificate of death for Milford Robert Howard. Department of Public Health, Sacramento, California.

Certificate of death for Milford W. Howard. Department of Public Health, Sacramento, California.

Certificate of death for Perle Roberta Howard. Department of Public Health, Sacramento, California.

Certificate of death for Sally Howard. Department of Public Health, Sacramento, California.

Certificate of death for William Edgar Howard. Department of Public Health, Montgomery, Alabama.

263

Certificate of marriage for C. M. Howard and Jennie V. Morris. Marriage Book 8, page 52. Tuscaloosa County Probate Office, Tuscaloosa, Alabama.

Certificate of marriage for Milford W. Howard and Stella V. Harper. Marriage Book 32, page 256. Hamilton County Court House, Chattanooga, Tennessee.

Certificate of marriage for M. W. Howard and Sally A. Lankford. Marriage Record C, page 344. DeKalb County Probate Office, Fort Payne, Alabama.

Corporation Record, Vol. B, pages 351-353. DeKalb County Probate Office, Fort Payne, Alabama.

Deed Book 59, page 241. The Master Schools, Inc. to Sally Howard. DeKalb County Probate Office, Fort Payne, Alabama.

Deed Book 66, page 596. The Master Schools, Inc. to Claude M. Howard. DeKalb County Probate Office, Fort Payne, Alabama.

Deed Book 69, page 181. C. M. Howard, Trustee, to Myrtle H. McCormack. DeKalb County Probate Office, Fort Payne, Alabama.

Deed Book 73, page 361. Milford W. Howard to The Boy Scouts of America. DeKalb County Probate Office, Fort Payne, Alabama.

Deed Book 77, pages 469-470. The Master Schools, Inc. to M. W. Howard, Jennie Howard, and Morris Howard. DeKalb County Probate Office, Fort Payne, Alabama.

Deed Book 79, page 250. Boy Scouts of America to The Master Schools, Inc. DeKalb County Probate Office, Fort Payne, Alabama.

Deed Book 176, page 529. Claude M. and Margaret Howard to J. V. Curtis, Jr. DeKalb County Probate Office, Fort Payne, Alabama.

Deed Book 176, pages 555-556. C. M. Howard to Local Council of Boy Scouts. DeKalb County Probate Office, Fort Payne, Alabama.

Final Record N, pages 489-491. Myrtle Howard vs. Claude M. Howard DeKalb County Register's Office, Fort Payne, Alabama.

Final Record L, pages 395-397. Claude M. Howard vs. Jennie M. Howard. DeKalb County Probate Office, Fort Payne, Alabama.

Final Record O, pages 35-36. Milford W. Howard vs. Stella Vivian Howard. DeKalb County Register's Office, Fort Payne, Alabama.

Map Book 1, page 191. River Park Subdivision. DeKalb County Probate Office, Fort Payne, Alabama.

Map Book 2, page 69. Castle Rock Heights Subdivision. DeKalb County Probate Office, Fort Payne, Alabama.

Master Schools, Inc. Papers of incorporation, minutes, contracts, powers of attorney, last will and testament of Milford W. Howard, etc. Legal file belonging to Honorable W. M. Beck, Sr., Fort Payne, Alabama.

Minute Record F, page 405. Claude M. Howard vs. Jennie M. Howard. DeKalb County Register's Office, Fort Payne, Alabama.

Minute Record G, Page 86. Myrtle Howard vs. Claude M. Howard. DeKalb County Register's Office, Fort Payne, Alabama.

Minute Record G, pages 113-114. Milford W. Howard vs. Stella Vivian Howard. DeKalb County Register's Office, Fort Payne, Alabama.

Official Court Records of case No. 2212. E. Burton Cook, et al. vs. C. M. Howard, et al., Circuit Court in Equity. DeKalb County Register's Office, Fort Payne, Alabama.

Letters

Alpine Lodge to "Dear Doctor." Form letter mailed during 1930's. Copy in Howard Papers, DeKalb County Library, Fort Payne, Alabama.

Beck, W.M., to Jennie Howard, University, Alabama, January 29, 1940. Legal documents in possession of Honorable W. M. Beck, Sr., Fort Payne, Alabama.

Berry, Martha, to M. W. Howard, Los Angeles, December 23, 1921. In possession of Col. C. M. Howard, Columbus, Georgia.

Blanchard, Frederic W., to his family in Holbrook, Massachusetts. Collection of letters written from January 1, 1890, to June 7, 1891, in DeKalb County Library, Fort Payne, Alabama.

Denson, William H., to Thomas A. Street, Guntersville, April 22, 1894. Oliver Day Street Papers, University of Alabama, Tuscaloosa, Alabama.

Ewing, W. N., to Thomas G. Jones, Montgomery, July 15, 1892. Thomas Goode Jones Papers, Alabama Archives, Montgomery, Alabama.

Herring, J. L., to Claude M. Howard, Panama City, Florida, July 16, 1930. DeKalb County Court Records, Case 2212, Fort Payne, Alabama.

Howard, Claude, to Martha Miller, River Park, Alabama, July 3, 1930. DeKalb County Court Records, Case 2212, Fort Payne, Alabama.

Howard, Claude, to Martha Miller, River Park, Alabama, August 12, 1930. DeKalb County Court Records, Case 2212, Fort Payne, Alabama.

Howard, Jennie, to W. M. Beck, Fort Payne, Alabama, September 16, 1940. In possession of Honorable W. M. Beck, Sr., Fort Payne, Alabama.

Howard, Milford, to John B. Isbell, Fort Payne, June 23, 1920. Howard Papers, DeKalb County Library, Fort Payne, Alabama.

Howard, Milford, to Thomas G. Jones, Montgomery, December 29, 1891. Thomas Goode Jones Papers, Alabama Archives, Montgomery, Alabama.

Howard, Stella Vivian, to Dr. C. D. Killian, Fort Payne, December 29, 1937. Fort Payne *Journal*, January 5, 1938.

Isbell, John B., to O. D. Street, Guntersivlle, August 28, 1898. Oliver Day Street Papers, University of Alabama, Tuscaloosa, Alabama.

Justice, Dr. Brady R., to Elizabeth S. Howard, Fort Payne, June 25, 1976. Howard Papers, DeKalb County Library, Fort Payne, Alabama.

Lankford, Milford, to Mrs. Cliff Cochran, Fort Payne, February 21, 1974. In possession of Mrs. Cliff Cochran, Fort Payne, Alabama.

Lankford, Milford, to Elizabeth S. Howard, Fort Payne, February 20, 1975. Howard Papers, DeKalb County Library, Fort Payne, Alabama.

Littlefield, George E., to M. W. Howard, Los Angeles, September 12, 1921. In possession of Col. C. M. Howard, Columbus, Georgia.

Scott, John Milton, to Milford Howard, Los Angeles, September 1, 1921. In possession of Col. C. M. Howard, Columbus, Georgia.

Interviews

Beck, Judge W. M., Sr. Fort Payne, June 22, 1972.

Biddle, Mrs. Woodrow. Fort Payne, April 20, 1976.

Cash, Grady. Fort Payne, January 20, 1976.

Cochran, Mrs. Cliff. Fort Payne, February 8, 1975.

Cordell, Mr. & Mrs. James F., of Rome, Georgia. Fort Payne, August 6, 1972.

Crow, Paul. Mentone, Alabama, November 5, 1974.
Culpepper, Willie. Fort Payne, June 5, 1974.
Downer, J. A. Fort Payne, September 22, 1972.
Garrett, Bill. Fort Payne, March 20, 1973.
Gilliam, Dee. Fort Payne, March 7, 1973.
Haralson, Judge W. J. Fort Payne, January 9, 1974.
Hunt, Judge Richard. Fort Payne, January 9, 1974.
Isbell, Mr. & Mrs. John B., Jr. Fort Payne, March 17, 1975.
Kirk, Frank. Mentone, June 6, 1974.
Kirk, Mr. & Mrs. Frank. Mentone, July 20, 1974.
Pendergrass, Mrs. Maude. Fort Payne, February 7, 1975.
Sawyer, Mrs. Sarah P. Fort Payne, December 13, 1974.
Webb, Mrs. Lucile. Gadsden, January 8, 1974.
Wester, B. C. Mentone, May 15, 1973.
Wester, Mrs. B. C. Mentone, February 13, 1974.

Unpublished Materials

Harris, Alan D. "Campaigning in the Bloody Seventh; The Election of 1894 in the Seventh Congressional District." Paper read at annual meeting of Alabama Historical Association, Birmingham, Alabama, April 29, 1972.
Harris, Alan D. "The Political Career of Milford W. Howard, Populist Congressman From Alabama." Master's thesis, Auburn University, 1957.
Howard, Milford W. "Autobiography." Manuscript completed in 1930, in possession of Col. C. M. Howard, Columbus, Georgia.
Howard, Milford W. "Is Prayer Scientific?" Manuscript written in 1933, in possession of Col. C. M. Howard, Columbus, Georgia.
Howard, Milford W. "Vagabonding at Seventy." Manuscript completed in 1933, in possession of Col. C. M. Howard, Columbus, Georgia.
Howard, Milford W. "Wild Ass' Skin." Manuscript written in 1920, in possession of Col. C. M. Howard, Columbus, Georgia.
Metzger, Abram Boyce. "A History of Fort Payne, Alabama." Master's thesis, Auburn University, 1938.
Stephens, Maxine. "My Visit to Colonel Howard." School report prepared in 1928, in possession of Mrs. Maxine S. Walsh, Jackson, Alabama.

Miscellaneous Sources

Assorted newspaper clippings (undated and unidentified) kept in Milford Howard's billfold. In possession of Col. C. M. Howard, Columbus, Georgia.
Inscription on tombstone of Clarence Howard, Glenwood Cemetery, Fort Payne, Alabama.
Inscription on tombstone of H. C. Haralson, Glenwood Cemetery, Fort Payne, Alabama.
"The Murmurer." Series of articles by Milford Howard, written for unidentified newspaper during 1890's. In possession of Col. C. M. Howard, Columbus, Georgia.
Howard family Bible. In possession of Mrs. Charles Willard, Silver Spring, Maryland.

Index

268